BROADWAY
— TO —
HOLLYWOOD

'Move your bloody arse!'
shouts Eliza Doolittle at the
Ascot races in *My Fair Lady* on
stage (above, with Julie
Andrews) and on screen (right,
with Audrey Hepburn).

2294522 *Aylesworth T.G.* *Broadway to Hollywood.*

AYLESWORTH, T. G.

BROADWAY TO HOLLYWOOD - MUSICALS FROM

Please renew/return this item by the last date shown.

So that your telephone call is charged at local rate, please call the numbers as set out below:

	From Area codes 01923 or 0208:	From the rest of Herts:
Renewals:	01923 471373	01438 737373
Enquiries:	01923 471333	01438 737333
Minicom:	01923 471599	01438 737599

L32b

2 0 JUN 2002

0 9 SEP 2002

2 9 MAR 2003

- 5 SEP 2008

2 - NOV 2002
2 5 NOV 2002

- 3 NOV 2003
2 6 NOV 2003

1 6 DEC 2002

2 7 JAN 2004

0 6 JAN 2003

1 9 APR 2005

2 3 JAN 2003

L33

BROADWAY
TO
HOLLYWOOD
MUSICALS FROM STAGE TO SCREEN

THOMAS G. AYLESWORTH

HAMLYN

A Bison Book

Published 1985 by
Hamlyn Publishing
A division of The Hamlyn Publishing Group Ltd.
Bridge House, London Road
Twickenham, Middlesex

Copyright © 1985 Bison Books Ltd.

Produced by
Bison Books Ltd.
176 Old Brompton Road
London SW5
England

ISBN 0 600 50047 0

Printed in Belgium

Robert Preston played Harold
Hill in both the stage (right,
singing 'Seventy-Six
Trombones') and screen
(above, talking to the mayor's
wife played by Hermione
Gingold) versions of *The Music
Man.*

CONTENTS

PREFACE

Time was when it was easy to define the Broadway musical. Called musical comedies, they had little or no plot and a lot of music – usually of the hummable variety. And most of them were either swashbucklers, such as *Naughty Marietta* (1910) and *The Desert Song* (1929), or simple comedies such as *Of Thee I Sing* (1931) and *Little Johnny Jones* (1904). But over the years, the Broadway musical branched out. Some became operatic, like *The Most Happy Fella* (1965) and *Lost in the Stars* (1949). Others became musical tragedies, like *Street Scene* (1947) and *West Side Story* (1957). Still others became operettas, such as *My Fair Lady* (1956) and *Up in Central Park* (1945).

But whether we call them musicals, musical comedies, light operas or even operas, these Broadway productions have been popular for a long time. In 1903, more than 25 percent of the productions playing in New York were musicals – many of them billed as musical comedies. The rest were called musical farces, extravaganzas, spectacular fantasies, burlesque reviews and comic operas. At the latest count, of the 55 Broadway shows with the longest runs, 33 have been musicals, with *A Chorus Line* (1975 and still running) heading the list. Of these 33 shows, 22 have been made into films, and *A Chorus Line* is scheduled for release in 1985.

The appeal of the musical to a wide cross-section of the public is probably due to the fact that the musical is the most eclectic form of stagecraft. Musicals can steal from popular literature, as in *Guys and Dolls* (1950), and the classics, as in *Kiss Me, Kate* (1948). They can use classical music, as in *Kismet* (1953); rock music, as in *Hair* (1968); or jazz music, as in *Strike Up the Band* (1930). They cannibalize their own world of show business, as in *Funny Girl* (1964). Whatever it is, let's make a musical out of it. And the musical, like other forms of the performing arts, can reflect the contemporary scene and even make a social comment on the world around it.

It hasn't always been this way. There was a time when the stage musical dwelt in its own putty society of Ruritanian romances or Long Island tennis parties. But then came *Show Boat* (1927), in which the musical suddenly developed a

"Go ahead, Rose Marie — give it to 'em — and make 'em like it!"

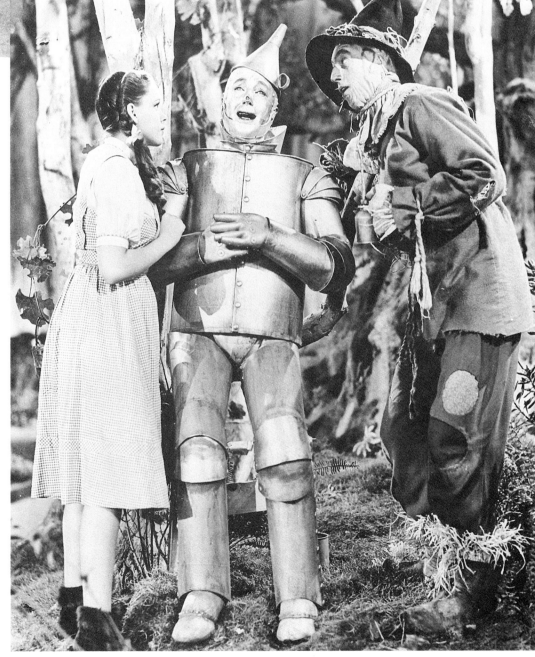

ABOVE: Fred Stone as the Scarecrow and David Montgomery as the Tin Woodman adrift in a boat in the Broadway version of *The Wizard of Oz* (1903).

RIGHT: Judy Garland as Dorothy, Jack Haley as the Tin Woodman and Ray Bolger as the Scarecrow in the film version of *The Wizard of Oz* (1939).

OPPOSITE: Jeanette MacDonald played the opera star in the 1935 film version of *Rose Marie*.

sense of artistry and even a conscience, telling the story of the rejection of the mulatto, Julie, by her white contemporaries. *Pal Joey* (1940) gave us the theme of the anti-hero. *West Side Story* (1957) probed into the world of the New York street gangs.

Another change seems to have occurred. It used to be that almost every musical of any consequence had a multitude of hit songs. Most of the songs from *Oklahoma!* (1943), *Carousel* (1945) and *The King and I* (1951) are remembered fondly 25 to 30 years later. But who remembers much more than the title song from *Hello Dolly!* (1964) and 'Send in the Clowns' from *A Little Night Music* (1973)? Indeed, in years past, the musical was put together for the composer – there were Cole Porter shows, Jerome Kern shows, Rodgers and Hart (or Hammerstein) shows, Irving Berlin shows, Jerome Kern shows, George and Ira Gershwin shows. And the show tunes were universally popular.

But not today. The emphasis is on the director. We think of Bob Fosse's *Pippin* (1972) rather than Stephen Schwartz's *Pippin*, or Michael Bennett's *A Chorus Line* (1975) rather than Marvin Hamlisch's *A Chorus Line*.

Since World War II, it has been the Broadway musical that has provided the Hollywood musical-film makers with a great deal of their material. There have been a few original musical films, such as *Funny Lady* (1975), but the Broadway stage represented a known commodity – the hit musical – and Hollywood producers have never taken too many chances. Also, long gone were the foreign musicals. The Parisian musical entertainments are not really exportable, and the Vienna Woods do not seem to be offering any more songs. The British still have a few talented song writers like Lionel Bart, Anthony Newley and Leslie Bricusse, but, by and large, it is Broadway that calls the tune for Hollywood.

Some Broadway musicals, however, could not really be made into film, and some others probably should not have been put in front of the cameras because they were too regional. *Fiorello!* (1959), a wonderful musical, was not filmed, probably because it was felt that only New Yorkers would be interested in the musical about their former mayor. Although it ran for 796 performances on Broadway, the Hollywood decision-makers were probably right. They made the wrong decision on the play *Up in Central Park* (1945),

BELOW: Barbra Streisand polishes the steps of the poorhouse in the film *On A Clear Day . . .* (1970).

RIGHT: Rex Harrison, as Henry Higgins, celebrates Eliza's triumph at the Ascot races in the filmed *My Fair Lady* (1964).

ABOVE: Aileen Quinn had the title role and Sandy played himself in the film version of *Annie*, released in 1982.

OPPOSITE: Shirley MacLaine certainly got a chance to strut her stuff in the film *Sweet Charity* (1969).

another charming Broadway musical. The film was released in 1948. It contained a story about the machinations of Boss Tweed's Tammany Hall gang in New York, and does anyone remember the movie?

There were quite a lot of agonizing decisions that had to be made in selecting the films and stage musicals to be used in this book. Agony number one was that there was room only for 'book musicals' – those with plots – and that meant losing some of the wonderful revues that traveled from Broadway to Hollywood. There went such things as *This Is the Army* (1942), *Call Me Mister* (1946), *New Faces of 1952* (1952), *The Band Wagon* (1931) and many others.

The second agonizing decision was to eliminate, because of the title of the book, those wonderful musicals that had appeared on Broadway but were not filmed in Hollywood. There went such gems as *Stop the World, I Want to Get Off* (1961), *The Threepenny Opera* (1954), *Oliver!* (1960) and *The Boy Friend* (1954).

Of course, there could be no Hollywood musical that later went to Broadway, and thus no *Seven Brides for Seven Brothers* and *Gigi*. Broadway musicals that had been totally emasculated of their music did not, of course, qualify either, so lost were such Broadway hits as *Irma la Douce* (1958) and *Fanny* (1954). They ended up just not being musical films at all.

Finally, many Broadway shows have spawned Hollywood musical films in which the plots have been completely rewritten, the songs have been replaced, or both. But still, Hollywood got its ideas from the legitimate theater, and these musicals were included. If they hadn't been, this would be a terribly tiny volume.

Just a word about the organization of the chapters. Each chapter covers a decade of movie making, and therefore, the Broadway shows are found in the chapter covering the release date of the film. To put the play in a chapter covering its premiere date would be cumbersome and confusing, inasmuch as finding the citation for *The Wizard of Oz*, for example, which was released to theaters in 1939, would necessitate looking in a chapter covering 1903, when the original stage version opened in New York.

Most Broadway musicals make good films. The camera, with its close-up shots, can make a poignant song more intimate; the wide screen can make a chorus routine more joyful and panoramic. This, then, is the story of those glorious Broadway musicals that made it to the silver screen.

THOMAS G AYLESWORTH
STAMFORD, CONNECTICUT

THE MUSICMAKERS

The composer was paramount for decades after the musical first traveled from Broadway to Hollywood. Blockbuster films like *Oklahoma!* and *The King and I* showcased many hit tunes that are still classics. Both stage and screen productions were closely identified with their composers – men like Richard Rodgers, Oscar Hammerstein II, Jerome Kern, Cole Porter, Kurt Weill, Meredith Willson, Irving Berlin, George Gershwin, Noel Coward, and many others. It is impossible to think of the musical genre without thinking first of them.

ABOVE: Irving Berlin and Ethel Merman running over some of the songs for *Call Me Madam* (1950).

ABOVE LEFT: The great George Gershwin (1889-1937).

LEFT: Meredith Willson (relaxing) confers with Harve Presnell, Dore Schary and Tammy Grimes.

LEFT: Sir Noel Coward (1899-1973), one of the most productive renaissance men of our time.

RIGHT: Kurt Weill (1900-1950) at the left, and Maxwell Anderson (1888-1959), at rehearsal.

LEFT: Cole Porter (1893-1964).

BELOW LEFT: Jerome Kern (1885-1945).

BELOW: Richard Rodgers, Joshua Logan and Oscar Hammerstein II.

RIGHT: John Boles, as the Red
Shadow, romances Carlotta
King in the film *The Desert
Song* (1929).

OPPOSITE: Joe E Brown greets
Marilyn Miller in the film
version of *Sally* (1929).

THE ADOLESCENT
TWENTIES

The challenge of radio helped stimulate the transition
from silent to sound movies: with the sound era came
the musical. It was inevitable that Hollywood would turn
to the New York theater district for much of its material.
Proven hits meant low risk for the studios, and musicals
provided maximum sound with minimal technical
problems. This was no small inducement in the days of
primitive sound equipment. In fact, the movies learned
to sing and dance before they really learned to talk.

The first sound film – that is, the first full-length feature movie to use the new Vitaphone Process – was, of course, *The Jazz Singer* (1927), starring Al Jolson. The revolution had happened. Manufacturers of the sound equipment were swamped with orders from exhibitors. By the end of the year, even the most confirmed skeptics realized that any sound film was attracting large crowds to any theater that showed it, and, of course, the best kind of sound film to show off the process was the musical.

It took Hollywood a couple of years to realize that the Broadway musical would be ideal for sound films, but when the idea dawned, movie moguls grabbed the rights to stage musical comedies with a vengeance. One of the first properties to appear on screen was *The Desert Song* (1929), taken from the stage show of the same name, first produced in 1926. It had a book by Otto Harbach, Oscar Hammerstein II and Frank Mandel, with lyrics by Harbach and Hammerstein and music by Sigmund Romberg. Directed by Arthur Hurley with dances by Bobby Connolly, it starred Vivienne Segal, Robert Halliday, Eddie Buzzell and William O'Neal. It was one of the hit stage musicals of the time, running for 465 performances.

The Desert Song was an unusual musical for the time because it had a modern setting – the 1925 revolt of the Riffs against the French Protectorate in Morocco. During its try-out in Wilmington, Delaware (titled *Lady Fair*), one critic was less than enthusiastic: 'With so many pleasant people in the cast and so much music, color and romance, I am perhaps ungrateful in regretting that, with the exception of one song called "It," the lyrics gave indication that W S Gilbert lived and died in vain.'

The Desert Song told the story of Margot, a gullible French girl who is unaware that her boy friend, Pierre Birabeau, the son of the French governor, is also 'the Red Shadow' – the leader of the Riffs. She doesn't recognize him even when he tries, as the Red Shadow, to lure her into the desert by singing what became the title song, also known as 'Blue Heaven.' Margot does go into the desert, but spurns the Red Shadow. He leaves the tent and returns as Pierre, but, wonder of wonders, now Margot says she loves the Red Shadow (leading ladies in swashbucklers were never long on brains). It takes her until the end of the show to realize that the two men are one and the same.

The movie version of *The Desert Song* (1929) starred John Boles, Carlotta King and Myrna Loy. It was filmed in a primitive two-color Technicolor process and kept most of the original score. In addition to the title song, there were the 'Riff Song,' 'French Marching Song,' 'Then You Will Know,' 'Song of the Brass Key,' 'Sabre Song,' 'Romance,' 'One Alone,' 'One Flower' and 'My Little Castagnette.'

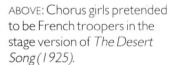

ABOVE: Chorus girls pretended to be French troopers in the stage version of *The Desert Song* (1925).

OPPOSITE: The film version of *The Desert Song* (1929) spared no expense in hiring actors and dancers and designing costumes and sets.

LEFT: The four Marx Brothers, Zeppo, Groucho, Chico and Harpo, mix it up in the film *The Cocoanuts* (1929). The studio publicity department let out the information that 'The Marx Brothers always sign their contracts in green ink and like to have the soles of their feet tickled.'

The Cocoanuts opened on Broadway in 1925 with a book by George S Kaufman and songs by Irving Berlin. Directed by Oscar Eagle with dances by Sammy Lee, it starred the Marx Brothers, Frances Williams, Margaret Dumont and Janet Velie, and ran for 276 performances.

The thin plot concerned the Florida real-estate boom of the 1920s, and Groucho played the part of Henry W Schlemmer, a crooked real-estate developer ('This property is only a stone's throw from the station.' 'Throw enough stones and he'll build a station.') In addition to his wheeling and dealing, Schlemmer also romances Mrs Potter (Dumont), hoping to get his hands on her money. Silent Sam (Harpo) eats telephones, tears up mail, steals the silver and chases every girl foolish enough to appear in the show. Chico plays Willie the Wop and Zeppo is Jamison – the only sane person in the cast. Some songs were: 'A Little Bungalow,' 'We Should Care,' 'Lucky Boy,' 'Florida by the Sea' and 'Monkey Doodle Doo.'

The movie version of The Cocoanuts (1929) was the Marx Brothers' first sound movie. This film eliminated many of the songs and added a new Irving Berlin tune, 'When My Dreams Come True.' Much of the action took place in the Hotel de Cocoanut, where Margaret Dumont was on hand, as was Kay Francis in her movie debut.

The stage musical version of Edna Ferber's novel Show Boat opened in December 1927 in Florenz Ziegfeld's theater – called, naturally, the Ziegfeld Theater – and it was a first for that great Broadway producer: his first non-revue. The book and lyrics were by Oscar Hammerstein II, the music by Jerome Kern, the direction by Zeke Colvan and the dances by Sammy Lee. There were more than 100 in the company, and the stars were Charles Winninger as Cap'n Andy of the show boat Cotton Blossom; Edna Mae Oliver as Parthy Ann Hawks, his wife; Sammy White as Frank; Eva Puck as Ellie; Helen Morgan as Julie La Verne, the mulatto; Norma Terris as

Magnolia, Andy and Parthy's beautiful daughter; Howard Marsh as Gaylord Ravenal, the gambler who romances Magnolia; Aunt Jemima as Queenie, the slave; and Jules Bledsoe as her husband Joe. It ran for 572 performances.

Paul Robeson had been announced to play Joe, whose big number is the heartrending 'Ol' Man River,' but he was unable to make it. Later, however, he was a smash hit in the London production, which starred Cedric Hardwicke as Cap'n Andy.

Many critics feel that the Broadway musical came of age with *Show Boat*. It was quite possibly the first musical that was more than a boy-meets-girl production. *Show Boat* had drama, characterization and plot development, plus tragedy, plus an anti-hero, plus a statement against slavery and racial prejudice, plus an integration of music and book, with the songs advancing the story line. Oddly enough, after this breakthrough, Jerome Kern and Oscar Hammerstein II seemed not to have gotten the message. Neither of them followed through, and both went back to the backstage musical genre in *Sweet Adeline* (1929) and the middle-European operetta style with *Music in the Air* (1932).

Show Boat had quite a history even before it opened. It was

LEFT: Paul Robeson as Joe in the London Company of *Show Boat*.

ABOVE: A melodramatic moment from the film *Show Boat* (1929).

RIGHT: Otis Harlan as Cap'n Andy.

OPPOSITE BELOW: Another melodrama from the stage version (1927).

Jerome Kern who approached Edna Ferber with the idea that a musical should be made from her 1926 novel. The book, of course, was an atmospheric story of life on a Mississippi River showboat in the 1880s. Ferber, believing that musical comedies had to be 'girlie' shows crammed with comedy and frivolous songs and dances, thought Kern was mad. But Kern explained that he was thinking of a new kind of musical that passed up the old methods, and Ferber assigned him the rights to go ahead. Kern had a problem. The conventional knowledge was that musical comedies were presented for diversion, not as enlightenment or art. It seemed that the only one who believed in Kern's idea was Oscar Hammer-

stein II, who was convinced with one phone call. They went to work. Hammerstein later said, 'We had fallen in love with it. We couldn't keep our hands off it. We acted out scenes together and planned the actual direction. We sang to each other. We had ourselves swooning.'

Somehow they convinced Florenz Ziegfeld to take a flyer, but things did not go smoothly. The play was not ready yet, but the Ziegfeld Theater had just been finished and something had to be put on there to start the cash flow. So Ziegfeld put in another musical – *Rio Rita* – which was so successful that *Show Boat* had to wait a year for the theater to be available. And what a success *Show Boat* was. It grossed about $50,000 per week for two years before going on tour from May 1929 to March 1930. Then there was another 180-performance run in New York. It played London and was translated into French to play Paris. Reviewers called it 'an American masterpiece' and 'a beautiful example of musical comedy.' Alan Dale, the critic, was overcome: '*Show Boat* is going to have a wonderful sail – no storms – no adverse winds – nothing to keep it from making port – goodness knows when.' Even today it is presented in hundreds of dinner theaters and high-school auditoriums every year.

with a protest implied.' Edna Ferber herself wrote about the first time that Kern played the song for her: 'The music mounted, mounted, and I give you my word my hair stood on end, the tears came to my eyes, and I breathed like a heroine in a melodrama. This was great music. This was music that would outlast Jerome Kern's day and mine.' And so it has.

Show Boat has often been revived on Broadway. The previously mentioned revival of 1930 starred Irene Dunne as Magnolia (she had been the understudy to the role in 1927 and was later to become a great movie star), Dennis King as Ravenal and (finally!) Paul Robeson as Joe. In 1946 there was a new production in New York starring Carol Bruce as Julie, Jan Clayton (who much later became the mother of Tommy Rettig on the 'Lassie' television series) as Magnolia, Charles Fredericks and Kenneth Spencer. There were also the revivals of 1948 and 1966. In 1954 *Show Boat* became part of the repertory of the New York City Opera for a time.

Of course Hollywood was not slow to adapt the musical to the screen. The first version was premiered in 1929, starring Joseph Schildkraut, Laura La Plante, Otis Harlan and Emily Fitzroy as, respectively, Gaylord Ravenal, Magnolia, Cap'n Andy and Parthy Ann. It was a strange film – so strange that it was not a hit at all. It was filmed as a silent picture to which songs and dialogue were added for a sound version. But the big mistake was in tacking on a prologue featuring several members of the original stage production singing their

ABOVE: Magnolia becomes the toast of Chicago in the film *Show Boat* (1929).

RIGHT: Carol Bruce (left) and Jan Clayton in the stage revival of *Show Boat* (1946).

The play opens with the arrival of the *Cotton Blossom* in Natchez, Mississippi, and the festive crowds are on hand at the dock singing 'Cotton Blossom.' Cap'n Andy tells the folks to return for the show in the evening, and Gaylord Ravenal sights Magnolia. They are certainly interested in each other, to the tune of 'Make Believe.' Ravenal leaves and Magnolia asks Joe, the black stevedore, his opinion of the gambler. Joe won't commit himself and tells her to ask the Mississippi River. He sings 'Ol' Man River.'

Meanwhile, Julie and Queenie talk of their respective men – Steve and Joe – and Julie sings 'Can't Help Lovin' Dat Man.' The sheriff finds out that Julie is a mulatto and her husband Steve is white – a clear case of miscegenation. The two are forced off the ship, and, since they had played the leads in the showboat performance, they are replaced by Gaylord and Magnolia, who sing 'You Are Love.' Ravenal proposes and Magnolia accepts.

Years go by, and Ravenal deserts Magnolia, who is forced to seek a job at a music hall in Chicago where the star turns out to be Julie, who sings 'Bill' (the song that Helen Morgan made her own after introducing it in the original stage production). Julie lets Magnolia take her place, but she is a flop until Cap'n Andy, who shows up in the audience, tells her to sing Charles K Harris's 'After the Ball' (the only song in the score not written by Kern and Hammerstein). Andy convinces Magnolia to return to the *Cotton Blossom* and a repentant Ravenal shows up.

The most famous of the songs – 'Ol' Man River' – was so remarkable in capturing the style of the spiritual that many people think of it as an American folk song. Hammerstein later wrote: 'Here is a song sung by a character who is a rugged and untutored philosopher. It is a song of resignation

songs. This 18-minute spot had Tess Gardella and the Jubilee Singers with 'C'mon Folks' and 'Hey Feller.' Helen Morgan sang 'Bill' and 'Can't Help Lovin' Dat Man.' Jules Bledsoe and a chorus sang 'Ol' Man River.'

No reason was given for this prologue, but it made the picture that followed, to say the least, an anticlimax. Laura La Plante, the silent screen leading lady, had to have her voice dubbed by Eva Olivetti. Schildkraut, a fine actor who kept his Austrian accent until he died in 1964, was horribly miscast as the Southern riverboat gambler. Only Alma Rubens, as Julie, was consistent. Her personal life gave her interpretation vitality. She was to die four years later, a drug addict, in the California Institute for the Insane.

ABOVE: Buddy Ebsen (in white) leads a dance in a stage revival of *Show Boat*.

TOP: Charles Winninger played Cap'n Andy in the 1936 remake of the film *Show Boat*.

It didn't help the film to have several of the classic songs from the play removed and songs by other composers inserted. The substitutions included: 'The Lonesome Road' by Gene Austin (a popular crooner of the day, most famous for his rendition of 'My Blue Heaven') and Nathaniel Shilkret (later to conduct very minor classical pops recordings for RCA Victor records); 'Here Comes That Showboat' by Maceo Pinkard and Billy Rose (later to become a flamboyant producer of his own musicals); 'Love Sings a Song in my Heart' by Joseph Cherniavsky and Clarence J Marks; 'Coon, Coon, Coon' (believe it or not) by Gene Jefferson and Leo Friedmann; 'Down South' by Sigmund Spaeth (later to become a prominent musicologist) and William H Myddleton; and the traditional spirituals 'I've Got Shoes' and 'Deep River.' Fortunately, *Show Boat* was remade more than once, but more of that later.

Rio Rita, the show that bumped *Show Boat* out of the Ziegfeld Theater in 1927, was strictly in the tradition of the old *Desert Song*. This time it concerned the identity of a disguised bandit known as 'the Kinkajou.' There was also the idea that he might be the brother of the heroine, Rita. In the play, Texas Ranger Jim, played by J Harold Murray, is in love with Rita, played by Ethelind Terry. Also in the cast were Bert Wheeler and Robert Woolsey, destined to become one of the top film-comedy teams of the early 1930s. But the main thing was the music. The songs by Harry Tierney and Joseph McCarthy included the title song, 'River Song,' 'If You're in Love You'll Waltz,' 'The Ranger's Song' ('You'd Better Look Out for the Lone Star Rangers Texas Way'), 'Following the Sun Around,' 'Out on the Loose' and many Mexican dances.

The 1929 film version of *Rio Rita* was made in 24 days, but it still retained the spirit of the play and was the most successful and remunerative musical picture to that date. Like the Broadway musical, the plot was nothing and the opulence was everything. The last half of the film was shot in two-color Technicolor and it starred John Boles, that stalwart American singer; Bebe Daniels, who had been in movies since 1908 at the age of seven; and Wheeler and Woolsey, re-creating their stage roles in their first talking picture. The film kept the original score and added one other Tierney-McCarthy number – 'You're Always in My Arms.'

BELOW: Chorus girls from the movie *Rio Rita* (1929).

LEFT: Stage hijinks from *Rio Rita* (1927).

OPPOSITE: John Boles and Bebe Daniels in a tender moment from the filmed adaptation of *Rio Rita* (1929).

Something terrible happened to Cole Porter's musical comedy *Paris* (1928). It was the story of a mother who doesn't want her son to marry a chorus girl and takes him off to Paris. Even though the Broadway musical had run for 195 performances, the Hollywood producers were afraid of the sophisticated Porter songs. So they tossed them out and used songs by Al Bryan and Ed Ward in the 1929 film version. These songs included 'Crystal Girl,' 'Miss Wonderful,' 'Paris,' 'I Wonder What Is Really on His Mind,' 'I'm a Little Negative,' 'Somebody Might Like You' and 'My Lover' ('Master of My Heart').

Starring in the roles they introduced on Broadway were Irene Bordoni (as the chorus girl) and Jack Buchanan. Also in the cast were Jason Robards (obviously the father of Jason Robards Jr) as the son, and ZaSu Pitts. The studio tried everything – Vitaphone sound and two-color Technicolor sequences – but the movie was a flop. It needed Cole Porter.

Early in the century there was a brash young performer-creator who was going to integrate vaudeville and musical comedy and come up with a new kind of American theater. His name was George M Cohan. He had been a part of his family's vaudeville act, 'The Four Cohans,' since he was nine years old, but he had ambitions that did not include sharing the billing with three other people, even though they were relatives. In 1902 he introduced himself to Broadway with two productions developed from his vaudeville sketches. They were flops. But he finally made it in 1904 as coproducer, with Sam H Harris, of *Little Johnny Jones*. As critic Arthur Jackson later said: 'As a musician he was no Kern, his lyrics would never bear comparison with a Gershwin or a Hammerstein, and his often jingoistic libretti would land with a dull thud on the stage of today. But what Cohan did was to inject the Broadway stage with the vitality and brashness of vaudeville, to emphasize his own gifts as singer, dancer, actor, writer and personality *par excellence*, and, perhaps most important of all in retrospect, to create an audience for the "book" musical in a musical theater attuned by habit and environment to extravaganzas and operettas.'

Little Johnny Jones was the story of an American jockey who goes to England and wins the Derby. It was as simple as that. But it was filled with chauvinism, and the audience

ABOVE: Eddie Buzzell played the title role of a jockey in the film version of *Little Johnny Jones* (1929).

OPPOSITE TOP: Jack Buchanan in the film *Paris* (1929).
RIGHT: Irene Bordoni and Buchanan in *Paris*.

24

cheered when the Yankee showed the British a thing or two. When filmed in 1929, it featured Eddie Buzzell in the title role, and, although not a winner, it at least came in in the place position. All but two of the Cohan songs had been removed ('Give My Regards to Broadway' and 'Yankee Doodle Boy'), and perhaps that was all to the good, since the rest sounded dated even in 1929. Songs that were added were: 'Painting the Clouds With Sunshine' by Al Dubin and Joe Burke, 'Straight, Place and Show' by Herman Ruby and M K Jerome, 'Go Find Somebody to Love' by Herb Magidson and Michael Cleary and 'My Paradise' by Magidson and James Cavanaugh.

Marilyn Miller, the legendary musical-comedy star who could fill a theater no matter what she was in, was the star of the Broadway musical *Sally* in 1920. It had a book by Guy Bolton, and the lyrics by Clifford Grey and Buddy de Sylva were set to music by Jerome Kern. Directed by Edward Royce with additional ballet music by Victor Herbert, *Sally* ran for 570 performances. Starring with Miller were Walter Catlett, Leon Errol and Stanley Ridges.

The story wasn't much. Leon Errol played the part of Connie, a waiter at the Elm Tree Inn who had taken a little dishwasher, Sally (Miller), under his wing. Connie, a former Balkan grand duke exiled by a revolution, helps Sally crash a huge party at the Long Island estate of wealthy Otis Hooper (Catlett). She poses as a Russian dancer, and her performance there sets her off on a dancing career that leads to the Ziegfeld Follies. She meets and marries the wealthy Blair Farquar (Irving Fisher). The end.

The hit song – still a classic – 'Look for the Silver Lining,' was not written for *Sally*. Indeed, it had had a checkered past. It was first written for a proposed musical comedy called *Brewster's Millions*, which told the story of a man who has to

RIGHT: Catlett in the stage *Sally* (1920).

BELOW: The Broadway *Sally*.

BOTTOM: Miller in Hollywood to make *Sally* (1929).

OPPOSITE TOP: Joe E Brown loves Marilyn Miller in the picture version of *Sally* (1929).

OPPOSITE BOTTOM: *Sally*'s Hollywood wedding.

spend a million dollars quickly if he is to come into a major inheritance (later made into a non-musical film in 1945 with Dennis O'Keefe, June Havoc and Eddie 'Rochester' Anderson). But the projected musical was never produced. The song's next appearance was in a trifling little musical comedy called *Good Morning, Dearie* (1919). But it wasn't until Marilyn Miller sang it in *Sally* that the song caught on. She captured the audience with it and made it her own. *Sally* was certainly her greatest hit. Other popular songs from the musical play were 'The Church 'Round the Corner,' 'Sally,' 'Whip-poor-will' and 'Wild Rose.'

Warner Brothers/First National lured Marilyn Miller to Hollywood to make the screen version of *Sally* (1929), and they spared no expense with the film, lavishing a fortune in hopes of repeating its Broadway success. According to the film's publicity flacks, Sally was helped on her way to Broadway by '150 beauties in the largest indoor scene ever photographed in color ... 36 Albertina Rasch girls who dance more perfectly than other choruses can clog ... an orchestra of 110 to play the song hits that *Sally* made famous, and many new numbers added for the screen production.' Also in the cast were Joe E Brown, the comedian with the giant mouth; Ford Sterling, one of the leading Keystone Kops; and Pert Kelton, who would finally gain recognition as a comedienne 28 years later as Mrs Paroo in *The Music Man* (1957).

Other songs in the film were 'Walking Off Those Balkan Blues,' 'After Business Hours' (That Certain Business Begins), 'All I Want to Do, Do, Do, Is Dance,' 'If I'm Dreaming Don't Wake Me Up Too Soon' and 'What Will I Do Without You?'.

The 1920s had come to a triumphant end with *Sally*. But much more was to come in the next decade.

LEFT: Paul Robeson in the 1936 film treatment of *Show Boat*.

OPPOSITE: One of those incredible chorus numbers by Busby Berkeley – *Whoopee* (1930).

THE EXTRAVAGANT THIRTIES

During the 1930s musicals came into their own as the great escape from the Great Depression. Lavish costumes and sets, glittering stars and production numbers, songs that raised hopes of a happier day to come – all these packed theaters despite the scarcity of spending money. The entertainment business challenged hard times with the cry 'Let's put on a show!' and the public responded wholeheartedly.

As Hollywood entered the third decade of the twentieth century, film makers began robbing the musical theater in earnest. One of the first musical films of the 1930s was also one of the more unusual. *Gypsy Love* had first appeared on Broadway in 1911, starring Marguerite Sylva. It was a frothy and silly vehicle about a bandit gang in the mountains of southern Russia, with music by Franz Lehar.

·MGM decided to do a film based on that operetta, retitling it *The Rogue Song* (1930) and sparing no expense. First of all, the most famous baritone of the Metropolitan Opera Company of that time, Lawrence Tibbett, was enticed to California to play the role of Yegor, the chief of the bandits. His was the most powerful voice ever heard in films until then, he was an American (so the audience could understand the lyrics when he sang) and he was not too bad an actor.

The Rogue Song was an all-Technicolor feature, though, of course, in just the available two-color process. Dmitri Tiomkin (later to win three Academy Awards for his music) was hired to write the ballet score that was performed by Albertina Rasch's Ballet Company. Oddly enough, the film was directed by Lionel Barrymore.

One of the highlights of the picture was a scene in which Princess Vera (Catherine Dale Owen) whips Yegor, who sings louder with each stroke. Stan Laurel and Oliver Hardy were also in the cast. Some of the songs were 'When I'm Looking at You,' 'Song of the Shirt' (not to be confused with the aria from *La Bòheme*, 'Vecchia Zimarra' or 'Old Coat') and 'Rogue Song' by Herbert Stothart and Clifford Grey, plus 'The White Dove' by Lehar and Grey.

One of the big Broadway hits of 1925 was *No, No, Nanette*,

ABOVE: Leola Luery and Phil Brannon on stage in *Gypsy Love* (1911).

LEFT: Lawrence Tibbett surprises Catherine Dale Owen as her dueña sleeps in *The Rogue Song* (1930).

BELOW: Stan Laurel (left) and Oliver Hardy in *The Rogue Song*.

with its book by Otto Harbach and Frank Mandel, lyrics by Irving Caesar and Otto Harbach and music by Vincent Youmans. Directed by H H Frazee, with dances by Sammy Lee, it featured Louise Groody, Charles Winninger, Wellington Cross, Mary Lawlor and John Barker. It ran for 321 performances.

The musical had had a disastrous tryout in Detroit, and something had to be done, including a new libretto and some new lyrics. Indeed, the two most popular songs from the show, 'Tea for Two' and 'I Want to Be Happy,' plus two others, were added before it opened in Chicago. The music for 'Tea For Two' was written in one night, and Youmans made

ABOVE: Claire and Littlefield in the 1930 movie *No, No, Nanette*.

LEFT: Broadway's *No, No, Nanette* (1925).

BELOW: Nanette (Bernice Claire) with Alexander Gray.

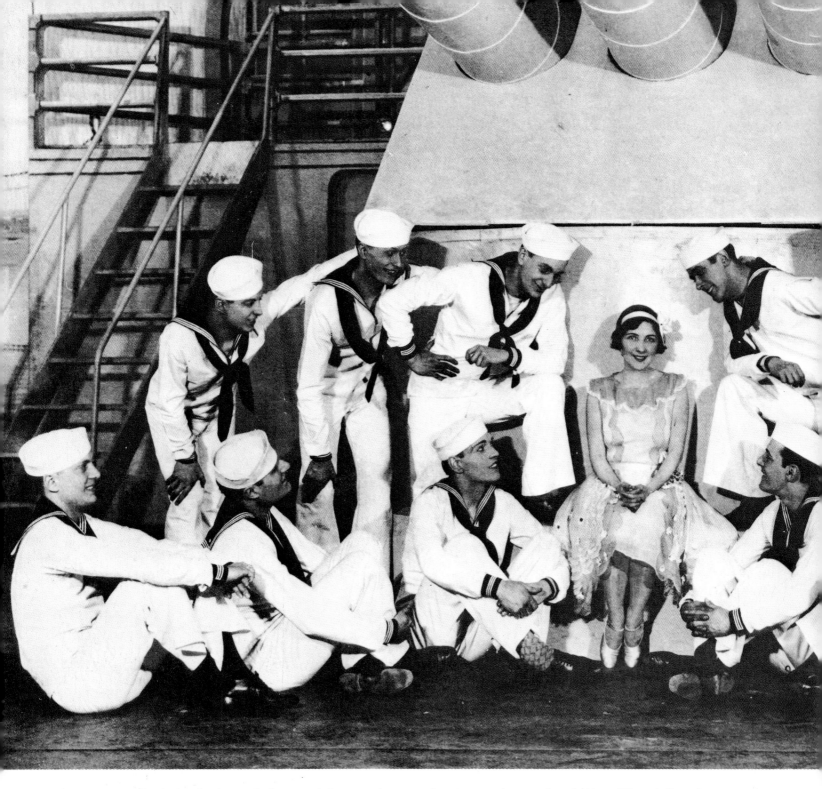

Caesar write the lyrics in the early hours of the morning.

The work paid off, and *Nanette* played to packed houses in Chicago for a year before going on to Broadway. Later there was a London Company (which ran for 665 performances) and 17 other companies in Europe, South America, New Zealand, the Philippines and China.

As usual, there wasn't much of a plot. Billy Early (Cross), a publisher of Bibles, has a daughter named Nanette (Groody), who is engaged to Tom (Barker). On a holiday in Atlantic City, Billy finds three girls who need his help: Betty from Boston (Beatrice Lee), Flora from San Francisco (Edna Whistler) and Winnie from Washington (Lawlor). Meanwhile, his lawyer, Jimmy Smith (Winninger), is chasing Nanette. She disappears from the hotel for a night and Tom is concerned. Everything turns out all right when Billy's wife appears to pay off the girls and Tom forgives Nanette.

No, No, Nanette was revived on Broadway in 1971. The backers and producers were so confident of its success that they invested more than half a million dollars, but even they were surprised by the public response to this dated vehicle of the Roaring Twenties. Busby Berkeley directed the production, which starred Ruby Keeler and a chorus line of 22 girls. When Keeler, who had been retired for some 30 years, started tap-dancing to 'I Want to Be Happy,' the audience cheered and screamed.

The reviewer for the New York *Daily News* wrote a love letter to the production: 'Dear Busby Berkeley, Ruby Keeler, Jack Gilford, Patsy Kelly, Helen Gallagher, Bobby Van, the two pianos, the orchestra, etc. – whoever you are and everyone connected with Broadway's revival of 1925's *No, No, Nanette*. You, collectively, are darlings. I have never attended an opening night that generated more enthusiasm, and may I say I whooped, applauded and otherwise cheered with all the others? I could not have been happier if I had been a backer.'

Hollywood did a fine job transferring all this enthusiasm to

Polly Walker and Jack Oakie. Some of the songs were 'Sometimes I'm Happy,' 'Hallelujah' and 'Why, Oh Why' by Youmans, Grey and Robin; 'Keeping Myself for You' by Youmans and Sidney Clare; 'More Than You Know' by Youmans, Edward Eliscu and Billy Rose; and 'I Know That You Know' by Youmans and Anne Caldwell.

The Vagabond King opened on Broadway in 1925. It was a musical play based on J H McCarthy's romance novel, *If I Were King* (one of the few book titles that used the subjunctive mood), which, in turn, had been a romanticized version of the exploits of François Villon, the fifteenth-century French vagabond-poet. The musical had a book by Brian Hooker and W H Post, who also wrote the lyrics for the music of Rudolf Friml. Directed by Max Figman with dances by Julian Alfred, the play starred Dennis King and Carolyn Thompson and lasted for 511 performances on Broadway and 480 in London's West End.

LEFT: A scene from the Broadway production of *Hit the Deck* (1927).

RIGHT: Dennis King as Francois Villon, on stage in *The Vagabond King* (1925).

BELOW: When *The Vagabond King* was filmed in 1930, Dennis King repeated his stage role. Here he is with Lillian Roth, who played his old love, Huguette.

the screen in 1930. Shot in the primitive Technicolor of the time, the film starred Bernice Claire as Nanette. Also in the cast were Alexander Gray, Lilyan Tashman, ZaSu Pitts, Louise Fazenda and Lucien Littlefield. In addition to the title song, 'Tea For Two' and 'I Want to Be Happy,' by Youmans and Caesar, the film featured 'Dance of the Wooden Shoes' by Ned Washington, Herb Magidson and Michael Cleary, 'As Long As I'm With You' by Grant Clarke and Harry Akst and 'King of the Air' and 'Dancing to Heaven' by Al Bryan and Ed Ward.

Hit the Deck opened on Broadway in 1927 with a book by Herbert Fields, music by Vincent Youmans and lyrics by Clifford Grey, Leo Robin and Irving Caesar. It featured Charles King, Louise Groody and Stella Mayhew and ran for 352 performances. The musical had virtually no plot; it centered on LooLoo, who owned a coffee shop, and her romance with a sailor named Bilge.

The screen version of *Hit the Deck* was made in 1930 with

King played Villon, the leader of a group of vagabonds in the Paris of King Louis XI. Louis decides to make Villon king for a day in order to embarrass one of the ladies of the court, Katherine de Vaucelles (Thompson). Villon has orders to manage to win the hand of the fair Katherine in that one day or lose his head. The two fall in love, but meanwhile the Duke of Burgundy has sent his troops to Paris to overthrow the king. In the end, it is necessary for Villon to gather his vagabonds together to help the king. Burgundy is defeated and Louis grants permission for Villon and Katherine to be married.

One of the most rousing songs to be found in the musical theater was the chorus of Villon's followers, 'Song of the Vagabonds.' And Villon's love ballad to Katherine, 'Only a Rose,' is still being sung. In addition, the other hits were 'Some Day,' 'Waltz Huguette' and 'Love Me Tonight.'

Dennis King repeated his stage role in the first movie version of *The Vagabond King* (1930). The direction was static – the work of the German director Ludwig Berger – and apart from the beautiful music and the two-color Technicolor, there was little to recommend it. Jeanette MacDonald was Katherine, O P Heggie was King Louis and Lillian Roth was Huguette, Villon's former girl friend. The songs and musical numbers included 'Love for Sale' (not to be confused with Cole Porter's more suggestive song of the same name), 'Love Me Tonight,' 'Only a Rose,' 'Some Day' and 'Song of the Vagabonds' by Friml and Brian Hooker; and 'If I Were King,' 'King Louis' and 'Mary, Queen of Heaven' by Sam Coslow, Leo Robin and Newell Chase.

One of the stage flops of 1928 was *Rainbow*, a musical about a United States Army scout who breaks out of prison where he was being held on a murder charge, joins the Gold Rush of 1849 and finds happiness. (This is not to be confused with the show *Rainbow* of 1972, a rock musical with book, music and lyrics by James Rado.) But the play had traces of what later became *Oklahoma!* and *Paint Your Wagon*. Perhaps when Oscar Hammerstein II became so enthusiastic about *Oklahoma!*, he knew what had gone wrong with his earlier turkey, which lasted a mere 30 performances. *Rainbow* had music by Vincent Youmans and a book and lyrics by Hammerstein, Laurence Stallings and Edward Eliscu.

Hollywood changed the vehicle's name from *Rainbow* to *Song of the West* (1930). It starred John Boles and Vivienne

Segal, who were hindered by poor sound recording, a bad script by Harvey Thew and lazy direction by Ray Enright. Joe E Brown played a guitar in the film, and, for once, was forced to die in a picture. The film's songs included 'The Bride Was Dressed in White,' 'Hay Straw,' 'West Wind' (not to be confused with the 'West Wind' by Kurt Weill and Ogden Nash from *One Touch of Venus* in 1943, coincidentally sung on

ABOVE: Louise Brown and Allan Prior in the Broadway musical *Rainbow* (1928).

OPPOSITE: One of the lavish chorus numbers from the motion picture *The Cuckoos* (1930).

LEFT: Vivienne Segal, Joe E Brown and John Boles in a saloon in *Song of the West* (1930).

stage by John Boles) and 'The One Girl' by Youmans and Hammerstein. Grant Clarke and Harry Akst contributed 'Come Back to Me,' a title that would be used by Alan Jay Lerner and Burton Lane for a different song in *On a Clear Day You Can See Forever* (1965).

One of the big hits on Broadway in 1926 has been virtually forgotten. It was *The Ramblers*, and it played for 289 performances – quite a long run for that time. The broad comedy combined various elements of spiritualism, moviemaking, crime fiction and westerns. The music was by Harry Ruby, the lyrics by Bert Kalmar and the book by Kalmar and Guy Bolton.

For some reason, in its transition to the screen, *The Ramblers* became *The Cuckoos* (1930). It starred Bert Wheeler and Robert Woolsey with their anything-goes personalities. The film was just one piece of spirited high-jinks after another about the kidnapping of a wealthy girl by a nobleman. Wheeler and Woolsey played a couple of needy fortune tellers. Also

in the cast were June Clyde, Hugh Trevor and Dorothy Lee. The songs included 'I Loved You So Much,' 'Knock Knees,' 'Looking for the Limelight in Your Eyes' and 'All Alone Monday' by Kalmar and Ruby; 'Dancing the Devil Away' by Kalmar, Ruby and Otto Harbach; 'Wherever You Are' by Charles Tobias and Cliff Friend; and 'If I Were a Travelling Salesman' (there's that subjunctive mood again) by Al Dubin and Joe Burke.

One of the oddities of the 1925 Broadway season was *Song of the Flame* – in which George Gershwin fell in with bad companions (bad for him, at least). Gershwin wrote the music with Herbert Stothart, and the book and lyrics were by Otto Harbach and Oscar Hammerstein II. Stothart, Harbach and Hammerstein were old operetta hands, and Gershwin had to play the game. The result was an operetta in *echt-*Russian style, a story of peasants versus nobility leading to a happy ending in Paris. It was not exactly a flop, playing 219 performances, but it did demonstrate that the operetta-style musical was not George Gershwin's cup of tea – or, in this case, glass of tea.

In 1930, Hollywood was unable to resist the idea of filming an operetta, so *Song of the Flame* came out that year. Bernice Claire played the part of a peasant girl known as 'the Flame,' who causes a Russian revolution by singing 'Song of the Flame.' A subplot involved her love affair with a Russian Prince (Alexander Gray) and how she saved his life by agreeing to submit to the sexual demands of an evil peasant revolutionary (Noah Beery Sr, singing, no less). The Technicolor production even went to wide screen at one point, but the story was sappy, the direction unremarkable.

The Hollywood people kept two of the original songs from the stage musical – 'The Cossack Love Song' and 'Song of the Flame' by Hammerstein, Stothard, Gershwin and Harbach. Other numbers were 'Petrograd,' 'Liberty Song,' 'The Goose Hangs High,' 'Passing Fancy' and 'One Little Drink' by Grant Clarke, Harry Akst and Ed Ward, and 'When Love Calls' by Ed Ward.

Spring Is Here lasted only three months on Broadway in 1929. It was a lyrical romance with music by Richard Rodgers and lyrics by Lorenz Hart, from a book by Owen Davis. The

star was Glen Hunter, who was also a leading man in the movies.

When it was made into a film by First National in 1930, *Spring Is Here* had been rewritten by James A Starr. In the movie, Bernice Claire was the daughter of Ford Sterling (formerly one of the leading Keystone Kops), who wants her to marry one brother when she prefers the other. Also starring were Louise Fazenda, Inez Courtney and Frank Albertson. Among the songs were 'Spring Is Here in Person' (not to be confused with 'Spring Is Here [Why Doesn't My Heart Go Dancing?]' which was another Rodgers and Hart song written for the film *I Married an Angel* in 1942); 'Yours Sincerely,' 'Rich Man, Poor Man,' 'Baby's Awake Now' and 'With a Song in My Heart' by Rodgers and Hart; and 'Cryin' for the Carolines,' 'Have a Little Faith in Me,' 'Baby, Baby' and 'How Shall I Tell?' by Sam Lewis, Joe Young and Harry Warren.

A combination of broad comedy, sporting satire and romance, *Hold Everything* opened on Broadway in 1928 and ran for 413 performances. It told the story of a society girl who comes between a boxer and his girl friend and had music by Buddy de Sylva, Ray Henderson, Lew Brown and a book by de Sylva and John McGowen.

OPPOSITE TOP AND BOTTOM: Bernard Gorcey with Dorothy MacKaye in the Broadway musical *Song of the Flame* (1925); a chorus number from the film *Song of the Flame* (1930).

ABOVE RIGHT: Joe E Brown and Sally O'Neil in the film *Hold Everything* (1930).

BELOW: Delmar Davis, Gus Shy and Bessie Love in the film version of *Good News* (1930).

When it appeared as a movie in 1930, it had been rewritten as a vehicle for Joe E Brown, who played Gink Shiner (get it?), the boxer. Winnie Lightner played his girl friend, and there was a guest star playing the part of the heavyweight champion Georges LaVerne – it was the real-life light heavyweight champion Georges Carpentier, who held the title from 1920 to 1922. Unfortunately, the original score was scrapped and a new one written by Al Dubin and Joe Burke that included such forgettables as 'Take It on the Chin,' 'When Little Red Roses Get the Blues for You,' 'Sing a Little Theme Song,' 'Physically Fit,' 'Girls We Remember,' 'All Alone Together' and 'Isn't This a Cockeyed World?'

The quintessential college musical, *Good News*, opened on Broadway in 1927 for a 557-performance run. With a book

Singleton and star in all those *Blondie* movies, eventually becoming president of the Screen Actors Guild. For some reason, several numbers were yanked – 'The Best Things in Life Are Free,' 'Lucky in Love' and 'That's How You Know We're Co-Eds.' Retained were 'The Varsity Drag,' 'He's a Lady's Man,' 'Good News,' 'Tait Song' and 'Students Are We.' Then there were other songs that were stuck in: 'If You're Not Kissing Me' and 'Football' by Arthur Freed and Nacio Herb Brown, 'I Feel Pessimistic' by J Russell Robinson and George Waggner and 'Gee But I'd Like to Make You Happy' by Reggie Montgomery.

Follow Thru opened on Broadway in 1929 and ran for 403 performances; in London, where it was more properly called *Follow Through*, it lasted for 148. It was a 1920s youth comedy set in a country club, where a man-hungry heroine chases a shy hero, with a subsidiary romance between a golf champion and a female contender. The songs were by Buddy de Sylva, Lew Brown and Ray Henderson, and the book was by de Sylva and Lawrence Schwab.

The Technicolor film version of *Follow Thru* came out in 1930 and starred Jack Haley in the role that he had created on Broadway the year before – the shy hero. The heroine was Nancy Carroll; Charles 'Buddy' Rogers (Mary Pickford's last husband) was the golf pro and Zelma O'Neal was the girl who chased him. Some of the songs in the film were 'Button Up Your Overcoat,' 'Then I'll Have Time for You' and 'I Want to Be Bad' by de Sylva, Brown and Henderson; 'A Peach of a Pair' by George Marion Jr and Richard A Whiting; and 'It Must Be You' by Edward Eliscu and Manning Sherwin.

Present Arms premiered on Broadway in 1928 and had what must have been the silliest plot of any musical that year. A United States Marine private poses as a captain to impress a beautiful English lady, but is discovered and court-

LEFT: Jack Haley and Zelma O'Neal in the film version of *Follow Thru* (1930).

BELOW: Gaile Beverly and Frank Woods in the Broadway musical *Present Arms* (1928).

by Lawrence Schwab and Buddy de Sylva, lyrics by de Sylva and Lew Brown and music by Ray Henderson, it was the story of a college boy on a 1920s campus where football is more important than academic learning. *Good News* starred John Price Jones, Mary Lawlor, Zelma O'Neal, Inez Courtney and Gus Shy, and was directed by Edgar MacGregor with dances by Bobby Connolly.

The ushers in the theater wore college jerseys. And the pit band wore college sweaters and entered through the rear of the theater, leading cheers as they marched down the aisles to the pit.

Tom Marlowe (Jones), the captain of the Tait College football team, can't play in the game with Colton College unless he passes an astronomy test. He is coached by Constance Lane (Lawlor), passes the exam, regains his place on the team, wins the big game and gets the girl.

Some of the hit songs were 'The Girls of Pi Beta Phi,' 'The Varsity Drag,' 'Flaming Youth,' 'The Best Things in Life Are Free,' 'Lucky in Love' and 'Just Imagine.'

The movie version of 1930 starred Stanley Smith and Mary Lawlor (who repeated her stage role as the ugly-duckling tutor), Bessie Love, Cliff Edwards, Lola Lane and an actress named Dorothy McNulty who would go on to become Penny

martialed. He finally triumphs over a German pineapple farmer by saving lives in a shipwreck. The score was by Richard Rodgers and Lorenz Hart, the book was by Herbert Fields and the show lasted 155 performances.

Dance director for the show was Busby Berkeley, and *Present Arms* turned out to be quite a personal venture for him. During the out-of-town tryouts, the actor playing the comedy lead was fired and the part was offered to Berkeley. He played a marine sergeant for nine weeks on Broadway, but it didn't always go easy. Berkeley recalled opening night: 'I launched into my first song, "You Took Advantage of Me," and after the first chorus my mind went blank. I couldn't remember a line, but I had to keep on singing. I concocted some lines like:

When I was walking down the street,
I saw a little bird who called "tweet-tweet,"
I shook my head and said instead,
'Cause you took advantage of me.

It was awful, but I got through it; I can still see poor Larry Hart running up and down in the wings, almost apoplectic. He already had a reputation for witty, poetic lyrics, and here I was ruining his marvelous lines. But I drew a lot of laughs from the audience that night and he later forgave me.'

Present Arms made its film debut in 1930 under the miserable title *Leathernecking* (it was released in Great Britain under its original title). Most of the original score had been excised, but it was filmed in two-color Technicolor. Ken Murray was the private, and Irene Dunne was the beautiful English lady. Also in the cast were several famous comedians: Benny Rubin, Eddie Foy Jr, Ned Sparks and Louise Fazenda.

Two songs were kept from the original stage play: 'You Took Advantage of Me' and 'A Kiss For Cinderella.' The new songs in the film were 'All My Life,' 'Careless Kisses,' 'Evening Star' and 'Nice and So Peculiar' by Benny Davis and Harry Akst. 'Shake It Off and Smile' was the work of Sidney Clare

and Oscar Levant (a fine pianist, wit and hypochondriac who was best known as a disciple of George Gershwin, and later a resident genius on the radio show 'Information, Please').

Rodgers and Hart's *Heads Up* lasted on Broadway for only 144 performances in 1929. The book by John McGowan and Paul Gerard Smith was pretty routine. When *Heads Up* appeared as a film in 1930, it hadn't been improved. Charles 'Buddy' Rogers was a Coast Guard officer who is trying to win the love of pretty Margaret Breen by exposing his rival as a fugitive bootlegger. Also in the cast were Victor Moore and Helen Kane (the 'boop-boop-a-doop girl'). Two songs were

ABOVE: Victor Moore and Helen Kane were in supporting roles in the movie version of *Heads Up* (1930).

Jack Whitney, Robert Glecker (the captain) and Victor Moore on stage in the production of *Heads Up* (1929).

ABOVE: Eddie Foy Jr and Irene Dunne in an army camp scene from the movie *Leathernecking* (1930).

RIGHT: An imitation Busby Berkeley number directed by Pearl Eaton from *Leathernecking*. It combined futuristic settings and costumes with a modernistic South Sea Islands dance by the Pearl Eaton Chorus. The set was designed by Max Ree.

kept from the original; 'My Man Is on the Make' and 'A Ship Without a Sail.' Director Victor Schertzinger also stuck in one of his own songs – 'If I Knew You Better.'

Whoopee was one of the musical hits on Broadway in 1928. When it finally closed, it had run 379 performances. It had a book by William Anthony McGuire based on Owen Davis's Broadway comedy *The Nervous Wreck*. Lyrics were by Gus Kahn, music by Walter Donaldson. *Whoopee* was produced by Florenz Ziegfeld and directed by McGuire, with dances by Seymour Felix. It starred Eddie Cantor, Ruth Etting and Tamara Geva.

The story is about a hypochondriac, Henry Williams (Cantor), who packs up his pills and goes out west to improve his health. He arrives at the Bar M Ranch at Mission Rest and gets involved with a girl and some Indians. The plot involves the romance between Wanenis (Paul Gregory), who is believed to be a halfbreed, and Sally Morgan (Frances Upton). She is supposed to marry Sheriff Bob Wells (Jack Rutherford), but she escapes with Henry to an Indian reservation. It turns out that Wanenis is not an Indian, and both Henry and the sheriff lose the girl.

Ziegfeld had originally wanted to star Ruby Keeler opposite Cantor. Since she was then famous only for her night club work, this would have advanced her career. But Keeler's new husband, Al Jolson, had to go to Hollywood to make a picture and convinced Ruby that she had to go with him. She was replaced by Ruth Etting, a newcomer who was catapulted into the big time in *Whoopee*. Indeed, her best-known number in the show was the song that became permanently identified with her – 'Love Me or Leave Me.' When her screen biography was filmed in 1955, starring Doris Day, it was titled after this song. Etting also sang 'I'm Bringing a Red, Red Rose.'

Whoopee ran for about a year on Broadway; it could have had a much longer run, since even at the end it was playing to packed audiences. The problem was that Ziegfeld had gone broke in the Wall Street Crash of 1929 and had to sell the movie rights to the play to Sam Goldwyn, the Hollywood producer. He also had to close the show to allow Cantor to act as consultant for, and as the star of, the movie.

Although listed as co-producer with Goldwyn on the screen credits, Ziegfeld's participation was nominal. The two men had formed a joint corporation to produce *Whoopee*, but Ziegfeld insisted on top billing in the corporation's title, so Goldwyn kept him off the soundstages.

The picture was released by United Artists in 1930 and Cantor, of course, sang his great hit, 'Makin' Whoopee.' He also introduced another song that had been written just for the film: 'My Baby Just Cares for Me' by Gus Kahn and Walter Donaldson. The song was the idea of Goldwyn, who demanded that the words and music be completed in just one day. The story goes that when Kahn and Donaldson brought it to Goldwyn, the producer asked if the song was suitable for dancing. To prove it was, Kahn hummed the melody, grabbed Goldwyn and danced with him around his office.

Goldwyn was nervous about the film. Not only was it to be in color, but this was his first musical movie. He knew he would need particular help with the choreography and staging and he, Cantor and Ziegfeld decided on Busby Berkeley.

Berkeley was working on *Lew Leslie's International Review* at the time and was called by the William Morris Agency and asked if he wanted to go to Hollywood. Berkeley explained what happened next:

I told them I was not at all interested. I had seen a few film musicals and I hadn't been impressed; they looked terribly static and restricted. But the Morris people kept hounding me. I finally said, "All right, you get me a great star, a great producer, and a great property and I might consider it," They replied, "You want a great star? How about Eddie Cantor?" I nodded. "You want a great producer? How about Florenz Ziegfeld and Sam Goldwyn together?" I blinked. "You want a great property? How about *Whoopee*?" With a barrage like that there wasn't much I could do but agree. I doubted that such a deal existed, but the Morris people invited me to their office to talk with Goldwyn on the telephone. Goldwyn confirmed that he had indeed bought *Whoopee*, which had been a great success on Broadway, with Cantor starring and Ziegfeld producing, and that Cantor and Ziegfeld had been signed for the film and wanted me to direct the musical sequences. All that remained now was to settle on a salary. I was then getting $1000 a week in New York and I figured that if they wanted me in Hollywood I could get $1500 a week. But Goldwyn was a shrewd dealer, and $1000 a week was as much as he was prepared to pay. As I was haggling with him, someone nudged me with a cane: "Go on, Buzz, take the thousand. What do you care? They've got a golf course out there five minutes from the studio, the ocean at your back door, beautiful beaches, sunshine every day. Take the thousand." I turned around and saw Al Jolson. With his prodding, I accepted Goldwyn's offer, and I often kidded him for talking me into taking less than I might have got if he hadn't been there.

Busby Berkeley and his new bride were met in the Los Angeles Union Station by people from the William Morris Agency and ensconced in the Hollywood Roosevelt Hotel.

OPPOSITE TOP: Some of the fake Indian chorines from the film version of *Whoopee* (1930).

LEFT: The star of *Whoopee*, both on stage and on film, was Eddie Cantor, who played Henry Williams, the hypochondriac.

RIGHT: The end of one of those patented Busby Berkeley chorus numbers in *Whoopee* (1930). This was Berkeley's first film.

Later they were taken to the studio to meet Samuel Goldwyn. Berkeley told the story:

He was very cordial and said he felt happy to have me with him on his first musical venture. He asked me what my first step would be, and I told him "girls." He smiled at this and told me the choice was entirely mine. Like everyone else, I doubt if he considered picking girls for the chorus more work than one would think. Actually, you had to look for more than pretty faces and shapely limbs. The girls needed intelligence, coordination, and the ability to understand intricate routines – plus good endurance, since the work was long and tiring. In choosing girls, I found that I could tell a great deal about them from their eyes – something people are unwilling to believe. Among the first girls I picked for *Whoopee* were Betty Grable, then only fifteen, Virginia Bruce, and Claire Dodd.

At this point Berkeley knew practically nothing about making moving pictures, but he wasn't about to admit that. Fortunately, Goldwyn advised him to spend several weeks wandering around the studio – just observing and learning. Berkeley told of that time:

I realized, of course, that the technique was entirely different from the stage. In pictures you see everything through the eye of the camera. Unlike the theater, where your eyes can roam at will, the director and his cameraman decide where the viewer will look. It was obvious to me that film musicals so far had been disappointing because no one thought of imaginative things to do with the camera. With my reputation as a man who came up with unique ideas, I now desperately tried to think of some. My total ignorance of photography and the completely alien environment made it difficult to keep up a facade of assurance. The art director of *Whoopee*, Richard Day, happened to notice me looking at a camera with obvious puzzlement and gave me a piece of advice that helped me greatly. "Buzz, they try to make a big secret out of this little box, but it's no mystery at all. All you have to remember is that the camera has only one eye, not two. You can see a lot with two eyes, but hold your hand over one and it cuts your area of vision." This was very simple advice but it made all the difference. I started planning my numbers with one eye in mind.

Berkeley's reputation as an innovator grew with his next move at the Goldwyn studio. As he recalled it:

It was then customary for the film's director to take over when it came to the actual shooting of the numbers, and I was supposed to step aside. I had never worked that way on Broadway and I wasn't going to work like that now. I went to Goldwyn and told him I wanted to film my own numbers. He hedged and asked me if I thought I could handle it. I replied, "Mr Goldwyn, I don't think I can, I *know* I can." This kind of confidence seemed to impress him, and I got his permission. When I walked on the set to start

shooting, I saw four cameras and four crews. This was something else I didn't know about, and I asked my assistant for an explanation. He told me the standard technique was for a routine to be filmed from four directions, and that the cutter would assemble the shots, make a selection, and put the scene together. With another show of confidence I announced, "Oh? Well, it's not my technique. I use only one camera, so let the others go." I finally got my way, and during my entire career in films I have never used more than one camera on anything. My idea was to plan every shot and edit in the camera.

The score for the film dropped all the songs from the play except for 'Makin' Whoopee.' Kahn and Donaldson were hired to compose other songs to fill in. This practice of dropping and adding songs was to become standard in the 1930s and 1940s, when a stage musical was made into a film. Many filmgoers who had also seen the stage version were puzzled by the removal of some of their favorite songs. The

OPPOSITE: Some of Berkeley's chorus girls from *Whoopee* (1930). The one at the bottom right is – Virginia Bruce.

RIGHT: William O'Neal played Phillippe in the stage version of *The New Moon* which opened on Broadway in 1928.

reason was a simple one – money. Many Hollywood studios either owned or were affiliated with music publishing houses, and royalties from songs written especially for the films went to the studios directly, instead of to the Broadway backers and composers.

In the film's opening sequence, a very young Betty Grable leads the chorus. This was the first time ever that chorines were filmed in close-up because, as Berkeley said to Goldwyn, 'We've got these beautiful girls, why not let the public see them?' The film also starred Eleanor Hunt as Sally, Paul Gregory as Wanenis, John (formerly Jack) Rutherford repeating his stage role as the sheriff and Ethel Shutta in the Ruth Etting role of Mary Custer.

The songs that were added were: 'Mission Number,' 'A Girlfriend of a Boyfriend of Mine,' 'Makin' Waffles,' 'My Baby Just Cares for Me,' 'Stetson' and 'The Song of the Setting Sun' by Donaldson and Kahn, and 'I'll Still Belong to You' by Nacio Herb Brown and Edward Eliscu.

One of the most durable of all Broadway hits, *The New Moon*, premiered in 1928. It had a book and lyrics by Oscar Hammerstein II, Frank Mandel and Lawrence Schwab, and music by the great Sigmund Romberg. Romberg had been a staff composer for the Schuberts in their Winter Garden Theater in the early part of the twentieth century, turning out forgettable hack music. But he was fired by none other than Al Jolson, who insisted on creating his own hits, cutting himself in as co-composer and then plugging the songs. (It was just such an arrangement that got George Gershwin his

first break. Jolson cut himself in on the song 'Swanee,' which he used in his 1919 Broadway musical *Sinbad*.) Romberg resisted the arrangement and was let go. But he had learned stagecraft at the Winter Garden, and he went on to become one of America's favorite operetta composers, with his *Maytime* (1917), *Blossom Time* (1921), *The Student Prince* (1924), *The Desert Song* (1926) and this production, *The New Moon*. The Broadway production, with its dances by Bobby Connolly, starred Evelyn Herbert, Robert Halliday and William O'Neal. It ran for 509 performances.

The New Moon was based on the life of a real person – according to the program: 'A musical romance of the Spanish Main ... founded on the life of Robert Misson, a French aristocrat whose autobiography was written in the late eighteenth century.' Misson (Halliday), the aristocrat turned revolutionary, is hiding in New Orleans in 1792 as a bondservant to M Beaunoir, a ship owner. The ship *New Moon* brings

OPPOSITE TOP: Emily Fitzroy,
Adolphe Menjou, Roland
Young and Grace Moore in the
ballroom scene from the
picture *New Moon* (1930).

OPPOSITE BOTTOM: Moore as
Princess Tanya Strogoff and
Lawrence Tibbett as
Lieutenant Michael Petroff in
New Moon – the movie.

RIGHT: Marilyn Miller went to
Hollywood to film her stage
triumph, *Sunny* (1930).

BELOW: A scene from the
Broadway version of *Sunny*
(1925) with Clifton Webb and
Marilyn Miller.

Ribaud (Max Figman) with secret orders from the French king to capture Misson. In the meantime, Misson has fallen in love with Beaunoir's daughter, Marianne (Herbert), as has Paul Duval, the captain of the *New Moon*. Misson's friend Philippe (O'Neal) warns him that love brings danger. Misson gets the sailors to fight for liberty.

Later, at a ball, Misson is in costume when Marianne confesses to friends that one kiss is being reserved for the right man, and she falls in love with the disguised Misson. Duval captures Misson and takes him to the *New Moon*. Later Marianne pretends to want to see Duval and comes aboard. She sends a tender note to Misson, who leads a successful mutiny and sails the ship to an island where a free government is set up. French ships arrive at the island to announce the French Revolution. Misson and Marianne are free and romance blossoms.

Some of the songs were: 'Lover Come Back to Me,' 'One Kiss,' 'Wanting You,' 'Softly, As in a Morning Sunrise' and 'Stout-Hearted Men.'

For some reason, the film version of *The New Moon*, now called simply *New Moon* (1930), transposed the story from New Orleans to Russia and from the eighteenth to the twentieth century. It starred two of the best voices ever to grace the soundstage – Lawrence Tibbett as Lieutenant Michael Petroff and Grace Moore as Princess Tanya Strogoff. This time, Tanya falls in love with Michael, even though she is engaged to a Russian governor called Brusiloff (Adolphe Menjou). Also in the cast were Roland Young, Guy Shy and Emily Fitzroy. The classic songs in the film were: 'Lover Come Back to Me,' 'One Kiss,' 'Stout-Hearted Men,' 'Wanting You,' 'Marianne,' 'Funny Little Sailor Men,' 'Farmer's Daughter' and 'What Is Your Price, Madame?'

Marilyn Miller's triumphs included the 1925 musical comedy *Sunny*, with book and lyrics by Oscar Hammerstein II and music by Jerome Kern. Directed by Hassard Short, with dances by Julian Mitchell, David Bennett and others, it featured Miller, Jack Donahue, Mary Hay, Clifton Webb, Joseph Cawthorn and George Olsen and his Orchestra. *Sunny* ran for 517 performances.

RIGHT: Marilyn Miller flanked by admirers after a circus performance in the film version of *Sunny* (1930).

BELOW:Paul Frawley with Marilyn Miller on the Broadway stage in *Sunny* (1925).

This was the first musical in which Kern and Hammerstein teamed up. Hammerstein later described *Sunny* as:

One of those tailor-made affairs in which [we] ... contrived to fit a collection of important theatrical talents. Our job was to tell a story with a cast that had been assembled as if for a revue. Charles Dillingham, the producer, had signed Cliff Edwards, who sang songs and played the ukelele and was known as "Ukelele Ike" [He was

later the voice of Jiminy Cricket in the Walt Disney film *Pinnochio* (1940)]. His contract required that he do his speciality between ten o'clock and ten-fifteen! So we had to construct our story in such a way that Ukelele Ike could come out and perform during that time and still not interfere with the continuity. In addition to Marilyn Miller, the star, there was Jack Donahue, a famous dancing comedian, and Clifton Webb and Mary Hay, who were a leading dance team of the time; Joseph Cawthorn, a star comedian; Esther Howard, another; Paul Frawley, the leading juvenile. In addition to the orchestra in the pit, we also had to take care of George Olsen's dance band on the stage. Well, we put it all together and it was a big hit.

Of course, with all those elements, the plot was complicated – it had to be – but it was essentially a showcase for Marilyn Miller: for her glamor and for her gifts in singing and dancing. She played Sunny Peters, a circus horseback rider in Southampton, England. A World-War-I US Army regiment from New York shows up, singing 'Sunny.' Love springs up between Sunny and Tom Warren (Frawley), one of the soldiers. Tom is now returning home, and Sunny cannot accompany him unless she remarries Jim Deming, the circus owner (Donahue), whom she divorced a few years earlier. She won't do this, and stows away aboard the ship that Tom is taking home.

One of the most unusual songs in all musical comedy appears in *Sunny*. It is 'Who?' – Sunny and Tom's love duet. It was a problem for Hammerstein to write lyrics for the song, since the refrain began with a single note held for two-and-a-quarter measures (or nine beats). It was impossible to use a phrase for such an extended melodic line, and if a single word were to be used, it had to be a word strong enough to sustain interest through five repetitions. The problem was solved with the word 'who,' and Kern always said that the selection of this word was responsible for the song's success. But he also added that Miller was the song's 'editor, critic, handicapper, clocker, tout and winner.'

The film version of *Sunny* appeared in 1930, starring the irrepressible Marilyn Miller, with Joe Donahue as the man she marries, plus Lawrence Gray, O P Heggie, Inez Courtney, Barbara Bedford, Judith Visselli and Clyde Cook. In addition to 'Sunny' and 'Who?,' the score included 'Two Little Love Birds,' 'D'ya Love Me?' and 'I Was Alone.'

The musical comedy *Manhattan Mary*, with music and lyrics by Buddy de Sylva, Lew Brown and Ray Henderson and a book by de Sylva, opened in 1927. The film version was released in 1930 with a new title, *Follow the Leader*. In it, Ed Wynn played a former acrobat turned waiter who finds himself elected the leader of a notorious gang called the 'Hudson Dunster' – something that could happen only in a musical comedy. Ginger Rogers starred with him as a singer looking for her first break on Broadway. Also in the cast were Stanley Smith, Lou Holtz, Lida Kane and a promising newcomer, Ethel Merman, who had been a last-minute substitute for Ruth Etting. In this role, she got to sing the fast-moving Sammy Fain-Irving Kahal number 'Satan's Holiday.' Other songs included 'Broadway' and 'The Heart of the World' by de Sylva, Brown and Henderson, from the original Broadway show, and 'Brother, Just Laugh It Off' by E Y Harburg, Arthur Schwartz and Ralph Rainger.

Mademoiselle Modiste was first seen on Broadway in 1905, with a book and lyrics by Henry Blossom and music by the father of American operetta, Victor Herbert, the Irish-born cellist who turned conductor and composer. It was directed by Fred G Latham and starred Fritzi Scheff, who had her greatest triumph singing 'Kiss Me Again,' William Pruette, Pauline Frederick and Walter Percival. The show had a run of 202 performances. It was revived in 1913 with Peggy Wood replacing Scheff, and there was another revival in 1929.

FRONT ROW, LEFT TO RIGHT: Tammany Young, Jack LaRue, Ed Wynn and James C Morton – *Follow the Leader* (1930).

1287-66

"THE MASCOT OF THE TROOP"

OPPOSITE TOP: Fritzi Scheff stands on a drum in a poster for the musical *Madamoiselle Modiste* (1905).

OPPOSITE BOTTOM: Fritzi Scheff tends to William Pruett in the stage version of *Madamoiselle Modiste* (1905).

FAR RIGHT: Miriam Hopkins and Maurice Chevalier starred in the film version of *The Waltz Dream*, retitled *The Smiling Lieutenant* (1931).

RIGHT: Fritzi Scheff, the belle of Broadway.

Before the Broadway opening, the show tried out in Washington, DC, and was seen by Theodore Roosevelt and his wife while they were tenants in the White House.

The story was typically musical comedy, set in Paris at Mme Cecile's hat shop on the Rue de la Paix, where Fifi (Scheff) works. She is in love with Captain Etienne de Bouvray (Pruette), but his family forbids him to marry a shopgirl. An American millionaire, Hiram Bent (Claude Gillingwater), becomes interested in Fifi and pays for her singing lessons. Fifi then becomes famous as 'Mme Bellini.' She sings at a charity affair at the Bouvray castle and impresses the Comte Henri de Bouvray (Percival) so much that he allows her to marry Etienne.

Fritzi Scheff had been a second-rate prima donna at the Metropolitan Opera, but this established her as a musical-comedy star. Oddly enough, her big hit, 'Kiss Me Again,' had not been written for this show. It was written in 1903 and put aside by Herbert, who resurrected it to go along with 'The Mascot of the Troop,' 'The Time and the Place and the Girl,' 'I

Want What I Want When I Want It,' and 'The Nightingale and the Star.'

The Hollywood version of *Mademoiselle Modiste*, retitled *Kiss Me Again*, was released in 1930. Walter Pidgeon and Bernice Claire were the stars, and they were supported by Edward Everett Horton, Claude Gillingwater and Frank McHugh. The film was shot in primitive Technicolor, and some new songs were included – 'When the Cat's Away,' 'If I Were on the Stage' and 'Love Me, Love My Dog.'

The first production of Oscar Straus's operetta *Ein Walzertraum* was unveiled in 1907 in Vienna, where it outdrew *The Merry Widow*. New companies were formed in Paris, London and New York, and the stars of the American production, now called *The Waltz Dream*, were Edward Johnson and Sophie Brandt. Johnson went on to become a leading singer with the Metropolitan Opera Company, and, still later, the head of that institution. The New York production kept the Straus score, adding lyrics by Clifford Grey and one completely new song, 'The Gay Lothario,' by Jerome Kern.

When Hollywood released it in 1931, *The Waltz Dream* had become *The Smiling Lieutenant*. Starring in the film were Maurice Chevalier, Miriam Hopkins, Claudette Colbert, Charles Ruggles and George Barbier. The songs included 'Toujours L'Amour,' 'In the Army,' 'Breakfast Table Love,' 'Jazz Up Your Lingerie,' 'Live for Today,' 'While Hearts Are Singing' and 'One More Hour of Love.'

In the film, Princess Anna (Hopkins) of tiny Flausenthurm visits Austria and falls in love with a dashing young lieutenant (Chevalier) of the Imperial Guard, whom she wants to marry. The lieutenant is a skirt-chasing fellow whose latest love is the very co-operative Franzi (Colbert), the leader of an all-girl orchestra. So far, so ridiculous.

Despite his liking for the ladies, the lieutenant simply isn't interested in the princess and consents to marry her only to avoid all sorts of nasty international complications. With such a lack of enthusiasm on his part, the marriage, as anyone could guess, is in trouble – that is, until Franzi, pretty well over her affair with Chevalier and finding that she likes

the princess, teaches the frustrated young woman a few tricks in the womanly art of captivating a man. The advice works, and they all live happily ever after.

Cole Porter's *Fifty Million Frenchmen* opened on Broadway in 1929, but not before it had had a stormy time in preparation. Irving Berlin, who was supposed to be the co-producer, withdrew before the project reached the planning table. Then, just as Warner Brothers put up the money, Porter and Herbert Fields (who was the writer of the book for the musical) were fined and suspended for six months by the Dramatists Guild for making a picture deal without the Guild's permission. After that, the director (Monty Woolley, no less) had a terrible time integrating the book, with its many varied scenes, into the production schedule. He ended up having to split the company into four units, each rehearsing in a different theater. The sets by Norman Bel Geddes

(father of Barbara Bel Geddes, who became a fine Broadway and film actress, then spent several years as a fixture on the television series 'Dallas') were so cumbersome that seven railroad cars were needed to ship them out of town for tryouts. When the sets got to Boston, it was found that the Colonial Theater there could not accommodate them, which caused a two-day delay in opening the show; rehearsals continued until one hour before curtain time. But the Boston audience and the critics raved.

The story was not over, however. *Fifty Million Frenchmen* opened in New York at the height of the stock-market crash, and the New York critics were not as enthusiastic as those in Boston. To help stimulate business, a full-page advertisement was placed in the newspapers on 19 December, quoting Irving Berlin, who called it 'The best musical comedy I have seen in years. More laughs than I have heard in a long

time. One of the best collections of song numbers I have listened to. It's worth the price of admission to hear Cole Porter's lyrics.' The show lasted 254 performances, which in those days represented a neat profit.

Porter, from a well-to-do family in Peru, Indiana, went off to Yale and never looked back on his Hoosier home. Until 1928, this urbane composer-lyricist, who had led the way to sophistication in Broadway and Hollywood productions, did most of his song-writing in Paris, Venice and on the Riviera. Then he made New York his home base, when he took an apartment at the Waldorf-Astoria Hotel.

The Broadway version of *Fifty Million Frenchmen* starred William Gaxton, Genevieve Tobin, Helen Broderick (the mother of a young man who would later win an Academy Award under the name of Broderick Crawford) and Evelyn Hoey, and was a spoof of American tourists in France. Violet Hildegarde (Broderick) was a bored American looking for shocking experiences; one of her favorite pastimes was sending risqué postcards back home. Peter Forbes (Gaxton), a wealthy playboy, falls in love with Looloo Carroll (Tobin), who is from Terre Haute (a little Hoosier joke from Porter). Forbes bets $25,000 that he can live for a month in Paris without any funds. He gets a job as a guide, becomes a gigolo and an Arabian magician, and wins both the bet and the girl.

Florenz Ziegfeld turned out to be a better judge of chorus girls than of music when he told the producer of *Fifty Million Frenchmen* that the show did not have 'one singable melody.' He must have been asleep when Gaxton sang 'You've Got That Thing' and 'You Do Something to Me.' For that matter, the other songs weren't too shabby – 'Find Me a Primitive Man,' 'I Worship You' and 'The Tale of an Oyster.' George Jean Nathan (admittedly a fellow Hoosier), the great drama critic, said 'When it comes to lyrics, this Cole Porter is so far ahead of the other boys in New York that there is just no race at all.'

Warner Brothers brought Gaxton and Broderick west to star in the film version of *Fifty Million Frenchmen* (1931), and the supporting stars included the comedy team of Ole Olsen and Chic Johnson, who would later become stars on their own in such zany shows as *Hellzapoppin* (1938) and in many movies like *Crazy House* (1942). Six songs were used from the stage show and, for some reason or other, another was added – George M Cohan's 'You Remind Me of My Mother.'

ABOVE: William Gaxton in a romantic moment from the film *Fifty Million Frenchmen* (1931).

OPPOSITE: Ole Olsen (left) and Chic Johnson steal a ride on a Paris cab in the film version of *Fifty Million Frenchmen*.

LEFT: Gaxton and his human piano in the stage version of *Fifty Million Frenchmen* (1929).

FAR LEFT: Genevieve Tobin co-starred with Gaxton on Broadway in *Fifty Million Frenchmen*.

Flying High opened on Broadway in 1930 with a book by Buddy de Sylva and Jack McGowen, lyrics by de Sylva and Lew Brown and music by Ray Henderson. The director was Edward Clark Lilley, and the choreographer was Bobby Connolly. It starred Oscar Shaw, Bert Lahr, Grace Brinkley and Kate Smith, and had a run of 357 performances.

The story, as usual, was simple and a little silly. Tod Addison (Shaw) was a flyer in a transcontinental race, which he wins; he also wins Eileen Cassidy (Brinkley), whom he met when his plane landed on top of her New York apartment house. Rusty Krause (Lahr) was a pilot who steals the plane of Tod's rival. Not knowing how to get it down, he wins an all-time record for keeping a plane in the air. Kate Smith played the part of Pansy Sparks, Rusty's girl friend. Some of the songs were 'I'll Know Him,' 'Red Hot Chicago,' 'Without Love,' 'Thank Your Father,' 'Good for You, Bad for Me,' 'Wasn't It Beautiful?' and 'Mrs Krause's Blue-Eyed Baby Boy.'

The film version of *Flying High* (titled *Happy Landing* in Britain) was released in 1931. The original score was

ABOVE: Bert Lahr as Rusty, and Kate Smith as Pansy, were in love in the stage production of *Flying High* (1930).

BELOW: Lahr re-created his stage role in the movie *Flying High* (1931). With him here is Charlotte Greenwood.

dumped, with the exception of the title song, in favor of a cluster of forgettable songs by Jimmy McHugh and Dorothy Fields, including 'Happy Landing' and 'We'll Dance Till Dawn.' But the movie introduced Bert Lahr to film audiences.

Also in the cast were Pat O'Brien, Charlotte Greenwood, Kathryn Crawford, Charles Winninger, Guy Kibbee and, before her days as a Hollywood gossip columnist, Hedda Hopper. Busby Berkeley choreographed two dance sequences for the movie.

The Gershwins' *Girl Crazy* opened on Broadway in 1930, with music by George, lyrics by Ira and a book by Guy Bolton and John McGowan. The director was Alexander Leftwich and the dances were by George Hale. The show ran for 272 performances.

Starring in *Girl Crazy* were Allen Kearns and Willie Howard. It also featured 19-year-old Ginger Rogers, a peppy young thing who introduced 'Embraceable You' and 'But Not For Me.' Then there was a 21-year-old ex-typist named Ethel Agnes Zimmerman, who had changed her name to Ethel Merman; she introduced 'I Got Rhythm,' the song that she used as her signature for more than 50 years, until her death in 1984.

Ethel Merman had a quality that can never again spring spontaneously into being. Call it classicalism, call it Olympian simplicity, call it God's pure untainted socko, but call it Merman. The world felt it immediately when she stepped onstage trumpeting 'I Got Rhythm' – holding one note of an entire incredible 16-bar chorus. She never took a singing lesson, but she immortalized more great tunes than anyone else in her 14 Broadway shows, including Cole Porter's *Anything Goes* (1934), Irving Berlin's *Annie Get Your Gun* (1946) and Jule Styne and Stephen Sondheim's *Gypsy* (1959). It was

said that in 'You're the Top' she gave muscle tone to Porter's sophistication; in 'There's No Business Like Show Business' she gave a Himalayan grandeur to Berlin's sentiment; and in 'Everything's Coming Up Roses' she turned *Gypsy*'s hard-driving Rose into the Mother Courage of Broadway. Merman even amazed the legendary conductor Arturo Toscanini, who said, 'Hers is not a human voice.'

Girl Crazy's story, as was usual for the musicals of the day, was a simple, perhaps idiotic, one. Danny Churchill (Kearns) is a Park Avenue playboy who is sent by his father to Custerville, Arizona, to get him away from temptation and women. He makes the trip across the country in a taxi driven by Gieber Goldfarb (Howard). Churchill turns Custerville into Sin City by opening a dude ranch staffed by showgirls and installing a gambling room. But he falls in love with the town postmistress, Molly Gray (Rogers). Merman played the role

of Kate Fothergill, wife of the gambling den's manager.

Among the songs were 'Sam and Delilah,' 'Boy, What Love Has Done to Me' and 'Bidin' My Time.' In the pit band for the show were soon-to-become Hall of Famers: Benny Goodman, Glenn Miller, Red Nichols, Gene Krupa, Jack Teagarden and Jimmy Dorsey.

When the film *Girl Crazy* came out in 1932, it featured a revised book by Herman Mankiewicz and starred the comedy team of Bert Wheeler (who played the cab driver) and Robert Woolsey (who was his passenger). Somehow, Wheeler finds himself elected sheriff of Custerville. Also in the film were Mitzi Green, Eddie Quillan, Stanley Fields, Dorothy Lee, Kitty Kelly, Arline Judge and Chris Pin Martin. The movie contained some of the songs from the original – 'Could You Use Me?' 'But Not For Me,' 'Embraceable You,' 'Sam and Delilah' and 'I Got Rhythm' – and the Gershwins wrote a brand new song for the picture, 'You've Got What Gets Me.'

But musical films had been suffering ever since the end of 1930, partly because they had been done to death, partly because audiences found that not even musicals could take their minds off the Great Depression – especially when they

ABOVE: Robert Woolsey, Arline
Judge and Stanley Fields in the
Hollywood version of *Girl
Crazy*, released in 1932.

RIGHT: Robert Woolsey, Eddie
Quillan, Kitty Kelly, Dorothy
Lee, Mitzi Green and Bert
Wheeler in the film *Girl Crazy*.

were dated operettas featuring unknowns from the stage whose vocal qualifications failed to make up for their visual inadequacies. In 1931 the death knell was sounded by a movie critic writing about a now-forgotten musical: 'Here is a reminder of the dear dead days that we thought beyond recall. For this is a musical extravaganza, replete with prancing chorines, low comics and "backstage" stuff. The picture must have been long delayed in release, for all its much-touted principals have by now gone back to the obscurity from whence they came.'

Obviously, the infant movie musical had overplayed its hand. The public was fed to the teeth with one partly or fully Technicolor song-and-dance epic after another. With the Depression hitting its depths, moviegoers, doling out their money one coin at a time, decided to spend no more of what little they had for entertainment on a tiresome, overexposed product. Grosses plunged.

The overexposure itself was bad enough, but there was something more behind the fall from grace. In its first years, the musical had pulled in audiences because sound was such a novelty. Now the novelty had worn off. The days of indiscriminate ticket-buying were over. Sound was an established fact of life and had to be accompanied up there on the

Joan Crawford, Johnny Mack Brown and Cliff Edwards. It featured songs with lyrics by Billy Rose and Edward Eliscu and music by Vincent Youmans. It was scrapped after ten days' shooting. Admittedly, it had also flopped in its 1929 stage version (36 performances), but despite its lack of success, three of its songs became standards – 'Great Day,' 'More Than You Know' and 'Without a Song.'

Another musical, *The March of Time*, designed as *The Hollywood Revue of 1930*, was given up as hopeless when it was near completion. It was finally finished in 1933 and called *Broadway to Hollywood*. Most of the revue part of the film was tossed out, but that left room for a dramatic story line. Starring were Frank Morgan (later to be the Wizard of Oz), Jackie Cooper, Jimmy Durante, Nelson Eddy (in his debut – he sang one song) and Mickey Rooney. In addition, two Marion Davies musicals were aborted – *The Five O'Clock Girl* and *Rosalie* – both Broadway transplants.

The next Broadway show that would be picked up by Hollywood, after the musical-film comeback ushered in by *42nd Street* (1933), was *The Cat and the Fiddle*, which had opened in New York in 1931. An operetta by Jerome Kern and Otto Harbach, it ran for a hefty 395 performances. It was a tale of the war between classical and popular music, in which the hero is a classical composer and the heroine a popular songwriter.

Otto Harbach also wrote the book. The director was José Ruben and the dance numbers were by Albertina Rasch. It starred Odette Myrtil, George Meader, Georges Metaxa and Bettina Hall.

LEFT: Hall, Metaxa and Meader: Broadway's *Cat and the Fiddle* (1931).

BELOW: MacDonald and Novarro: the film *Cat and the Fiddle*.

screen by those basic ingredients always needed to draw an audience – well-acted, well-told, well-produced stories. The musical, appearing in one form after another, simply hadn't filled the bill, too often sacrificing plot and character for the singing and dancing, too often sacrificing quality in the rush to get to the market and too often – no fault of its own, really, in the primitive days of a new technology – coming up with sound that was unacceptable except as a novelty.

With the downfall of the musicals, some fine projects were dropped. *Great Day* had gone into production in 1930 with

ABOVE: The glamorous Dolores Del Rio in a romantic moment with Dick Powell in the film *Wonder Bar* (1934).

RIGHT: Dolores Del Rio as Ynes and Ricardo Cortez as Harry, the dance team that entertains at the *Wonder Bar*.

OPPOSITE FAR RIGHT: A jealous Al Jolson, the owner of the *Wonder Bar*, eyes Ricardo Cortez as he and Dolores Del Rio take a bow after one of their numbers. A worried Dick Powell (to the rear), the band singer, looks on.

After *Show Boat*, Kern had wanted another musical that would break with tradition, eliminating chorus girls, production numbers and comedy routines. So *The Cat and the Fiddle* was set in twentieth-century Brussels. Shirley Sheridan (Hall) is an American popular-music composer in Brussels to study music. She meets Victor Florescu (Meader), who is a classical composer. They live in adjoining apartments and irritate each other with their music.

When *The Cat and the Fiddle* reached the screen in 1934, it had been modified by Samuel and Bella Spewack. The book had to be rewritten, because on stage the two had been 'living in sin' and trouble was expected from the Hays Office. The finale was filmed in three-color Technicolor.

This was Jeanette MacDonald's first big musical for MGM, but the real star of the movie was the dashing Ramon Novarro, playing the classical composer who meets MacDonald in Brussels and falls in love. But he is not a success, while she is, so he feels compelled to leave her. Naturally, they are reunited when, just before the premiere of his first operetta, the female lead (shades of *42nd Street*) walks out and Mac-

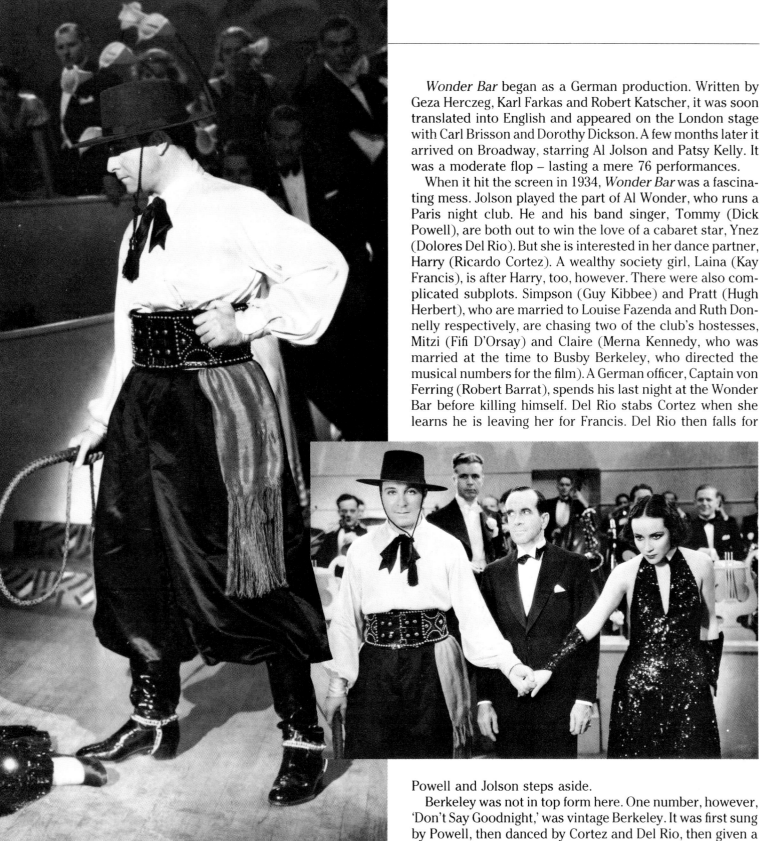

Wonder Bar began as a German production. Written by Geza Herczeg, Karl Farkas and Robert Katscher, it was soon translated into English and appeared on the London stage with Carl Brisson and Dorothy Dickson. A few months later it arrived on Broadway, starring Al Jolson and Patsy Kelly. It was a moderate flop – lasting a mere 76 performances.

When it hit the screen in 1934, *Wonder Bar* was a fascinating mess. Jolson played the part of Al Wonder, who runs a Paris night club. He and his band singer, Tommy (Dick Powell), are both out to win the love of a cabaret star, Ynez (Dolores Del Rio). But she is interested in her dance partner, Harry (Ricardo Cortez). A wealthy society girl, Laina (Kay Francis), is after Harry, too, however. There were also complicated subplots. Simpson (Guy Kibbee) and Pratt (Hugh Herbert), who are married to Louise Fazenda and Ruth Donnelly respectively, are chasing two of the club's hostesses, Mitzi (Fifi D'Orsay) and Claire (Merna Kennedy, who was married at the time to Busby Berkeley, who directed the musical numbers for the film). A German officer, Captain von Ferring (Robert Barrat), spends his last night at the Wonder Bar before killing himself. Del Rio stabs Cortez when she learns he is leaving her for Francis. Del Rio then falls for

Powell and Jolson steps aside.

Berkeley was not in top form here. One number, however, 'Don't Say Goodnight,' was vintage Berkeley. It was first sung by Powell, then danced by Cortez and Del Rio, then given a fantasy treatment. As Berkeley told it, 'I had them build me 60 tall, white, moveable columns, to move against a black background. The columns were on separate tracks, independent of each other and all controlled electrically. I had a hundred dancers dance with the columns. Then they all disappeared, and in their place was a huge forest of silver trees with a white reindeer running around. To get the effect I wanted, I built an octagon of mirrors – each 28 feet high and 12 feet wide – and inside this octad a revolving platform 24 feet in diameter. When I was drawing up my plans for this, everyone at the studio thought I had lost my mind. Even Sol Polito, one of the best cameramen I ever worked with, couldn't figure out how I was going to photograph a production from the inside without the camera being seen. Actually, when I

Donald throws herself into the breach by taking over the singing.

Also in the cast of *The Cat and the Fiddle* were Charles Butterworth, as a harpist who is never asked to play his instrument, and Frank Morgan as a girl chaser, plus Jean Hersholt, Vivienne Segal, Frank Conroy and Henry Armetta. The songs include 'The Night Was Made for Love,' 'The Breeze Kissed Your Hair,' 'One Moment Alone,' 'Impressions in a Harlem Flat,' 'Poor Pierrot,' 'She Didn't Say "Yes",' 'A New Love Is Old,' 'The Crystal Candelabra,' 'Ha! Cha Cha' and 'Try to Forget.'

RIGHT: The 1925 film version of *The Merry Widow*, with John Gilbert and Mae Murray. It was a silent.

BELOW: The 'Maxim's' number from the Broadway version of *The Merry Widow* (1907).

OPPOSITE TOP: A sad Maurice Chevalier and the Maxim's girls in the film *The Merry Widow* (1934). At far left is a young Sterling Holloway.

OPPOSITE BOTTOM: MacDonald and Chevalier.

figured it out in my office using eight little compacts – the kind girls carry in their handbags – I discovered there was a way of moving at the center of the mirrors without being reflected.'

But, as far as taste is concerned, Berkeley hit rock bottom in the same film. In a number called 'Going to Heaven on a Mule,' Jolson, in blackface, plays the part of a Southern field hand who loves his mule so much that when he dies he takes the beast to Heaven with him. He passes St Peter's Pearly Gates and enters Paradise, singing to the accompaniment of 200 children, also in blackface, who compose the angel choir. Other songs in the film were 'Why Do I Dream These Dreams?,' 'Vive La France,' 'Tango Del Rio' and 'Wonder Bar.'

The Merry Widow, Franz Lehar's masterpiece, premiered in Vienna in 1905 as *Die lustige witwe*. At first, it was not a tremendous success, and the producers had to distribute free tickets. But by the fiftieth performance, business had picked up, and by 1907 it had been produced in almost every city in the English-speaking world. It ran for 778 performances in London and 416 in New York. After the Broadway opening on 21 October 1907, a Merry Widow craze swept the United States. 'Merry Widow' hats were put on sale, as were Merry Widow corsets, trains for ladies' gowns, lunches, cigarettes and cocktails.

The Merry Widow opened, with a Spanish translation, in Buenos Aires, Argentina, in 1907 and was soon playing in five different theaters there in five different languages at the same time. Altogether, it has been translated into 25 languages, has been performed more than a quarter of a million times, and has supplied the theme for three ballets, a 'Holiday on Ice' show, a 1907 Swedish short subject and three Hollywood films.

The third and best movie version of *The Merry Widow* (1934) starred Maurice Chevalier and Jeanette MacDonald and was directed by Ernst Lubitsch. All three of them had been stolen from Paramount by Metro-Goldwyn-Mayer. The

result was one of the great screen musicals of all time. Despite its lavish production techniques, it managed to retain that delicate 'Lubitsch Touch' which characterized the director's best work.

The German-born Lubitsch, a successful stage actor and screen director in Europe before coming to Hollywood to direct Mary Pickford in *Rosita* (1923), was undoubtedly the most impressive of the early movie-musical directors. The fact is, he was impressive in any assignment he took on, whether it was a musical, a drama or a comedy. It was, however, in comedy – and its musical counterpart – that he earned his greatest fame, displaying both a talent for satire and a deft ability for handling sophisticated themes. Like most other directors of the late 1920s, Lubitsch was not experienced with musicals when he first took them on, but, having brushed them with his distinctive skill, they emerged as the very best that the early musicals had to offer.

Lubitsch musicals, from beginning to end, were delightful, risqué puffs of froth. Their main themes were sex and money, with the former a charming game played by those who had ample supplies of the latter. Always involved were fairy-tale characters: debonair, lavishly uniformed guardsmen with roving eyes who became the love targets of queens and princesses from imaginary little European countries.

That such characters and locales were selected for the plots was no accident. Lubitsch understood that Americans liked sex and money, but he understood just as well that, should his pictures be given an American setting, the bluenose side of the American character might well surface with annoyance and demand a retribution at the film's end that simply wouldn't work in a happy musical. He was dead right. Coming out of Hollywood at the time was a stream of sexually accented pictures, and not a few scandals. This eventually led to a moviegoers' revolt and the establishment of the ridiculously strict Will Hays Motion Picture Production Code in 1930.

The Merry Widow was also the end of the most interesting part of Jeanette MacDonald's career. She had been the only singer in pictures who could sing with her tongue in her cheek. But when she started her eight-operetta partnership with Nelson Eddy, although she still retained a certain amount of sauce, it was no longer characterized by sexual innuendo but by sentimentality. Although Chevalier had wanted Grace Moore as the widow, MacDonald was irresistibly charming.

Also in the cast were Edward Everett Horton, Una Merkel, George Barbier, Minna Gombell, Ruth Channing, Sterling

OPPOSITE TOP: *The Gay Divorcée* (1934).

OPPOSITE BOTTOM: *The Gay Divorce* (1932).

Astaire and Rogers dance 'The Continental' in *The Gay Divorcée*. It won the best-song Oscar.

Holloway, Donald Meek, Akim Tamiroff and Herman Bing. With a few changes in the supporting cast, a French version, *La Veuve Joyeuse*, was shot at the same time. The lyrics were redone by professionals. The lilting 'Merry Widow Waltz' had lyrics by Lorenz Hart, as did 'Girls Girls Girls,' 'Vilia,' 'Maxim's,' 'Melody of Laughter' and 'If Widows Were Rich.' Gus Kahn contributed the words to 'Tonight Will Teach Me to Forget.'

The Gay Divorce hit Broadway in 1932 with a book by Dwight Taylor, which he had adapted from a play by Kenneth Webb and Samuel Hoffenstein from an unproduced play by J Hartley Manners. It had words and music by Cole Porter and was directed by Howard Lindsay, with dance numbers by Carl Randall and Barbara Newberry. The stars were Fred Astaire (in his first musical-comedy appearance without his sister Adele), Luella Gear, Eric Blore, Erik Rhodes and Claire Luce. It ran a respectable 248 performances.

Basically, *The Gay Divorce* was a bedroom farce. Mimi (Luce) wants to divorce her husband because he is so dull. She sets off for an English resort, hoping to be compromised so that her husband will sue for the divorce. The person who has been selected as her lover (Rhodes) has been given a password, which Guy (Astaire) intercepts. A cunning lad, he meets Mimi by passing himself off as the co-respondent. Naturally, he wins her.

Porter had liked the original play so much that he began writing songs for it before he was under contract to do the score. He got the idea for the show's hit song, 'Night and Day,' from hearing a Mohammedan muezzin cry the hour of prayer in Morocco. Other songs from the show were 'After You, Who?,' 'Mister and Missus Fitch,' 'I Still Love the Red, White and Blue,' 'I've Got You in My Mind' and 'You're in Love.'

When the film version appeared in 1934, Pandro S Berman, the 29-year-old producer, had thrown out all the songs except 'Night and Day.' Inserted was what would become a perennial favorite, however – the 17-minute production number 'The Continental' by Herb Magidson and Con Conrad. It was created just for Fred Astaire and Ginger Rogers to dance to.

By decree of the Hays Office, the movie was retitled *The Gay Divorcée*, apparently because Hollywood feared to intimate that divorces could become happy arrangements. The picture had the empty-headed 'mistaken identity' plot, but that didn't matter. The truth was that no one in the audience cared about the plot. They went to the theater to see Fred and Ginger dance. The film did have some comedy, too. There was Erik Rhodes as the stage Italian, Eric Blore as the stage English butler, Edward Everett Horton doing his double-takes and a very young Betty Grable.

The choreographer for the movie was one Hermes Panagiotopulos, better known under his professional name of Hermes Pan. He worked with Astaire and Rogers in later films and deserved a lot of the credit for their wonderful dance numbers.

The Gay Divorcée set the tone for all of the Astaire-Rogers movies. Fred, alias Guy Holden, sees Ginger and it seems to be love at first glance. He pursues her hither and yon through a glamorous resort hotel. She resists, but all one has to do is see them dance to know that he'll get her. This was no Broadway-backstage musical where dances had nothing to do with the story line, such as it was. It was when Fred and Ginger danced that audiences saw how they felt about each other. All the sensuality missing in the dialogue emerged when they were on the ballroom floor. The film was a breakthrough for musicals. For the first time, not the songs, but the dances, conveyed emotion. No wonder Fred and Ginger didn't bother with the obligatory Hollywood romantic kiss. They didn't need it.

The picture presented them in two extraordinarily good dance numbers – the aforementioned 'The Continental,' which was the first song to win an Academy Award, and 'Night and Day.' For the Astaire-Rogers team, and for the development of the musical film, 'Night and Day' was a far more significant accomplishment. Danced in an art deco ballroom, it established a dramatic story line – the girl reluctantly beginning to dance with the amorous young man, then eventually surrendering herself to him as the music and their partnership in it flow on – that was to be a hallmark of their own best numbers. And, allowing very human emotions to show through a dance routine as it did, it was a theme that, with all the variations that reluctance changed into exultation can achieve, has been used time and time again by

BELOW: Hall, Slezak, Carrington and Carminati on stage in *Music in the Air* (1932).

Slezak as Karl and Carrington as Sieglinde on their trip to Munich – *Music in the Air*.

Fox made the film version of *Music in the Air* (1934) with Gloria Swanson as a German opera star and John Boles as an opera lyricist. Obviously, they are suspicious of each other.

musicals through the years. No wonder that Astaire later had his legs insured for a million dollars.

Also in *The Gay Divorcée* were Betty Grable's renditions of 'Let's K-nock K-nees' and 'Don't Let it Bother You' by Mack Gordon and Harry Revel, and the Magidson and Conrad song 'Needle In a Haystack.'

Music In the Air, with music by Jerome Kern and lyrics by Oscar Hammerstein II, opened on Broadway in 1932. The production was directed by Hammerstein and Kern and starred Walter Slezak, Katherine Carrington, Tullio Carminati and Al Shean and ran for 342 performances.

The setting was the Bavarian town of Edendorf, where Dr Walter Lessing (Shean) teaches music and conducts the local choral society. His daughter Sieglinde (Carrington) and the schoolmaster, Karl Reder (Slezak), are in love. Karl writes the lyrics for Lessing's song, 'I've Told Every Little Star,' and he and Sieglinde go to Munich on foot to have it published. In Munich, Karl flirts with Frieda Hatzfeld, an operetta star (Natalie Hall), and Sieglinde befriends an opera librettist, Bruno Mahler (Carminati), who asks her to appear in his opera. Sieglinde fails as a performer, Frieda becomes bored with Karl, and Sieglinde and Karl go back to Edendorf.

Some of the other songs were 'Tingle Tangle,' 'Egern on the Tegern Sea' and 'The Song Is You.' But when the movie was made in 1934, starring Gloria Swanson and John Boles,

only six of the original numbers were kept.

Swanson played the part of the German prima donna and Boles's role was that of an opera lyricist rather than a librettist. The schoolmaster was played by Douglass Montgomery (with a singing voice dubbed by James O'Brien), and the young girl was played by June Lang (vocals dubbed by Betty Hiestand). Al Shean repeated his Broadway role as the father. Also in the cast were Reginald Owen, Joseph Cawthorn, Hobart Bosworth and Marjorie Main (later to become Ma Kettle). The six songs that remained were 'I've Told Every Little Star,' 'There's a Hill Beyond a Hill.' 'One More Dance,' 'The Song Is You,' 'We Belong Together' and 'I'm So Eager.'

One of the Broadway hits of 1903 was *Babes In Toyland*, with its book and lyrics by Glen MacDonough and its music by Victor Herbert. Directed by Julian Mitchell, it starred William Norris, Bessie Wynn, George W Denham and Mabel Barrison. It lasted for 192 performances.

Actually, the story was a rip-off of another Broadway musical of that same year – *The Wizard of Oz* (more of that later). In this case, the setting was changed from the Land of Oz to Mother Goose Land and Toyland to introduce charac-

ters from fairy tales, children's storybooks and nursery rhymes. Toys were even brought to life. But it had the tremendous asset of Herbert's music – one of his most tuneful scores.

Alan and Jane (Norris and Barrison) are shipwrecked on the shores of Mother Goose Land and meet Jack and Jill, Tom Thumb, Bo-Peep, Red Riding Hood, Tommy Tucker, etc. Their Uncle Barnaby (who was trying to steal their estate by getting them shipwrecked in the first place) forecloses the mortgage on Mother Hubbard's house, but is thrown in a pond. Barnaby hires two evil characters to get the children lost in the Forest of No Return, but they are saved by gypsies. The children now come to Toyland, a country ruled by the tyrant Toymaker. Toymaker brings the toys to life, but they plot against him, and he is overthrown and everybody lives happily ever after.

Among the hits were 'Toyland,' 'The March of the Toys,' 'I Can't Do That Sum,' 'Go To Sleep, Slumber Deep' and 'Rock-a-Bye Baby.'

Stan Laurel and Oliver Hardy starred in the 1934 movie version of *Babes In Toyland.* Produced by Hal Roach of 'Our Gang' comedy fame, it was a delight. Laurel and Hardy played Stannie Dum and Ollie Dee, a couple of toymakers. Laurel makes a terrible mistake. Instead of making 600 soldiers one foot high, he makes 100 soldiers six feet high. But things turn out all right. When the walls of Toyland are stormed by Bogeymen, the huge toy soldiers repel them.

Also in the cast were Charlotte Henry (Bo-Peep), Felix Knight (Tom-Tom), Johnny Downs (Little Boy Blue), Jean Darling (Curly Locks), Virginia Karns (Mother Goose), Florence Roberts (Widow Peep) and Alice Dahl (Miss Muffet). The songs included 'Toyland,' 'Don't Cry, Bo-Peep.' 'A Castle in Spain,' 'I Can't Do That Sum,' 'Go to Sleep, Slumber Deep' and 'March of the Toys' from the original stage musical, and 'Who's Afraid of the Big Bad Wolf' by Ann Ronell and Frank Churchill.

Perhaps it was the influence of the immensely popular Jeanette MacDonald-Nelson Eddy films of the time, but Hollywood seemed to change course a bit in the last half of the

1930s. Silly-plotted sophisticated Broadway musicals seemed to give way to silly-plotted costumed Broadway operettas. One of the exceptions to this trend was *Roberta*.

Roberta, with its book and lyrics by Otto Harbach and its music by Jerome Kern, opened on Broadway in 1933. Directed by Hassard Short and choreographed by José Limón, it featured Tamara, Raymond E (later Ray) Middleton, Fay Templeton, George Murphy (later a US Senator), Lyda Roberti, Bob Hope, and, in small roles, Sidney Greenstreet and Fred MacMurray.

Kern was the one to see the possibilities in a musical based on Alice Duer Miller's novel *Gowns by Roberta*, and that was the title under which it began out-of-town tryouts in Philadelphia. It was a flop there. Max Gordon, the producer, realized that he had to redo the whole production, and he called in Hassard Short to direct and doctor the play. The show was restaged, the costumes and the sets thrown out in favor of more lavish gowns and scenery. Still, it didn't do well when it opened in New York. The critics accused it of being boring – just a musical fashion show. But when one of its hit songs, 'Smoke Gets In Your Eyes,' began to be heard on the radio, business picked up and the show ran for 295 performances.

The story was about an All-American klutzy fullback, John Kent (Middleton), who is jilted by his girl friend, the debutante Sophie Teal (Roberti). Still carrying the torch, he tries to forget by going to Paris with his friend Huckleberry Haines (Bob Hope, in his first good role on Broadway). Kent's Aunt Minnie (Templeton), known in Paris as Roberta, the *coutouriere*, runs a salon. For some reason, she lets Kent take over as manager, with the aid of the shop's chief designer, the Russian expatriate Stephanie (Tamara). Love

ABOVE: The Toymaker threatens Bo-Peep (Charlotte Henry) in the movie version of *Babes in Toyland* (1934).

OPPOSITE TOP: A scene in the Toymaker's factory in the Broadway production of *Babes in Toyland* (1903).

OPPOSITE BOTTOM: William Norris and Mabel Barrison starred as Alan and Jane in the stage production of *Babes in Toyland* (1903).

RIGHT: Stan Laurel, as Stannie Dum, points to one of the six-foot-tall wooden soldiers while Oliver Hardy, as Ollie Dee, gapes in amazement, in the film version of *Babes in Toyland* (1934).

blooms between the two, despite the reappearance of Sophie, who has changed her mind about the football player. The salon is a roaring success and it turns out that Stephanie is really a Russian princess.

Face it: it was dull. But the score contained some of the most memorable songs in the history of Broadway, including three masterpieces. The first was 'Smoke Gets in Your Eyes,' which Kern had written, not for *Roberta*, but as a theme for a radio series that never got off the drawing board. When a song was needed to reflect Stephanie's memories of her childhood, Kern pulled the melody out of his trunk and Harbach wrote the lyrics to it. Everyone hated it because Kern had set it to strict march tempo, but when he gave it a slower tempo and a more sentimental mood, it was recognized as the musical wonder that it is. The other two classics were 'Yesterdays' and 'The Touch of Your Hand.' Bob Hope's rendition of 'You're Devastating' was also a winner.

Roberta's cast was a strange one, with one has-been and several newcomers. Fay Templeton, who had been a musical-comedy star for years, was coaxed out of retirement for this, her last show. She was no longer a leading lady, and

weighed some 250 pounds. Indeed, Harbach wrote her part so that she could perform most of the role sitting down. On the newcomers' side, Tamara had been discovered working at the Kretchma, a New York Russian restaurant. Bob Hope was found by Max Gordon doing a comedy act in vaudeville at the Palace Theater in New York. (The story goes that when Gordon asked Kern about getting Hope to play Huckleberry Haines, Kern retorted, 'What are you trying to do, palm off one of your old vaudevillians on me?')

Three members of the cast were complete unknowns who were yet to make their mark. Sidney Greenstreet, long before *Casablanca* and *The Maltese Falcon*, played the tiny part of Lord Delves, one of Roberta's friends. On stage was a jazz band, 'The California Collegians,' one of whose members was saxophonist Fred MacMurray. The smallest role was played by George Murphy, who went completely unnoticed. Who would have thought that he would have a long career as a song-and-dance man in Hollywood and end up becoming a United States Senator?

The film version of *Roberta* appeared in 1935, and it was dull, too. But it had the advantage of the wonderful dancing of Fred Astaire and Ginger Rogers. Officially, they were not the stars – Irene Dunne and Randolph Scott were – but they stole the picture. Fred, with his thin voice and thinning hair, seemed to pass through a magical transformation when he danced. He became the most attractive, most elegant, most debonair human being on earth. If he had danced with Helen of Troy, it would have been hard to keep one's eyes off him and on her. So it was a tribute to Ginger Rogers that she not

ABOVE: Bob Hope, Ray Middleton, Lyda Roberti and Sidney Greenstreet in the original cast of the Broadway production of *Roberta* (1933).

OPPOSITE: Bob Hope plays and sings for Fay Templeton (seated), as (left to right) Ray Middleton, Tamara and George Murphy look on in Broadway's *Roberta*.

RIGHT: Although Fred Astaire and Ginger Rogers stole the show, top billing went to Irene Dunne and Randolph Scott in the film version of *Roberta* (1935).

only did not fade from view, but added a tart glamor uniquely her own.

Two songs were added by Kern and lyricist Dorothy Fields – 'Lovely to Look At,' which became a standard, and 'I Won't Dance' (but, of course, Fred did), which was not new, but was resurrected, with new lyrics by Fields, from the score of *Three Sisters*, a Kern-Oscar Hammerstein II Broadway flop of 1934. 'Indiana' by Ballard MacDonald and James Hanley was stuck in. The songs retained from the original Broadway show were 'Smoke Gets in Your Eyes,' 'Yesterdays' and 'I'll Be Hard to Handle,' but the latter song had new lyrics by Bernard Dougall. Pandro S Berman had struck again.

Victor Herbert's *Naughty Marietta* premiered on Broadway in 1910. With a book and lyrics by Rida Johnson Young, it was directed by Jacques Coini and starred Emma Trentini and Orville Harrold. It ran for 136 performances, with a story set in New Orleans in 1780, when the city was under Spanish rule. Captain Richard Warrington (Harrold) and his troops are looking for a pirate named Bras-Pique. Warrington meets Marietta (Trentini), a Neapolitan lady of noble birth who has fled from her wedding in Italy to join a group of girls en route to Louisiana to marry New World planters. In the meantime, Adah (Marie Duchene), a slave of Etienne Grandet (Edward Martindale), the son of the lieutenant governor, realizes that she loves her master. At a ball, Etienne falls in love with Marietta, and auctions off Adah to Warrington, who intends to free her. Marietta doesn't understand his intentions, so she decides to marry Etienne. Then she finds out that Etienne is really Bras-Pique, as does Warrington. Etienne escapes and Warrington wins Marietta to the tune of 'Ah! Sweet Mystery of Life.'

In addition to 'Ah! Sweet Mystery . . . ,' there were other great songs. Among them were 'Tramp, Tramp, Tramp,' 'Italian Street Song,' ' 'Neath the Southern Moon' and 'I'm Falling in Love with Someone.'

Orville Harrold sings 'I'm Falling in Love with Someone' to Emma Trentini in the 1910 Broadway version of *Naughty Marietta* (1910).

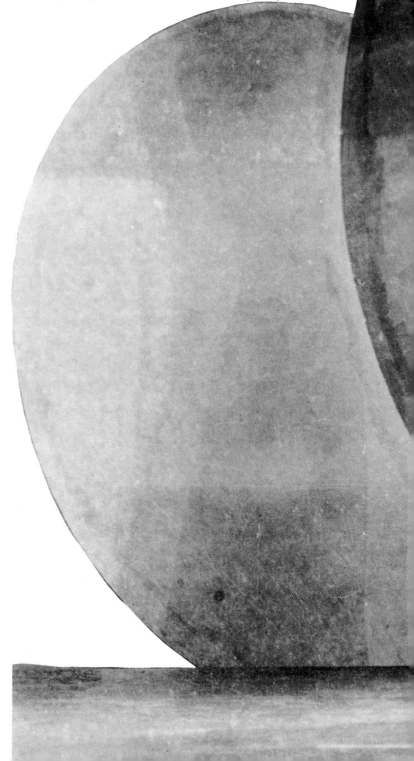

The show stoppers in action: Fred Astaire and Ginger Rogers dance in the film version of Jerome Kern's *Roberta* (1935).

The film, which appeared in 1935, kept only those five songs from the original, and still had to add new lyrics by Gus Kahn for 'Tramp, Tramp, Tramp' and ''Neath the Southern Moon.' MGM had bought the rights to the Broadway show earlier, hoping to star Marion Davies as Marietta. But when the beginning of the decade brought its musical-film slump, it was shelved. The operetta, however, was a favorite of Louis B Mayer, and by the time it was safe to have movies sing again, so was Jeanette MacDonald. But Mayer knew he was taking a chance when he filmed it, and hired W S Van Dyke II as the director – he was known as 'One-Take Woody' and brought things in under budget. Mayer hired Nelson Eddy as the leading man. Eddy had been under contract to MGM for two years and had been in films for a grand total of seven minutes.

This was the first of eight pictures that MacDonald made with Eddy. She was never to get beyond her sugary persona as Eddy's soprano. The mix, however, between these two and their saccharine romantic stories spelled 'gold mine' for Metro-Goldwyn-Mayer.

Marietta was only Eddy's fourth film, but he became a star. He was blond. He sang baritone. And the film made more money for the studio than had any musical up to that time. Considering everything, especially Eddy's lack of screen experience, the venture had been a risky one. But *Naughty Marietta* paid handsome dividends when it was released.

TOP: Elsa Lanchester and Frank Morgan appeared with Nelson Eddy in the film *Naughty Marietta*.

ABOVE: Jeanette MacDonald and Nelson Eddy in their first film together – *Naughty Marietta* (1935).

RIGHT: Bing Crosby, the stowaway, masquerades as a steward, which surprises Merman and Ruggles in the film version of *Anything Goes* (1936).

BELOW: Ethel Merman and chorus belting out 'Blow, Gabriel, Blow' in the Broadway show *Anything Goes* (1934).

Somehow, the disparate singers – MacDonald vivacious and Eddy almost hopelessly wooden (a problem that was to dog him throughout his career) – charmed audiences as a team, perhaps because of their youthful attractiveness (he was 34, she was 28), perhaps because their voices, both so genuinely good, blended to near perfection. They were immediately given the sickeningly sweet tag 'the Singing Sweethearts,' and spent much of the next seven years working together.

In the film version of *Naughty Marietta*, the title character became a French princess who is escaping her marriage to a Spanish grandee. Frank Morgan was the governor of Louisiana, and others in the cast were Elsa Lanchester, Douglass Dumbrille, Joseph Cawthorn, Walter Kingsford, Harold Huber, Edward Brophy and Akim Tamiroff. Other songs in the movie were 'Chansonette,' 'Antoinette and Anatola,' 'Prayer,' 'The Owl and the Bob Cat' and 'Mon Ami Pierrot,' a traditional French folk song. The sound engineer, Douglas Shearer (brother of Norma Shearer), won the

second of his 12 Academy Awards for the recording of the sound track.

Anything Goes, with a book by Guy Bolton and P G Wodehouse revised by Howard Lindsay and Russel Crouse, songs by Cole Porter and dances by Robert Alton, opened on Broadway in 1934. It starred Ethel Merman, William Gaxton, Victor Moore and Bettina Hall and ran for 420 performances. This was the vehicle in which Porter really made Ethel Merman a star.

Vinton Freedley, the producer, had asked Bolton and Wodehouse to come up with a musical book about some screwball characters on a gambling ship that is wrecked on the high seas. But then, on 8 September 1934, the *Morro Castle* went up in flames off the coast of New Jersey, and 134 people were killed. Suddenly it was felt that shipwrecks could not be the subject of musical comedy. Lindsay and Crouse were asked to prepare a new text, and this was the first of their many splendid collaborations.

They came up with a plot in which Reno Sweeney (Merman), a night-club entertainer, is in unrequited love with Billy Crocker (Gaxton), and is taking a trip to Europe on a luxury liner in order to forget him. Crocker shows up as an unlisted passenger who has sneaked on board to say good-bye to his new girl friend, Hope Harcourt (Hall). He has stayed on board without ticket or passport, not to mention luggage. But a ticket and passport are given to him by another passenger – Public Enemy Number 13 (Moore) – who is masquerading as the Reverend Doctor Moon in order to flee from the law. (The credentials became available when one of Moon's criminal confederates failed to show up on the boat.) Meanwhile, the FBI in Washington sends a message to the captain that Moon is as harmless as a sponge. Moon is insulted, since he wants to be promoted from Number 13 to Number 1: 'I can't understand this administration,' he complains.

Silly though the story line was, the Porter songs in *Anything Goes* were spectacular. Russel Crouse said of the score: 'All I can say is that no doubt Ludwig von Beethoven, Johann Sebastian Bach, Wolfgang Amadeus Mozart, Richard Wagner ... Josef Hayden and Francis Scott Key could have marched into the room and I wouldn't have looked up.'

But when the musical was made into a film in 1936, only four of the original songs were kept, in addition to 'All Through the Night,' which was used as background music only. The four were 'You're the Top,' 'I Get a Kick out of You,' 'Anything Goes' and 'There'll Always Be a Lady Fair.' In the ads, it was billed as 'Cole Porter's *Anything Goes*,' but in fact it was 60 percent the work of Hoagy Carmichael, Frederick Holland, Richard Whiting, Leo Robin and Edward Heyman. Eight Porter songs had been deep-sixed. Some of the new songs were the eminently forgettable 'Sailor Beware' by Whiting and Robin, 'Shanghai-De-Ho' and 'My Heart and I' by Hollander and Robin, and 'Moonburn' by Heyman and Carmichael.

As far as the cast was concerned, Ethel Merman was in there pitching, re-creating her stage role as Reno Sweeney.

But substituting Charles Ruggles for Victor Moore was a terrible mistake. And Bing Crosby was not the one to use in place of William Gaxton. In short, it lacked sparkle, and sparkle was the thing most needed to overcome the silliness of the plot. Also in the cast were Ida Lupino, Arthur Treacher and Margaret Dumont.

Rose Marie had been a big hit in 1924, lasting for 557 performances. With its book and lyrics by Otto Harbach and Oscar Hammerstein II and its music by Rudolf Friml and Herbert Stothart, it soon became one of the classic operettas of all time. Directed by Paul Dickey with dances by David Bennett, it starred Dennis King, Mary Ellis, William Kent and Arthur Deagon.

The story goes that Arthur Hammerstein, the producer, came up with the idea that the Canadian Rockies would make a good setting for an operetta – he was probably

OPPOSITE TOP: Ethel Merman leads the chorus in the 'Shanghai-De-Ho' number in the movie *Anything Goes* (1936).

RIGHT: Jeanette MacDonald and Nelson Eddy singing and romancing on the shores of Lake Tahoe (standing in for Canada) in the motion picture version of *Rose Marie* (1936).

BELOW: William Gaxton as Billy, Ethel Merman as Reno and Victor Moore as Moon were the stars on Broadway in *Anything Goes* (1934).

thinking of the magnificent sets that could be created. Then it occurred to him that using the Royal Canadian Mounted Police in the show would add some color to the costumes (besides, their uniforms were already designed). Hammerstein went to Otto Harbach to work out a libretto for him, and Harbach, in turn, invited Arthur Hammerstein's nephew, Oscar Hammerstein II, to collaborate with him. Friml and Stothart wrote the music, and the rest is history. Successful as *Rose Marie* was, it remains the only musical comedy set in the Canadian Rockies.

Rose Marie La Flamme (Ellis) is a singer at Lady Jane's Hotel and a favorite with the Mounties and fur trappers who make up her audiences. Ed Hawley (Frank Green), a trader, loves her, but she is in love with Jim Kenyon (King), a young man who has gone west to seek his fortune. Hawley tries to frame Kenyon by suggesting that he has killed an Indian brave, although he knows that the brave was killed by one of his (Hawley's) Indian girl friends. (Incidentally, *Rose Marie* was the first American musical to involve a murder.) Rose Marie, suspecting that Hawley can exonerate Kenyon, offers herself to him if he will clear Jim of the charges. Then come the Mounties, led by Sergeant Malone (Deagon). They clear Jim and discredit Hawley. Love triumphs over all.

The reviews were mixed. The *New York Telegram* gave it a left-handed compliment: 'Its plot clings together sufficiently to sustain interest.' But the New York *Tribune* raved: 'A bon-voyage basket of musical shows. There is drama and

melodrama, musical comedy, grand opera, and opéra-comique.... A beautiful composite photograph of a three-ring circus ... [with] the most entrancing music it has long been our privilege to hear.' Mary Ellis had been a soprano with the Metropolitan Opera Company, and Arthur Hornblow, the critic, was thrilled. 'She establishes herself as the peer of any musical-show star in the country.' Among the songs were 'Indian Love Call,' 'Rose Marie,' 'The Door of My Dreams,' 'The Mounties' and 'Totem Tom-Tom.'

While it was running its 16 months on Broadway, *Rose Marie* had four touring companies, one of which brought the production back to Broadway in 1927.

The 1936 filmed version of *Rose Marie* starred Nelson Eddy and Jeanette MacDonald. This was not the first time that the operetta had appeared on screen, but the 1928 Joan Crawford vehicle had had a drastically altered plot, and music but no singing. This time around, the part of Rose Marie had been intended for Grace Moore, the American opera star, but she had prior commitments. The studio couldn't wait for her, because the outdoor scenes were to be shot at Lake Tahoe – giving a breadth to 'Totem Tom-Tom' and 'Indian Love Call' – and the film had to be made in the summer, before the snow began to fall.

The plot was changed so that Eddy, the Mountie, could be Rose Marie's boy friend. Rose Marie's role was changed from Rose Marie La Flamme, the backwoods singer, to Rose Marie La Flor, the Canadian opera star. She is strictly a high-class lady who goes to the wilds of Canada because her brother is there, having escaped from jail and murdered a Mountie. En route, MacDonald meets Eddy, the Mountie who is tracking down her brother. In this film everybody wins except the brother. He has to go to jail again.

In *Rose Marie*, a young actor in his second picture was tapped as a future star – James Stewart. But another young actor, in his fifth picture, was hardly noticed – David Niven.

ABOVE: An 1844 lithograph of a scene from *The Bohemian Girl* (1843), with Arthur Seguin as Devilshoof, Frazer as Thaddeus and Mrs Seguin as Arline.

RIGHT: Stan Laurel (left) and Oliver Hardy played gypsies in the movie version of *The Bohemian Girl* (1936).

OPPOSITE: Jeanette MacDonald played the title role in the 1936 filming of *Rose Marie* – as an opera star.

For us today it is hard to take 'Indian Love Call' seriously. But that doesn't make us right and millions of people in 1936 wrong. It just means that styles have changed. 'When I'm calling you-ou-ou-ou-ou-ou-ou' is rather laughable in the 1980s, but it set a lot of hearts pounding in 1936. Nelson Eddy and Jeanette MacDonald were trained singers. They were supposed to bring culture to the audience. Compared to them, Busby Berkeley, Astaire, and Rogers were low-brows. It was also all right to be drippingly romantic in the mid-1930s, when people were not embarrassed by love.

Only a few songs were kept from the original: 'Rose Marie,' 'Indian Love Call,' 'The Mounties' and 'Totem Tom-Tom.' 'Finaletto,' also from the original, had new lyrics by Gus Kahn. Added were 'Pardon Me, Madame,' by Herbert Stothart and Gus Kahn; 'Dinah' by Harry Akst, Sam Lewis and Joe Young; 'Some of These Days' by Shelton Brooks; and '*Tes Yeux*' by Rene Alphonse Rabey. Three songs that would have been perfect vehicles for MacDonald's voice were left out – 'Door of My Dreams,' 'Pretty Things' and 'Minuet of the Minute.' Thrown in to show off her voice were a so-so selection of arias from Puccini's *Tosca* and Gounod's *Romeo and Juliet.*

On stage, *The Bohemian Girl* went back to 1843. It was the work of Alfred Bunn, who wrote the book, and Michael William Balfe, an English composer who had been called 'the British Bellini.' It was said that his frankly Italian operas had nothing to do with operetta, but his best moments had an Italian flashiness or a sweet Irish simplicity. At any rate, *The Bohemian Girl* so impressed William S Gilbert that he edited a vocal score for a London publisher in his pre-Gilbert-and-Sullivan days. It was a worldwide success, and is still occasionally performed.

When it hit the screen in 1936, *The Bohemian Girl* bore little resemblance in plot to the original. Stan Laurel and Oliver Hardy played two gypsies who adopted a little girl. The girl, played by Darla Hunt, who was so appealing in the 'Our Gang' comedies, turned out to be a princess. In the cast were Jacqueline Wells, Joy Hodges, James Finlayson, Mae Busch, Antonio Moreno, Harry Bowers and Thelma Todd.

Many of the songs by Balfe and Bunn were classics: 'I Dreamt That I Dwelt in Marble Halls,' 'Then You'll Remember Me,' 'The Heart Bowed Down' and 'But Memory Is the Only Friend That Grief Can Call Its Own.' Added was 'Heart of a Gypsy' by Nathaniel Shilkret and Robert Shayon.

Hit the Deck, the 1927 Broadway musical that had been first transferred to the screen in 1930, was refurbished as a film in 1936, renamed *Follow the Fleet*, and turned over to Astaire and Rogers to work their magic. Fred was a dancer who had joined the Navy. Ginger was a former dance partner of his now working in a San Francisco dance hall. They get together again in a dance contest and proceed to win a fund-raising show for the benefit of a worn-out schooner.

In *Follow the Fleet*, Rogers was permitted to do a solo tapdance – her only one in films with Astaire. And for the first time, Fred was permitted to dance in something other than white tie and tails (except in the 'Let's Face the Music and Dance' number). Randolph Scott and Harriet Hilliard (later to marry Ozzie Nelson and star with him in the 'Ozzie and Harriet' television series) played supporting parts, and Betty Grable appeared again.

Other numbers in the Irving Berlin score were 'Let Your-

Fred Astaire, as a former dancer who had joined the Navy, and Ginger Rogers, as his one-time partner, are reunited in a dance hall in *Hit the Deck* – the motion picture of 1936.

self Go,' 'I'm Putting All My Eggs in One Basket,' 'Get Thee Behind Me Satan,' 'But Where Are You,' 'We Saw the Sea' and 'I'd Rather Lead a Band.'

The King Steps Out (1936) was an adaptation of a minor operetta of 1932 called *Cissy*, written by Gustav Holm, Ernest Decsey and Hulbert and Ernst Marishka, with music by Fritz Kreisler. It was a retelling of the courtship of Princess Elizabeth of Bavaria by the younger Emperor Franz-Josef of Austria. Grace Moore played the princess who rescues her sister (Frieda Inescourt) from an unwanted marriage to Franz-Josef (Franchot Tone), then pretends to be a dressmaker and eventually marries him.

Others in the cast were Walter Connolly as the King of Bavaria (described by his wife as 'a grease spot on the face of history'), Herman Bing as Pretzelberger, the owner of a restaurant, Raymond Walburn, Victor Jory, Elizabeth Risdon, Nana Bryant and Thurston Hall. The plot had been reworked by Sidney Buchman, wth Dorothy Felds adding new lyrics, borrowing some of the tunes from another Kreisler operetta, *Apple Blossoms*, which had appeared on Broadway in 1919. Among the songs were 'The Old Refrain,' 'Learn How to Lose,' 'Stars In My Eyes,' 'Madly in Love,' 'Soldier's March,' 'What Shall Remain?' and 'Call to Arms.'

ABOVE: Grace Moore and Franchot Tone in the film version of *The King Steps Out* (1936).
TOP: Herman Bing (left) and Walter Connolly in *The King Steps Out.*

LEFT: Hattie McDaniel as Queenie and Paul Robeson as Joe in the wonderful refilming of *Show Boat* (1936).

BOTTOM: A scene from a play on the stage of the *Cotton Blossom*, from the 1936 film *Show Boat*. Charles Winninger (in white trousers) was Cap'n Andy and Alan Jones (in black suit) was Gaylord Ravenal.

OPPOSITE: Grace Daniels and Peggy Wood in the Broadway production of *Maytime* (1917).

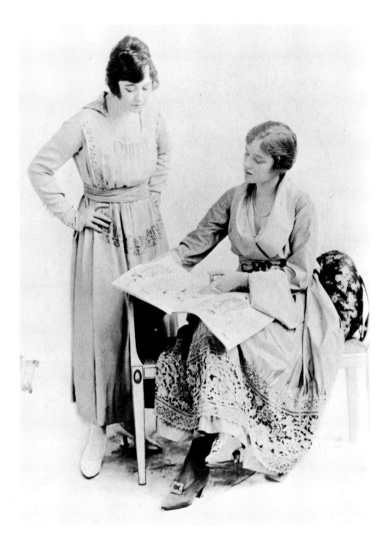

Show Boat was back on the screen again in 1936, directed by James Whale, probably best known for his *Frankenstein* (1931). This time around it starred Irene Dunne as Magnolia, Allan Jones as Ravenal, Charles Winninger as Cap'n Andy, Helen Morgan as Julie, Helen Westley as Parthenia Hawks, Queenie Smith as Ellie, Donald Cook as Steve (Julie's husband), Hattie McDaniel as Queenie and, finally, Paul Robeson as Joe. Oddly enough, all but Westley and Smith had appeared in various stage productions of the musical.

The adaptation of the film had been done by Oscar Hammerstein II himself, and, of course, it was quite faithful to the original. Three new Jerome Kern-Hammerstein songs were added: 'I Have the Room Above Her,' 'Ah Still Suits Me' and 'Gallivantin' Around.' The latter was sung by Irene Dunne in blackface. But for some reason, 'Why Do I Love You' was not used as a song, but as background music.

At any rate, the songs from the original were the thing. They included 'Cotton Blossom,' 'Cap'n Andy's Ballyhoo,' 'Where's the Mate for Me?,' 'Make Believe,' 'Ol' Man River,' 'Can't Help Lovin' Dat Man,' 'Mis'ry's Comin' Around,' 'You Are Love' and 'Bill.' Also included were 'Goodbye Ma Lady Love' by Joe Howard, 'At a Georgia Camp Meeting' by Kerry Mills, 'After the Ball' by Charles K Harris and 'Washington Post March' by John Philip Sousa.

One of the sensational operettas in the Germany and Austria of 1913 was Walter Kollo's *Wie einst im Mai*. It didn't take long for Sigmund Romberg to discover it, and, with music by Romberg and book and lyrics by Rida Johnson Young and Cyrus Wood, and dances by Allan K Foster, it

opened as *Maytime* on Broadway in 1917. Starring Peggy Wood (who would become an American television favorite playing Mama on the series 'I Remember Mama'), Charles Purcell and Willam Norris, it ran a respectable 492 performances. It was so popular that the Schuberts, who produced it, staged a second *Maytime* in the theater across the street, and the two companies played simultaneously.

Maytime had a more complicated plot than the average operetta of the time. The original German version told the story of two lovers in Berlin, but the American version switched the locale to New York City. The story was about the fortunes of a house in Washington Square during the course of 60 years. Ottilie Van Zandt (Wood) and Richard Wayne (Purcell) carry on a love affair from 1840 to the end of the century. Wayne's father had owned a mansion but had to turn it over to Colonel Van Zandt (Ottilie's father) in payment of a debt. Richard is now an apprentice on the estate. The two lovers find the deed to the mansion, blown from the Colonel's study into the garden. They bury it in a box with a finger ring, and pledge eternal love. Fifteen years later, Ottilie is forced to marry Claude, a gambler. Claude dies and Ottilie is penniless. By now Richard has earned a fortune and buys the mansion, deeding it to Ottilie anonymously. At the turn of the century, the mansion is turned into a dress shop managed by Ottilie's granddaughter (also played by Wood). Richard's grandson (played by Purcell) falls in love with her. Happiness comes only in the third generation. *Maytime* made Peggy Wood a star, and handkerchiefs dripped with tears.

Some of the most successful songs were 'Will You Remember?,' 'The Road to Paradise,' 'Jump Jim Crow' and 'Dancing Will Keep You Young.' When the film appeared in 1937, only one number was kept from the Romberg score – 'Will You Remember?' Producer Hunt Stromberg hated the Romberg music, so he had a new score prepared that stole heavily from the classics. There was 'Czarita,' based on themes from Tchaikovsky's *Fifth Symphony*; '[Virginia] Ham and Eggs,' an amalgam of various operatic arias, among them the 'Caro Nome' from *Rigoletto*; 'Now Is the Month of Maying,' a traditional song; 'Summer Is a Cumin In,' also traditional; 'Love's Old Sweet Song' by J L Molloy and G Clifton Bingham; 'Vive L'Opéra,' a folk song; 'Le Regiment de Sambre et Meuse' by Robert Planquette; 'Plantons la Vigne,' a traditional; 'Carry Me Back to Old Virginny' by James Bland; 'Santa Lucia,' a folk song; 'Les Filles de Cadiz' by Leo Delibes and an aria from *Les Huguenots* by Giacomo Meyerbeer.

Maytime (1937) was MacDonald and Eddy's most lavish movie yet. Of course the plot was changed, too. MacDonald was a great opera singer who had had a tragic love affair with a young baritone (Eddy). It was told in flashback, as the aged soprano Marcia Mornay talks to a young would-be singer (Lynne Carver). At the end, MacDonald and Eddy find each other again after spending years apart. Also in the cast were John Barrymore (playing MacDonald's manager in one of his last decent Hollywood roles), Herman Bing and Tom Brown.

The Firefly first appeared on Broadway in 1912, with a book and lyrics by Otto Harbach (who was spelling his name Haurbach at the time) and music by Rudolf Friml. Directed by Fred G Latham, it starred Emma Trentini, Roy Atwell and Audrey Maple and ran for 120 performances.

The Firefly was Friml's first stage score. He had written concert music and some songs, even a piano concerto.

ABOVE: Jeanette MacDonald as the opera singer and John Barrymore as her manager in the film version of *Maytime* (1937).

RIGHT: The great ballroom scene from the film *Maytime*.

Originally, Victor Herbert had been contracted to write the music, but he and the volatile Trentini had gotten into a feud, and Herbert backed out of the assignment. This was Friml's big chance.

The story was about Nina (Trentini), an Italian street singer, and Jack Travers (Atwell), whom she loves. Jack goes on a yachting trip to Bermuda, and Nina dresses up as a boy in order to get a job on board near Jack, but nothing happens. Two years later, Nina reappears as an opera prima donna and Jack falls in love with her and wins her hand.

It was the songs that stole the show – certainly the plot couldn't have. The score included 'Giannina Mia,' 'Love Is Like a Firefly,' 'The Dawn of Love,' 'When a Maid Comes Knocking at Your Heart' and 'Sympathy.'

Jeanette MacDonald took a vacation from Nelson Eddy in the 1937 film version of *The Firefly*. This time her co-star was Alan Jones (whose son, Jack, was later to become a popular singing heartthrob). The film jettisoned the Harbach plot and substituted a book by Frances Goodrich, Albert Hackett and

– proving that geniuses can sometimes write trash – Ogden Nash. Nina Maria (MacDonald) was a Spanish spy during the Napoleonic invasion of Spain; she spends her time trying to get information out of French Army officers. Don Diego (Jones) was a counterspy for the French. Nevertheless, Diego and Nina managed to get together enough to make beautiful music.

Most of Harbach's lyrics were thrown out – only his words to 'Giannina Mia,' 'Sympathy' and 'When a Maid Comes

Knocking at Your Door' remained. 'Love Is Like a Firefly,' 'A Woman's Kiss' and 'English March' had new lyrics by Bob Wright and Chet Forrest; 'He Who Loves and Runs Away' had lyrics by Gus Kahn; 'Danse Jeanette' had lyrics by Herbert Stothart; 'Para la Salud' was rearranged by Stothart. 'Ojos Rojos,' an Argentine folk song, was added, as was 'The Donkey Serenade,' one of the movie's biggest hits. It used the music from a Friml piano piece written in 1920 called 'Chanson,' adding lyrics by Bob Wright and Chet Forrest.

When *Rosalie* appeared on Boadway in 1928, it was billed as an operetta. The book was by Guy Bolton and William Anthony McGuire, and it had lyrics by Ira Gershwin and P G Wodehouse and music by George Gershwin and Sigmund Romberg. Produced by Florenz Ziegfeld and directed by McGuire, with dances by Seymour Felix, it starred Marilyn Miller, Bobbe Arnst, Frank Morgan and Jack Donahue. It ran a fantastic 327 performances.

ABOVE: Henry Vogel, Emma Trentini and Craig Campbell in a scene from the Broadway production of 1912 of the Haurbach-Friml operetta *The Firefly.*

OPPOSITE FAR LEFT: Jeanette MacDonald as the Spanish entertainer/spy in the film version of *The Firefly* (1937).

OPPOSITE BOTTOM RIGHT: Alan Jones and Jeanette MacDonald in *The Firefly.* They had appeared together the year before, in *Rose Marie* (1936), in which he had had a small part as her costar at the opera.

Bobbe Arnst was one of the stars on Broadway in *Rosalie* (1928).

ABOVE: Eleanor Powell in one of the gigantic dance numbers in the film version of *Rosalie* (1938).

RIGHT: Nelson Eddy (with sore leg) was 37 years old when he starred as the West Point football hero in the filmed *Rosalie* (1938).

OPPOSITE LEFT: Virginia Grey and Ray Bolger were juvenile leads in the movie *Rosalie* (1938).

OPPOSITE RIGHT: Nelson Eddy and Jeanette MacDonald on stage in the play-within-a-play sequence in the movie *Sweethearts* (1938).

Undoubtedly, George Gershwin's first big break on Broadway had been when his song 'Swanee' was picked up by Al Jolson and used in Jolson's *Sinbad* in 1919. But a case could be made for his work in *Rosalie*. Originally, Sigmund Romberg was to handle all the music for the show, but Ziegfeld demanded that he finish the whole score in three weeks, and Romberg couldn't meet the deadline. It was Romberg himself who suggested that Gershwin be brought in to help. In the final score, Romberg had written eight songs and Gershwin seven. 'How Long Has This Been Going On?' was unquestionably the most important Gershwin contribution – it became a classic. But it was not written for *Rosalie*, being a discard from the earlier Gershwin music *Funny Face* (1927). Three other songs were also former discards: 'Show Me the Town' (*Oh Kay!*, 1926), 'Beautiful Gypsy' (from the English produc-

tion of *Primrose* in 1924, when it had been titled 'Wait a Bit') and 'Yankee Doodle Rhythm' (*Strike Up the Band*, 1930). Truthfully, this was not a score of which either Gershwin or Romberg could be proud.

Rosalie was a typical operetta, involving the princess of a mythical kingdom. Marilyn Miller played Rosalie of Romanza, who falls in love with an American Army lieutenant from West Point, Richard Fay (Donahue). Of course the royal family of Romanza visits the United States, and of course Fay is the leader of the color guard and thus can get near Rosalie. But then Rosalie's father, King Cyril (Morgan), is forced to abdicate, and Fay is able to win Rosalie's hand in marriage.

When MGM released the film *Rosalie* (1937), Cole Porter had his revenge. After all those years of seeing his songs go down the drain when one of his musical comedies hit the screen, he finally won out. Gershwin and Romberg's *Rosalie* became Porter's *Rosalie*.

Eleanor Powell and Nelson Eddy (on one of his vacations from Jeanette MacDonald) replaced Marilyn Miller and Jack Donahue. One critic called the film 'a preposterous cross between operetta and campus musical.' Powell played Princess Rosalie of Romanza, but she was attending college in the United States, while Eddy was a college football hero, if one can believe that. Eddy saves Romanza from upheaval, and thus can marry Rosalie. There was a subplot involving Ray Bolger and Virginia Grey. Also in the cast were Ilona Massey, Edna May Oliver, Billy Gilbert, Reginald Owen, George Zucco, Jerry Colonna and William Demarest. In a strange twist, some of the footage from the unreleased 1930 film *Rosalie*, featuring Marion Davies, was used.

As it turned out, *Rosalie* was one of the biggest money-makers of the year, partly because of Powell's dancing, partly because of Eddy's singing, but mostly because of the music. From Cole Porter came 'I've a Strange New Rhythm in My Heart,' 'Rosalie,' 'In the Still of the Night,' 'Who Knows?,' 'Spring Is in the Air,' 'Why Should I Care?,' 'It's All Over But the Shouting' and 'To Love or not to Love.' In addition, there was '*M'Appari*' from Friedrich von Flotow's opera *Marta*. Then there were medleys incorporating bits from the following: 'On, Brave Old Army Team,' 'The Caissons Go Rolling Along,' 'Anchors Aweigh,' and John Philip Sousa's 'Washington Post March,' 'Stars and Stripes Forever,' '*Semper Fidelis*' and '*El Capitan*.' On the classical side were '*Addio*' ('Goodbye

Forever') by Paolo Tosti; 'The Polivitsian Dances' from Aleksandr Borodin's *Prince Igor*, part of Peter Ilich Tchaikovsky's *Swan Lake*; the 'Wedding March' from Felix Mendelssohn's *A Midsummer Night's Dream*; the traditional German university song '*Gaudeamus Igitur*', and 'Oh Promise Me' by Reginald DeKoven and Scott Clement.

One of Broadway's musical hits of 1913 was *Sweethearts*, a romantic operetta with a book by Harry B Smith and Fred de Gresac, lyrics by Robert B Smith and music by Victor Herbert. Directed by Frederick G Latham with dances by Charles S Morgan Jr, it ran for 136 performances. In the cast were Christie MacDonald, Tom McNaughton and Thomas Conkey.

The plot was typically inane. Indeed, an explanation had to be inserted in the program notes. 'The story of the opera is founded on the adventures of Princess Jeanne, daughter of King René of Naples, who reigned in the 15th century. Time has been changed to the present, the locale to the ancient city of Bruges, to which the little princess is carried for safety in time of war and is given the name of Silvie.'

At any rate, Silvie (MacDonald) is now a foundling raised by a woman who runs the 'Laundry of the White Geese.' Of course, Prince Franz of Zilania (Conkey) meets her and is smitten by her looks and charm. But for some reason she rejects him, perhaps because she feels that she cannot rise to so high a station. Lieutenant Karl (Edwin Wilson) also loves her, but she can't stand him because he is fickle. All ends well when everyone finds out that she is really the Crown Princess of Zilania, and she is willing to accept Franz's hand in what might have been an incestuous marriage.

Herbert F Peyser, a noted critic of the time, said: 'From first to last the music is utterly free from any suggestions of triviality. The abundant melodic flow is invariably marked by distinction, individuality and a quality of superlative charm.' There was no doubt that this operetta was vintage Herbert.

There were such numbers as 'The Angelus,' 'Every Lover Must Meet His Fate,' 'Pilgrims of Love' and 'Jeanette and Her Wooden Shoes.' Then there was the title song, 'Sweethearts,' which was written long before the operetta itself, having been found in one of Herbert's notebooks dating back to 1896. Another song, 'Pretty As a Picture,' was originally written to make fun of women's use of cosmetics; Herbert intended it as a comedy number. But he changed it into a sweet sentimental song in the operetta and had it sung by the chorus.

In the filmed version of *Sweethearts* (1938), the story was thrown out altogether and only seven songs were kept from the score; even those had new lyrics by Bob Wright and Chet Forrest. They were 'Sweethearts,' 'Every Lover Must Meet His Fate,' 'Jeanette and Her Wooden Shoes,' 'Summer Serenade,' 'Pretty As a Picture,' 'On Parade' and 'Game of Love.' Added were 'The Message to the Violet' and 'Keep it Dark' by Gustav Luders and Frank Pixley; 'Little Gray Home in the West' by Hermann Lohr; 'In the Convent They Never Taught Me That' by Herbert and Robert V Smith; and 'Happy Day' by Herbert Stothart, Wright and Forrest.

Sweethearts (1938) was the first MGM picture to use the new three-color Technicolor process – and the only Jeanette MacDonald-Nelson Eddy film in color. The plot was set in modern times, with the stars playing members of a musical-comedy team who become bored during the sixth year of a hit Broadway musical comedy, coincidentally called *Sweethearts*. Then an agent (Reginald Gardiner) lures them away to Hollywood, much to the disgust of their Broadway producer (Frank Morgan), writer (Mischa Auer) and composer (Herman Bing). But Hollywood comes near to destroying their marriage, and they separate. The happy ending

OPPOSITE TOP: Tony Martin, Alice Faye, Fred Allen, Joan Davis and Jimmy Durante in the movie *Sally, Irene and Mary* (1938).

OPPOSITE BOTTOM: Left to right, Marjorie Weaver, Joan Davis and Alice Faye in Hollywood's *Sally, Irene and Mary* (1938).

RIGHT: Marie Burke, H Reeves Smith, Marian Claire and Guy Robertson on stage in *The Great Waltz* (1934).

BELOW: Rainer and Gravet are reconciled, as Kruger and Shean look on in the film *The Great Waltz* (1938).

comes when they reunite and return to Broadway in triumph.

Dorothy Parker had been hired to add some acid wit to a sugary plot, and it came out as pretty good comedy. Legend has it that once, while she was working on the script, Parker leaned out of her window in the writers' building and shouted 'Let me out! I'm as sane as you are!'

Sally, Irene and Mary was a modest little Broadway musical of 1922. Directed by Frank Smithson, with a book by Eddie Dowling and Cyrus Wood, lyrics by Raymond Klages and music by J Fred Coots, it starred Eddie Dowling, Jean Brown, Kitty Flynn, Edna Morn and Hal Van Rensselaer. Modest though it was, it ran for 318 performances.

The story was about Jimmy Dugan (Dowling), a small-town plumber who loves Mary (Morn), the little girl next door. But Mary leaves for New York and shares an apartment with Irene (Flynn) and Sally (Brown) – all of them want to be actresses. A producer becomes interested in them, and within a year all three become stars. Although Mary is pursued by a rich man, for some reason she goes back to Jimmy. Among the songs were 'Time Will Tell,' 'I Wonder Why' and 'Do You Remember the Days?'.

The film version of *Sally, Irene and Mary* (1938) bore no relationship to the Broadway musical. With its new script by Harry Tugend and Jack Yellen, and its score by a committee, it told the story of singing manicurists and their ambitions to become Broadway stars. The leads were played by Alice Faye, Joan Davis and Marjorie Weaver, assisted by Tony Martin (then Faye's husband), Fred Allen, Jimmy Durante, Gregory Ratoff and Louise Hovick (the former stripper, Gypsy Rose Lee).

Among the songs were 'This Is Where I Came In' by Walter Bullock and Harold Spina; 'Got My Mind on Music' and 'Sweet As a Song' by Mack Gordon and Harry Revel; 'Half Moon on the Hudson,' 'I Could Use a Dream,' 'Who Stole the Jam?' and 'Help Wanted' by Bullock and Spina; and 'Hot Patatta' by Durante. Also added was a dance instrumental, 'Minuet in Jazz,' by Raymond Scott.

The Great Waltz, when it appeared on Broadway in 1934, was one of the first musical comedies to have lyrics set to the music of classical composers – this time the Strauss family – father and son. The book was by Moss Hart, adapted from libretti by A M Willner, Heinz Reichert, Ernst Marischka and Casell Garth, with lyrics by Desmond Carter. Directed by Hassard Short with dances by Albertina Rasch, it featured Guy Robertson, Marie Burke, Marion Claire and the great ballerina Alexandra Danilova. It ran 297 performances.

And what an extravaganza it was. It cost $250,000 to stage – an unheard-of figure for that time in the depths of the Great Depression. It had a chorus of 100 and a cast of 42 principals and supporting players, a ballet troupe of 40 and an orchestra of 53. Add to that a backstage crew of 90 and a total of 500 costumes.

The story, as usual, was banal. Johann Strauss Sr (H Reeves Smith) doesn't want his son, Johann Strauss Jr, (Robertson) to write waltzes – perhaps because of professional jealousy. The Russian Countess Olga (Burke) has the father waylaid, and the son takes his place at Dommayer's

LEFT: Dorothy and her pet cow, Imogene, come upon the Scarecrow in the stage production of *The Wizard of Oz* (1903). Anna Laughlin played Dorothy and the Scarecrow was Fred Stone.

OPPOSITE: The Scarecrow gives the Tin Woodman, played by David Montgomery, a refreshing dose of oil in Broadway's *Wizard of Oz* (1903).

BELOW: The Kansas farmers are terrified in the imaginative tornado scene in the stage version of *The Wizard of Oz*.

Gardens, where he conducts 'The Blue Danube Waltz.' Now the son has assumed the mantle of 'Waltz King of Vienna' and marries Therese (Claire) to the accompaniment of the 'Radetzky March.'

MGM's film version was released in 1938, with the music by Johann Strauss Jr rearranged and adapted by Dmitri Tiomkin, with new lyrics by Oscar Hammerstein II. Most of it was sung by the great soprano Miliza Korjus, who played a temptress of the now-married Strauss Jr (Fernand Gravet). His wife was Luise Rainer. Also in the cast were Hugh Herbert, Lionel Atwill, Herman Bing and Sig Ruman. Some of the songs were 'Voices of Spring,' *Du und Du*,' 'The Bat,' 'I'm in

Love With Vienna,' 'One Day When We Were Young,' 'Revolutionary March' and 'There'll Come a Time.'

One of the most successful Broadway musicals of 1903 was *The Wizard of Oz*. It ran for 293 performances. It was a musical fantasy, with book and lyrics by L Frank Baum, adapted from his own novel. The music was by A Baldwin Sloane and Paul Tietjens. Directed by Julian Mitchell, the cast included Fred Stone, David Montgomery, Grace Kimball and Bessie Wynn.

Baum had published his book *The Wonderful Wizard of Oz* just three years previously, but since it had sold some 100,000 copies in its first year, he thought it likely that it

OPPOSITE: Jack Haley, Bert Lahr, Judy Garland and Ray Bolger are told to go away by the Emerald City's gateman.

ABOVE: Dorothy comforts the Cowardly Lion in the film version of *The Wizard of Oz* (1939).

would go over as a Broadway musical. Legend has it that he had a filing cabinet with three drawers – 'A to G,' 'H to N' and 'O to Z.' The bottom drawer became the name of his mythical country.

The production opened the Majestic Theater in New York, and it was full of lavish sets and production numbers – just the thing to make a child's world of fantasy come alive. There was the tornado scene that opened the play, the poppy field, with chorus girls in large hats to make them look like flowers, and the beautiful courtyard of the Wizard's Palace.

The story was about Dorothy Dale (not Dorothy Gale) and her pet cow Imogene (not her pet dog Toto). They are carried by a tornado from their Kansas farm and deposited in a fairy garden, Oz, where Dorothy's house crashes on the cruel witch who has ruled the Munchkins. (Maybe they were the selected short subjects we have all heard about.) This sets the midget Munchkins free from the witch's spell, and the Good Witch of Oz gives Dorothy a ring (not a pair of ruby slippers) that will grant her two wishes. She wastes the first wish on a triviality, but with the second she brings to life the

scarecrow (Stone), who has lost his brains. Dorothy accompanies him on a search for the Wizard, who is the only one who can restore his brains. They are joined by the Tin Woodman (Montgomery), who has lost his heart. Finally, they find the Wizard (Bobby Gaylor) who gives back the Scarecrow's brains and the Woodman's heart.

Some of the best songs had music by Sloane – 'Niccolo's Piccolo' and 'The Medley of Nations.' But the two biggest hits were added after the musical had opened, and were written by other composers: 'Sammy' by James O'Day and Edward Hutchinson, and 'Hurray for Baffin's Bay' by Vincent Bryan and Charles Zimmermann.

The biggest Hollywood musical blockbuster of the 1930s was the screen version of *The Wizard of Oz* (1939), which was the most expensive production in MGM history up to that time, costing $3,200,000. It has never been off release since, and for many people it is an all-time favorite. Nothing could match the cinema magic wrought by this filming of Baum's children's classic. It starred Judy Garland, Ray Bolger, Bert Lahr, Jack Haley, Billie Burke (the widow of Florenz Ziegfeld played Glynda, the good witch, with a singing voice dubbed by Lorraine Bridges), the inimitable Margaret Hamilton (who had once been a kindergarten teacher) as the Wicked Witch of the West, and the equally inimitable Frank Morgan as the Wizard – not to mention the others in the cast of hundreds, 150 of them Munchkins. Here was a combination of sheer beauty, free-flying imagination and good fun that couldn't help but charm audiences.

Everything about the film had charm – the songs by Harold Arlen and E Y 'Yip' Harburg; the special effects like that marvelous yellow brick road, the Wizard's assorted magical contraptions and the Witch's skywriting; the 3210 costume changes, the 8428 separate make-ups and the 68 sets. The musical sequences included Garland singing 'Over the Rainbow,' Bolger dancing at his eccentric best as the Scarecrow, while trying to keep his straw inside his body where it belonged, and Lahr's Cowardly Lion plaintively growling 'If I Were King of the Forest.' Then there were the characterizations: Jack Haley's lonely and likeable Tin Woodman, Margaret Hamilton's evil, screeching Wicked Witch and Frank Morgan's all-stops-out portrayals of various Emerald City residents, among them the Wizard himself.

It was all the stuff of magic, and it worked critical and commercial magic for Metro-Goldwyn-Mayer. *The Wizard of Oz*, however, had the misfortune to come out in the same year as *Gone With The Wind* and so did not get the Academy Award for best picture of 1939, an honor that most likely would have come to it in any other year. But the 17-year-old Judy Garland received a special Oscar for the year's outstanding performance by a juvenile. An Academy Award went to Herbert Stothart for the picture's musical adaptation, and to Arlen and Harburg for the year's best song – 'Over the Rainbow.'

It took four directors working on the film to finally get it in the can. Richard Thorpe began the project, but was fired after 10 days because his footage lacked the fairy-tale feeling so necessary for the picture. George Cukor took over and lasted only three days because he thought that Garland should be outfitted with a blond wig and doll-face make-up (he must have had Shirley Temple on his mind). Victor Fleming entered the scene, and lasted long enough to get the credit as director of the movie. Then he had to leave to direct *Gone With the Wind* (for which he received the Oscar as best director), and King Vidor took over for the last 10 days to shoot the Kansas scenes.

The Wizard of Oz was the first of a series of musicals produced for MGM by Arthur Freed – musicals that would give that studio dominance in the field for many years. Freed, who encouraged and gave free rein to such people as Vincente Minnelli, Gene Kelly and Stanley Donen as directors, harbored a definite conception of what a musical ought to be. He saw it as an organic whole, an entertainment in which story, songs and dances were integrated and unified by a strong dramatic line. Songs, according to Freed's concept, must flow out of the dramatic material and advance the story, rather than serve merely as intermezzos between action that stops when music begins and resumes when the music has ended.

A song, no matter how tuneful or pleasure-giving, that did not advance the story had to be scrapped. Such a number was 'The Jitterbug' in *The Wizard of Oz*, a pretty senseless

OPPOSITE TOP: Dorothy (Judy Garland) is consoled by Glinda, the good Witch (Billie Burke), on her arrival in the Land of Oz – from the film version of *The Wizard of Oz* (1939).

OPPOSITE BOTTOM LEFT: The Scarecrow (Ray Bolger) tells Dorothy that he is missing a brain in *The Wizard of Oz*.

OPPOSITE BOTTOM RIGHT: Toto, the Scarecrow and Dorothy on their expedition in *The Wizard of Oz* – 'Follow the Yellow Brick Road.'

LEFT: The principals in *The Wizard of Oz* are terrified as they go through the haunted forest.

song and dance done by Garland, Haley, Bolger and Lahr in the middle of the forest. It was completely out of place. Composer Harold Arlen, however, was lurking behind the scenes with his 16mm movie camera, and preserved the number for posterity. This musical out-take was shown on a 'Ripley's Believe It or Not' television program in October 1983, and it would better have been completely forgotten.

The same thing almost happened to the picture's most famous and popular song, 'Over the Rainbow,' which the producer felt did not move the story line along. The idea of *The Wizard of Oz* without 'Over the Rainbow' brings tears to the eyes.

The other songs in the film included: 'Come Out, Come Out Wherever You Are,' 'It Really Was No Miracle,' 'Ding Dong the Witch Is Dead,' 'We Welcome You to Munchkinland,' 'Follow the Yellow Brick Road,' 'We're Off to See the Wizard,' 'If I Only Had a Brain (A Heart, the Nerve)' 'Lions and Tigers and Bears,' 'You're Out of the Woods,' 'The Merry Old Land of Oz' and 'Optimistic Voices.'

The film had everything going for it. It had a magnificent score that appealed to both children and adults. It had special architecture, special effects and the distortion of normal space-time. And it had Judy Garland. Her place in the history of the musical film is as important as that of Fred Astaire.

She got the lead in the movie by a fluke. MGM had wanted Shirley Temple, and they were willing to work a trade-off with 20th Century-Fox by borrowing Shirley in exchange for Jean Harlow and Clark Gable, who were working in the film *Saratoga* (1937) at the time. When Harlow died during the filming of that picture, the deal fell through and MGM decided to risk everything on Garland, who was then making a piddling $300 per week. She was, however, a blossoming 16-year-old when she was assigned the part, so the studio made special caps for her teeth, strapped her into a corset that hid her maturing figure, gave her a strict diet in which the studio commissary was told to feed her nothing but chicken soup, no matter how much she pleaded for banana splits, and thereby turned her into 11-year-old Dorothy Gale of Kansas.

The Wizard of Oz began in black and white in a bitterly real America of stern faces and endless plains. Dorothy, the innocent dreamer, was swirled from this place to a Technicolor dreamland 'somewhere over the rainbow.' Here she eluded evil, overcame enemies and found loving friends. *The Wizard of Oz*, like *Snow White and the Seven Dwarfs*, is one of those films on which people are brought up and which they never forget. Children and parents who see it year after year on television never seem to tire of it.

The special effects, created by Arnold Gillespie, were first-rate. One of the most inventive feats was the creation of the tornado in the picture. Gillespie tried many ways of photographing the great whirlwind that takes Dorothy to the Land of Oz, but everyone looked phoney until he hit upon the ingenious idea of blowing air from a fan through a woman's stocking. The resulting miniature 'twister' was so realistic that for years Metro-Goldwyn-Mayer used this footage in other movies that happened to have tornadoes in them.

Gillespie also used a lot of piano wire. How else to let the flying monkeys and the Wicked Witch become airborne? How else to hold up the Cowardly Lion's tail? There is a Hollywood story, probably apocryphal, about the accoun-tant who received several bills for piano wire during the making of the film. He paid the bills dutifully, but after he saw the movie, he complained that he hadn't seen any piano wire in the picture at all.

Near the end of *The Wizard of Oz*, the Wicked Witch of the West has finally captured Dorothy and her friends. Gleefully, the Witch sets fire to the Scarecrow. In an attempt to save her friend, Dorothy picks up a bucket of water and heaves it at him. Much of the water accidentally splashes on the Witch and, emitting a stream of shrieks and curses, the Witch begins melting ... melting ... melting ... until there is nothing left of her but an empty cloak and a hat. Dorothy has saved the day, thanks to a superb piece of special effects.

For this 'melting' effect, Margaret Hamilton stood on a small elevator platform built into the floor of the studio. The hem of her full-length witch's cloak was nailed to the floor of the set around the platform. When Dorothy threw the bucket of water on the Witch, the elevator platform began descending below the floor until it had lowered nearly six feet and the Witch had completely disappeared, leaving her clothing in a steamy pile. (Steam was provided courtesy of dry ice hidden in the hem of her cloak.)

Another special effect backfired badly. The Witch was made to appear and disappear by means of a trap door through which smoke and flames were sent up just before she materialized. The timing was just a little off, and the flames did not disappear completely before Margaret Hamilton came up. The fire melted the green copper-based paint that covered her face, giving her third-degree burns. She was

Ray Bolger confronts George Church with a pistol, as Tamara Geva looks on in horror, in the 'Slaughter on Tenth Avenue' ballet in Broadway's *On Your Toes* (1936).

OPPOSITE TOP: Bolger, Gear and Woolley on stage: *On Your Toes*.

OPPOSITE BOTTOM: *On Your Toes* was revived with Teeter and Makarova.

out recuperating for some three months.

Judy was not the only person in the picture who got the role as a second choice. The studio wanted Gale Sondergaard to play the Witch and Ray Bolger to play the Tin Woodman. Sondergaard wasn't available, and Bolger talked the casting director into making him the Scarecrow. The second choice for the Tin Woodman was Buddy Ebsen, but after a few scenes were shot, he became so allergic to the

silver make-up he had to wear that he almost died. So Jack Haley got the role. He also got sick, but, fortunately, he was able to stick it out.

Haley, Bolger and Lahr had another problem while making *The Wizard of Oz*. Because their strange make-up made it difficult to eat (Lahr's lion costume, for example, weighed 40 pounds), they had a run-in with the people at the studio commissary. They were asked to leave because of their terrible table manners and had to eat on the set.

As everyone knows, the result justified all the problems. *The Wizard of Oz* still stands today as one of the legendary pictures of all time.

On Your Toes was a most unusual musical comedy when it opened on Broadway in 1936. It was one of the first to incorporate ballet into the plot, and that was pretty esoteric

for those days. The book was by Lorenz Hart, Richard Rodgers and George Abbott, with lyrics by Hart and music by Rodgers. Directed by Worthington Miner with choreography by George Balanchine, it featured Ray Bolger, Tamara Geva, Doris Carson, Luella Gear and Monty Woolley, and ran for 315 performances.

Rodgers and Hart had prepared an outline for a motion-picture script about a Broadway hoofer involved with the Russian Ballet while they were working in Hollywood in the early 1930s. The idea was that Pandro S Berman should buy it for Fred Astaire, but the proposition was turned down. Later, the two sold the idea to the Schuberts for the talents of Ray Bolger. But by the time that Rodgers, Hart and Abbott had written the book, the production had been turned over to Dwight Deere Wiman.

The show opened with a pair of veteran vaudeville hoofers, Phil Dolan II and Lil, who have a typical vaudeville turn with 'Two-a-Day for Keith,' describing how things are on the Keith Vaudeville Circuit. They want their son, Phil Dolan III (Bolger), to follow a different and more ambitious career – something cultural, they hope. So Phil becomes a music instructor, explaining his interest in 'The Three B's.' Along the way, he meets an amateur female songwriter, Frankie Frayne (Carson), and they hit it off, even thinking of stealing away where no one can bother them in the hit song of the show, 'There's a Small Hotel.' But Phil is becoming more interested in ballet and meets and falls in love with a ballerina, Vera Barinova (Geva). Afraid that he will lose her, he joins the Russian Ballet and becomes involved in a production that is an absolute mess – 'La Princesse Zenobia' – based on the tales of Scheherazade.

This brings the ballet company close to bankruptcy, but it is saved when a friend of Phil's gives him the scenario for a modern ballet – 'Slaughter on Tenth Avenue.' Out of despera-

ABOVE: Tamara Geva as Princesse Zenobia in the Broadway musical *On Your Toes* (1936).

OPPOSITE: Eric Rhodes (Morrisine) and Vera Zorina (Vera) in the 'Princesse Zenobia' ballet in the film version of *On Your Toes*, which was released in 1939.

RIGHT: Lionel Atwill shakes Nelson Eddy's hand as Ilona Massey looks on. Cossack Prince Eddy has just joined the revolutionaries in the film *Balalaika* (1939).

tion, the troupe mounts the ballet, with Phil and Vera as the main dancers. The performance is a success, the Russian Ballet is saved and Phil realizes he loves Frankie rather than Vera.

Other interesting numbers in the production were 'Quiet Night' and 'Too Good for the Average Man.'

This was Balanchine's first experience on Broadway, and he did a tremendous job with both of his ballet sequences – 'La Princesse Zenobia,' a spoof of classical dance tradition, and 'Slaughter on Tenth Avenue,' a spoof of gangster movies. 'Slaughter' was about a dancer and his girl who are fleeing from gangsters and hide in a Tenth Avenue cafe. It ends with the girl being shot and the hoofer being saved by the police. It was a show-stopper then, and when *On Your Toes* was revived on Broadway in 1954, one critic said, 'A sizable number of jazz ballets have passed this way since it first appeared, but it ['Slaughter on Tenth Avenue'] still is something of a classic in its field, and the music Mr Rodgers wrote for it continues to seem one of the major achievements of his career.'

In the early 1980s, the show was revived on Broadway with Natalia Makarova as Vera, and this classical dancer said of her role, 'It's nice to get away from playing swans and other birds for a while.' The revival was so successful that a touring company was formed with Leslie Caron as Vera.

Vera Zorina played Vera in the film version of *On Your Toes* (1939). The plot was changed, and this time the American composer/dancer (Eddie Albert) was mistaken for a traitor by a visiting Russian ballet company. Apart from 'Slaughter,' it was remarkably dull. In addition, it had the 'Zenobia' ballet and (heard as background music only) 'There's a Small Hotel,' 'Quiet Night' and 'On Your Toes.'

One stage musical comedy that bypassed Broadway on its way to the screen was *Balalaika* (1936), which ran for 570 performances in London. Set in pre-Revolutionary Russia, it told the story of a romance between a Cossack officer and a

beautiful singer, and their reunion 20 years later in Paris. The book and lyrics were by Eric Maschwitz, the music by Bernard Grun and George Posford. Other songs by Robert Stolz were added to the score.

The film version of *Balalaika* (1939) was much altered – especially the score. It was still about the struggle in Russia between the nobility and the revolutionaries, but Hollywood, reflecting the concern of the United States for placating its Soviet ally against the growing Nazi threat, soft-pedaled the politics of the Russian Revolution and made a film that seemed like a Ruritanian romance. Nelson Eddy was Prince Peter Karagin. He is a Cossack, but he is pretending to be a peasant because he is in love with Lydia, a Revolutionary singer. Ilona Massey, the Hungarian touted as 'the new Dietrich,' whose first name is familiar to every crossword puzzle fan, appeared as Lydia in her first starring role in films. But she had two problems – she couldn't act and she couldn't sing. Only one song remained from the stage production: 'At the Balalaika,' but it had new lyrics by Bob Wright and Chet Forrest.

Other musical numbers included 'After the Service,' a traditional song; 'A Life for the Czar' by Michael Glinka; 'Ride, Cossack, Ride,' 'Tanya' and 'Wishing Episode (Mirror Mirror)' by Herbert Stothart, Wright and Forrest; 'Gorko,' traditional; 'Polonaise in A Flat, Opus 53' by Frederic Chopin; 'Song of the Volga Boatman,' traditional; *Chanson Bohéme,* *Chanson du Toreador,* and *Si Tu M'Aimes,* all from *Carmen,* by Georges Bizet; 'Shadows on the Sand' from *Scheherazade* by Nicolai Rimsky-Korsakov; 'God Save the Czar' by Alexei Lvov and Vasili Zhukovsky; *Stille Nacht* (Silent Night)' by Franz Gruber and Joseph Mohr; *Otchichornya,* traditional; 'Flow, Flow, White Wine' by Stothart and Gus Kahn; and 'The Magic of Your Love' By Franz Lehar.

Babes in Arms opened on Broadway in 1937, and it was the first musical by Rodgers and Hart in which they wrote the book without outside assistance. Of course, Rodgers also wrote the music and Hart the lyrics. Directed by Robert Sinclair with choreography by George Balanchine, it starred Mitzi Green, Wynn Murray and Ray Heatherton. Alfred Drake, long before his triumph in *Oklahoma!*, had a small role as Marshal Blackstone. And in the chorus (called 'The Gang' in the program notes) were two youngsters who were also to become famous – Robert Rounseville and Dan Dailey.

The plot of *Babes in Arms* – putting on a show in a barn – was refreshing because of the youth and talent of the cast. Most of the characters were actually adolescent; Green and Murray were only 16 at the time. It was a zestful, tuneful, brilliantly danced and sung affair filled with talented striplings and bubbling over with the freshness and energy of youth.

The story concerned the children of touring vaudevillians who have been left behind in Eastport, Long Island. The sheriff threatens them with work camp if their parents don't return. Money is the solution, so they put on a show – 'Lee Calhoun's Follies.' The show is a flop, but it is rescued by French flyer Rene Flambeau. Some of the great numbers were 'Where or When,' 'My Funny Valentine,' 'The Lady Is a Tramp,' 'Johnny One Note,' 'I Wish I Were in Love Again' and 'All at Once.'

The movie *Babes in Arms* (1939) was lyricist Arthur Freed's first effort as a producer and Busby Berkeley's first directorial job for Metro-Goldwyn-Mayer. It starred Mickey Rooney (then among the top 10 performers at the box office) and Judy Garland (fresh from her triumph in *The Wizard of Oz*), plus Charles Winninger, Guy Kibbee, June Preisser, Grace Hays and Betty Jaynes. Only three of the original songs were retained: 'Babes in Arms,' 'The Lady Is a Tramp' and 'Where or When.' Freed added some of his own songs, one new one called 'Good Morning' and two oldies: 'You Are My Lucky Star' and 'Broadway Rhythm,' all three with music by Nacio Herb Brown. Also in the film was a sprawling production number designed by Berkeley: 'God's Country' by E Y 'Yip' Harburg, Roger Edens and Harold Arlen.

Also thrown in were some ancient goodies, including 'I Cried for You' by Freed, Gus Arnheim and Abe Lyman; 'Ja-Da' by Bob Carleton; 'Rock-a-Bye, Baby' by Effie I Crockett; 'Si-

OPPOSITE TOP: The very young Wynn Murray, Mitzi Green and Alfred Drake in the stage musical *Babes in Arms* (1937).

OPPOSITE BOTTOM: Judy Garland and Mickey Rooney were the stars of the motion-picture adaptation of *Babes in Arms* (1939).

LEFT: George Tobias as a lunch-counter clerk waits on Nelson Eddy and Ilona Massey in the Hollywood version of *Balalaika* (1939).

lent Night' by Franz Gruber, 'Darktown Strutters Ball' by Shelton Brooks; 'I Like Opera, I Like Swing' and 'My Daddy Was A Minstrel Man' by Roger Edens; 'Oh! Susanna' by Stephen Foster; 'Ida, Sweet As Apple Cider' by Eddie Leonard and Eddie Munson; 'Moonlight Bay' by Edward Madeen and Percy Wenrich; 'I'm Just Wild About Harry' by Noble Sissle and Eubie Blake; and 'The Stars and Stripes Forever' by John Philip Sousa.

The story line remained pretty much unchanged except that the show the kids put on was a hit. The movie was a financial triumph and spawned a whole cycle of 'Come on kids, let's put on a show' musical pictures.

THE FLAG-WAVING
FORTIES

Show business went to war with the rest of the country in the 1940s, when the stars shared top billing with the American flag. Glamor queens doffed sequins and donned uniforms to entertain the troops while searching for their soldier or sailor boy friends in some most unlikely ports. Stage and screen musicals struck a patriotic note, but kept it upbeat, and a war-weary nation followed the Pied Piper into fantasyland.

LEFT: Nelson Eddy and opera diva Risë Stevens starred in the film *The Chocolate Soldier* (1941).

BELOW: Martha Raye and Joe Penner played a couple of slaves in the film *The Boys From Syracuse* (1940).

If the thirties was the decade for movie musicals that contained durable songs of quality, the forties was the decade that gave us great musical shows that endured as shows. Unfortunately, Broadway shows in the forties, just as had been the case in the thirties, were frequently manhandled by Hollywood. Story lines were changed, and many of the original Broadway scores were ditched in favor of inferior but more 'popular' material Probably the composers hardest hit were Cole Porter and Kurt Weill, whose music was super-sophisticated. It is possible that Porter could hardly recognize the film treatments of *Panama Hattie* (1942), *Du Barry Was a Lady* (1943) and *Mexican Hayride* (1949) as being related to his Broadway musicals, and Weill probably had the same problem with the Hollywood versions of his *Knickerbocker Holiday* (1944), *Lady in the Dark* (1944) and *One Touch of Venus* (1948).

Irene had burst upon the Broadway scene in 1919 and went on to set a record as the longest-running musical up to that time, lasting for an amazing 670 performances. With a book by James Montgomery, lyrics by Joseph McCarthy and music by Harry Tierney, it starred Edith Day, Walter Regan, Adele Rowland and Bobbie Watson. This archetypal shopgirl romance also had 17 road companies on tour at the same time, and when it was revived on Broadway and in London in the 1970s, it was still a rousing success.

The story was a rags-to-riches fable. Irene O'Dare (Day) is a shopgirl living in the slums of New York City. One day she makes a delivery to the home of the wealthy Donald Marshal (Regan), who is so impressed with her that he finds her a job as a model at the fashionable shop of the modiste Mme Lucy. Irene charms everyone at a party on Long Island, brings fame to Mme Lucy and marries Donald. The two biggest hits from the show were 'Alice Blue Gown' and 'Castle of Dreams.'

When the film version of *Irene* was released in 1940, most of the score was used only as background music. It starred Anna Neagle, Ray Milland, Alan Marshall, Roland Young, Billie Burke, May Robeson, Arthur Treacher and Marsha Hunt. The highlight of the film was the ball sequence, filmed in Technicolor, in which Neagle sang and danced to 'Alice Blue Gown.' Other songs were 'Irene,' 'Castle of Dreams,' 'There's Something in the Air,' 'Worthy of You' and 'Sweet

ABOVE: Neida Snow, Irene Ewight and Adele Ormiston as 'The Three Graces' in the Broadway hit *Irene* (1919).

RIGHT: Eddie Albert (left) as Antipholus of Syracuse and Jimmy Savo as Dromio, his servant, on the Broadway stage in *The Boys From Syracuse* (1938).

LEFT: Anna Neagle and Ray Milland in the 'Alice Blue Gown' number from the film version of *Irene* (1940).

Vermosa Brown.' Tierney and McCarthy wrote a new song for the film: 'You've Got Me Out on a Limb.'

Rodgers and Hart had another smash hit in 1938 – *The Boys From Syracuse* – with a book by George Abbott. Directed by Abbott with dances by George Balanchine, it starred Jimmy Savo, Teddy Hart (Lorenz Hart's brother), Eddie Albert, Ronald Graham, Muriel Angelus and Marcy Wescott. In a minor role – that of a tailor's apprentice – was Burl Ives. The show ran for 235 performances.

The idea of converting William Shakespeare's *A Comedy of Errors* into a Broadway musical was Rodgers'. He convinced Hart that the idea was a good one, and they asked Abbott to do the book. Abbot retained only two lines from the original Shakespeare; 'The venom clamours of a jealous woman/Poisons more deadly than a mad dog's tooth.' Abbot's slangy, decidedly non-Shakespearean dialogue helped lend this zany bedroom farce an atmosphere of sophisticated naughtiness.

Antipholus of Syracuse (Albert) comes to Ephesus with his servant Dromio (Savo). While there, they are confused with Antipholus of Ephesus (Graham) and his servant, Dromio of Ephesus (Hart). It turns out that the Antipholuses (or Antipholi) are twin brothers who were separated at birth, and that the Dromios also look alike. Everything gets mixed up in

RIGHT: Allan Marshall admires Anna Neagle, who has become a top model in the movie *Irene* (1940).

BELOW: Eddie Albert is smitten with Muriel Angelus, in the Broadway musical hit *The Boys From Syracuse* (1938).

amusing, irreverent and mildly bawdy situations.

The show had great songs: 'Sing for Your Supper,' 'Falling in Love With Love,' 'The Shortest Day of the Year,' 'You Have Cast Your Shadow on the Sea,' 'This Can't Be Love,' 'He and She,' 'What Can You Do with a Man?' and 'Oh Diogenes!'

The film version of *The Boys From Syracuse* (1940) starred Alan Jones as both Antipholuses and Joe Penner as both Dromios. Also in the cast were Martha Raye, Rosemary Lane, Charles Butterworth, Irene Hervey (Alan Jones's wife), Eric Blore, Alan Mowbray and Samuel S Hinds. Unfortunately, producer Jules Levey manhandled the score. Such songs as 'Sing for Your Supper,' 'Falling in Love With Love,' 'He and She' and 'This Can't Be Love' – all of them classics – were included only in shortened versions that didn't do them justice. Then Levey added such forgettable new tunes as 'Who Are You' and 'The Greeks Have No Word for It.'

The original stage version of *New Moon* had been set in New Orleans. When it was first made into a movie (1931), the scene shifted to twentieth-century Russia. But the remake of *New Moon* (1940), starring Jeanette MacDonald and Nelson Eddy, moved the locale back to New Orleans. Eddy had fattened up a bit in the five years since the dynamic duo had made *Naughty Marietta*, and some snide critics were beginning to call him 'the singing capon.' But the Romberg music saved this rather stodgy adaptation. Also in the cast were Mary Boland, George Zucco, H B Warner, Buster Keaton (in a small role) and MacDonald's wardrobe. She had 16 costume changes, involving 80 petticoats, and her most elaborate gown was an emerald-green creation (even though this was

a black-and-white movie) that weighed in at 35 pounds. The film was pure escapism and the public loved it.

Still in the score were 'Lover Come Back to Me,' 'Softly As in a Morning Sunrise,' 'Stout-Hearted Men,' 'Dance Your Cares Away,' 'The Way They Do It in Paris,' 'Shoes,' 'One Kiss,' 'Wanting You' and 'Marianne.' Added were Handel's '*Ombra Mai Fu*' and '*La Marseillaise.*'

One of the great musicals of all time premiered on Broadway in 1930. It was *Strike Up the Band*, with a book by George S Kaufman and Morrie Ryskind, music by George Gershwin and lyrics by Ira Gershwin. Directed by Alexander Leftwich, it featured Blanche Ring, Victor Moore, Bobby Clark and Doris Carson and ran for 191 performances.

The road to Broadway was a rocky one for this musical. The original book had been written by Kaufman, and it was a devastating satire on war and peacemaking efforts, big business and politics, written in the Gilbert and Sullivan vein. It originally starred Jimmy Savo and Vivienne Hart, but it closed in 1927 in its out-of-town tryout in Philadelphia. The critics had loved it, but the public stayed away in droves.

Late in 1929, producer Edgar Selwyn decided to have another shot at *Strike Up the Band*, but he knew he had to make the book less highbrow, more commercial. So he brought in Morrie Ryskind to rewrite it, and changes were made in both score and cast. It was still one of the most provocative and original musicals to hit Broadway in years. Critic William Bolitho said, 'Here is a bitter ... satirical

ABOVE: Antipholus (Alan Jones) sings 'Who Are You?' to his love Phyllis in the film version of *The Boys From Syracuse* (1940).

BELOW: Nelson Eddy and Jeanette MacDonald co-starred once again in the 1940 remake of the film version of *Naughty Marietta* (1940).

and Swiss hotel owners – the latter being able to raise their rates and use their hotels to house American troops. But not much fighting goes on.

Townsend discovers the secret signal of the Swiss Army – the yodel – and manages to get the whole Swiss Army captured. A Swiss spy is caught and admits that he was the one who committed the sabotage of putting Grade-B milk in Fletcher's cheese. The American soldiers return home to find that they can't get jobs. But they go back into the army when the Russians protest the new tariff on caviar.

LEFT: Paul McCullogh (left) and Bobby Clark ham it up on the stage in *Strike Up the Band* (1929).

BELOW: Mickey Rooney and his high-school dance band in the movie *Strike Up the Band* (1940).

attack on war, genuine propaganda at times, sung and danced on Broadway.'

The original plot was complicated. The United States imposes a tariff on cheese, which enrages the Swiss. Horace J Fletcher, owner of the American Cheese Company, has so much clout (and money) that he engineers a declaration of war on Switzerland. He also promises to finance the war if it is renamed 'The Horace J Fletcher Memorial War.' Jim Townsend, a newspaperman who is in love with Fletcher's daughter, finds out that Fletcher has been using Grade-B milk in his cheese. American patriots label Jim a traitor, and, to make matters worse, it is discovered that Jim owns a Swiss watch. The war starts, much to the delight of American warmongers

The new Ryskind-Kaufman version still packed a sting. This time Fletcher makes chocolates and the United States Government won't put a tariff on candy. He is so upset that his doctor gives him a sedative. The old yodel trick helps him to defeat the Swiss, and he is a national hero. (This time the newspapers report that his chocolates have Grade-B milk in them.)

Among the songs were 'A Typical Self-Made American,' 'The Unofficial Spokesman,' 'Entrance of the Swiss Army,' 'Soon,' 'I've Got a Crush on You' (which had actually been taken from a previous musical, *Treasure Girl* in 1928) and 'Strike Up the Band.' The 1927 version contained the famous 'The Man I Love,' but it was dropped. That was the second elimination for the song, since it had originally been written for and then left out of *Lady Be Good!* in 1924. *Strike Up the Band* was the first musical ever to win the Pulitzer Prize for drama.

The film *Strike Up the Band* (1940) bore virtually no relationship to the stage musical. Starring Mickey Rooney, Judy Garland and Paul Whiteman, it had a screenplay by John Monks Jr and Fred Finkelhoff, and producer Arthur Freed dumped all the songs except for the title tune. Substitutions included 'Our Love Affair' by Freed and Roger Edens and 'Drummer Boy,' 'Nobody,' 'Do the Conga' and 'Nell of New Rochelle' by Edens.

The plot was familiar – nice, decent All-American kids were having a hard time through no fault of their own. Rooney was the leader of a high-school band competing in Paul Whiteman's nationwide radio contest. There was enough sentimentality and good singing for any musical-picture fan. Judy's 'Do the Conga,' 'Nell of New Rochelle' and 'Our Love Affair' were tremendous.

Noel Coward wrote the book, the music and the lyrics for *Bitter Sweet* (1929), which ran for 151 performances on Broadway and an astonishing 697 in London. Coward had admitted that he was influenced in his writing by listening to phonograph records of *Die Fledermaus*. Casting was a bit of a

ABOVE: Ann Miller and Desi Arnaz in the film *Too Many Girls* (1940).

TOP: Desi Arnaz being held up after a hard night by Eddie Bracken (left) and Hal LeRoy, as Mary Westcott looks on with amusement – from the Broadway hit *Too Many Girls* (1939).

LEFT: Jeanette MacDonald (far right) in the motion picture *Bitter Sweet* (1940).

OPPOSITE TOP: Alan Jones and Evelyn Herbert in the American stage version of *Bitter Sweet* (1929).

OPPOSITE CENTER: Nelson Eddy and friend with Jeanette MacDonald in the movie version of *Bitter Sweet* (1940).

problem, at least insofar as who was to play Gertrude, the heroine. Sari Linden was supposed to star in the London production, but she had a limited voice, and the role fell to Peggy Wood. And with an American Gertrude in London, it seemed only fair to have a British Gertrude, Evelyn Laye, in New York.

The story was about an upper-class English maiden who, in 1875, escapes an arranged marriage and runs off to Vienna with her music teacher. She marries him and he is killed in a duel at the cafe where they work. Some of the fine songs in the show were 'If Love Were All,' 'Green Carnations,' 'Ladies of the Town,' 'Zigeuner,' 'Tokay,' 'Dear Little Cafe,' 'Kiss Me' and 'Tell Me What Is Love.'

It is said that Coward wept when he saw the film version of *Bitter Sweet* (1940) – not because he was so moved, but because he thought it was so dreadful. There were Nelson Eddy and Jeanette MacDonald singing cheek-by-jowl in this sweet, sweet adaptation, which was turned into just another vehicle for them. It was hard to believe that the 38-year-old MacDonald was a lass of 18, and it was impossible to believe that the chubby Eddy was a starving Viennese singing teacher. Also in the cast were George Sanders (who kills Eddy in the duel), Felix Bressart and Fay Holden.

For some reason, 'If Love Were All' – the most moving song that Coward ever wrote – was missing from the film, but

LEFT: Vera Zorina, the ballerina, in a typical angelic pose in the Broadway musical *I Married an Angel* (1938).

ABOVE: Nelson Eddy and entourage in a dream sequence in the film version of *I Married an Angel* (1942).

several Coward songs were there to relieve the boredom: 'Zigeuner,' 'I'll See You Again,' 'If You Could Only Come With Me,' 'What Is Love?' 'Tokay,' 'Love in Any Language' (with new lyrics by Gus Kahn), 'Dear Little Cafe,' 'Kiss Me' and 'Ladies of the Town.' Also thrown in was '*Una Voce Poco Fa*' from Rossini's *The Barber of Seville*.

One of the best campus musicals ever was *Too Many Girls*, which opened on Broadway in 1939, starring Mary Jane Walsh, Marcy Wescott, Eddie Bracken, Desi Arnaz, Diosa Costello, Hal LeRoy and Van Johnson. With a book by George Marion Jr, music by Richard Rogers and lyrics by Lorenz Hart, it told the story of a college in which the girls outnumbered the boys by ten to one, thus creating a problem – how to field a winning football team.

The songs included 'I Didn't Know What Time It Was,' 'Spic and Spanish,' 'Love Never Went to College,' ''Cause We All Got Cake,' 'Heroes in the Fall,' 'Pottawatomie' and 'Look Out.'

Producer-director George Abbott brought four members of the original cast, LeRoy, Arnaz, Bracken and Johnson, to Hollywood to film the screen version of *Too Many Girls*

LEFT: Anna Neagle and Ray Bolger dance it up in the film remake of *Sunny* (1941).

ABOVE: Anna Neagle and Victor Mature in the film remake of *No, No, Nanette* (1940).

extremely thin plot. Featuring Anna Neagle, Richard Carlson, Victor Mature, Roland Young, Helen Broderick, ZaSu Pitts and Eve Arden, the film was one of the clinkers of the year. If the audience paid close attention, they could hear snippets of 'Tea for Two,' 'I Want to Be Happy,' 'Where Has My Hubby Gone?' 'Take a Little One-Step' and 'No, No Nanette.'

Sunny was refilmed in 1941, rewritten to tell the tale of a circus performer (Anna Neagle, who was no Marilyn Miller) who marries a New Orleans aristocrat (John Carroll) despite his family's objections. Also featured in the film were Ray Bolger and Edward Everett Horton. Bolger and Jerome Kern's score stole the show.

Lady Be Good opened on Broadway in 1924. It was George Gershwin's second book musical (by Guy Bolton and Fred Thompson). Directed by Felix Edwards with dances by Sammy Lee and lyrics by Ira Gershwin, the cast featured Fred and Adele Astaire, Cliff 'Ukelele Ike' Edwards and Walter Catlett. It ran for 330 performances.

The story of *Lady Be Good* (originally called *Black Eyed Susan*) was a simple one. Fred and Adele were Dick and Susie Trevor, a brother-and-sister dance team who are not doing too well financially. Forced to entertain at private parties and the homes of friends, they still go broke and are evicted from their apartment. In one wonderful scene, when their furniture is thrown into the street, they arrange it around the corner lamp post. Dick chases a rich girl he doesn't like in hopes of getting her money, but Susie tries to rescue him by

(1940). Also in the cast were Lucille Ball, Richard Carlson, Ann Miller and Frances Langford. Ball was an heiress who is accompanied to a small Western college by her four football-hero bodyguards. Rodgers and Hart wrote an extra song especially for the film – 'You're Nearer.'

The Broadway musical *No, No Nanette* was refilmed in 1940. Unlike the 1930 version, this movie relegated its comfortable score to the background and concentrated on the

ABOVE AND RIGHT: Robert Young plays the piano for Eleanor Powell in the movie version of *Lady Be Good* (1941).

impersonating a Mexican widow for the purpose of getting an inheritance. She is assisted in this by a shady lawyer, J Watterson Watkins (Catlett). The plan fails, but all ends well.

In the score were such classics as 'Fascinatin' Rhythm,' 'So Am I,' 'The Half of It,' 'Oh, Lady Be Good' and 'Blues.'

When the film came out in 1941 it had an entirely new story and only a fragment of the original score. The producers kept 'Fascinatin' Rhythm' and 'Lady Be Good.' Added were 'You'll Never Know' by Roger Edens, 'Your Words and My Music' by Arthur Freed and Edens and 'The Last Time I Saw Paris' by Jerome Kern and Oscar Hammerstein II, which, ironically, won the Academy Award for the best song.

The movie *Lady Be Good*, which starred Eleanor Powell, Ann Sothern, Robert Young, Lionel Barrymore, John Carroll, Red Skelton and Dan Dailey, told the story of a pair of songwriters (Sothern and Young) who split up when their success goes to Young's head. They are reunited, and that's that.

Powell had star billing, but all she had to do was pop up now and then in a tap routine. She was at her best in the finale, 'Fascinatin' Rhythm,' with its eight grand pianos plus 100 male dancers in white tie and tails, the dancing Berry Brothers and singer Connie Russell.

Busby Berkeley, who directed the dances, had this to say about the number:

Eleanor was by far the finest female dancer we ever had in films, and a very hard-working perfectionist. This particular number was difficult for her because of the mechanics involved. She started the dance in front of a huge silver-beaded curtain, which circled to the left in a zig-zag course disclosing, on five-foot-high platforms, one grand piano after another. Eleanor followed, and as the curtain circled

each piano, a high-lift would move in, pick up the platform with the piano on it, and pull it back out of the way of the camera boom which was following Eleanor as she danced. All of this was filmed in one continuous shot until the last piano disappeared and the moving curtain revealed Eleanor in a huge circular set surrounded by the hundred boys, with a full orchestra in the background. Toward the end of this number, the boys would throw Eleanor like a pendulum down through the tunnel they formed, ending with a big close-up of her at the end of the shot. We rehearsed this trick over and over in order to get it right, and it was two in the morning by the time we finished. It was pretty bad for Eleanor physically; she was battered and bruised, but never complained. Not a whimper! She wouldn't give up until I had got what I wanted on film. After the preview of the picture she thanked me. I've known very few women that talented and that gracious.

Der tapfere Soldat, an operetta by Oscar Strauss, premiered in Vienna in 1908. By 1909, with English lyrics by Stanislaus Stange and retitled *The Chocolate Soldier*, it opened on Broadway, followed by a London production in 1910. The plot was based on the George Bernard Shaw pacifistic play *Arms and the Man*, but when Shaw was first approached for his permission to make it into a musical, he declined because he thought that if the musical were a success, people would forget his play. He finally agreed that the plot could be used, but none of the dialogue. He also stipulated 'that all advertising and programmes bear the legend that the play was "an unauthorized parody of Mr Bernard Shaw's play, *Arms and the Man*" and 'that he receives no royalties from it.'

The Chocolate Soldier was such a success that Louis B Mayer wanted to film it with Jeanette MacDonald and Nelson Eddy. But by now Shaw had realized his mistake and asked for a tremendous sum for the film rights. Mayer wanted to compromise, but the playwright wouldn't budge, saying, 'No, Mr Mayer, I fear we two will never understand each other. You're an idealist, you see, whereas I'm only a businessman.' Defeated, Mayer had to substitute the plot of Ferenc Molnár's play *The Guardsman*.

By the time the picture was released in 1941, MacDonald was replaced by opera star Risë Stevens. She and Eddy played two opera stars, husband and wife, who were appearing in a production of the original *Chocolate Soldier* – the typical 'play within a play' device. Eddy is so jealous that he disguises himself as a Cossack to test his wife's fidelity. This may have been Eddy's finest hour. It turned out that he had a

talent for light comedy, and Stevens was magnetic. Also, their voices seemed to blend together. Everything worked.

Among the songs were 'My Hero,' 'Sympathy,' 'The Flower Presentation,' 'Thank the Lord the War Is Over,' 'Ti-ra-la-la' and 'Seek the Spy' by Strauss and Stange; 'While My Lady Sleeps' by Bronislau Kaper and Gus Kahn; 'Song of the Flea' by Modest Moussorgsky and '*Mon Coeur S'Ouvre a Ta Voix*' from *Samson and Delilah* by Camille Saint Saëns.

One of Irving Berlin's longest-running shows – 444 performances – opened on Broadway in 1940. *Louisiana Purchase* had a book by Morrie Ryskind and words and music by

BELOW: Vera Zorina tries to trap Bob Hope in the film *Louisiana Purchase* (1942).

RIGHT: Bordoni, Gaxton and Moore in the play *Louisiana Purchase* (1940).

Berlin. Directed by Edgar MacGregor with dances by George Balanchine and Carl Randall, it starred William Gaxton, Victor Moore, Vera Zorina and Irene Bordoni.

Senator Oliver P Loganberry (Moore) goes to Louisiana to investigate the Louisiana Purchase Company and its shady lawyer Jim Taylor (Gaxton). He finds out about some under-the-table deals, and Jim tries to blackmail him to keep him silent. Marina van Lindon (Zorina), a dancer, and Mme Bordelaise (Bordoni) get the Senator drunk, and when Marina sits on his lap, pictures are taken. But the senator wins in the end.

Carol Bruce, in a subsidiary role, sang the title number, Other songs included 'It's a Lovely Day Tomorrow,' 'Latins Know How,' 'You're Lonely and I'm Lonely,' 'The Lord Done Fixed Up My Soul,' 'Sex Marches On' and 'What Chance Have I.' In the film version of *Louisiana Purchase* (1942), Moore, Zorina and Bordoni were brought in from Broadway, but Gaxton was replaced by Bob Hope. The highlight was the filibuster scene, in which Hope was a riot. Unfortunately, all but three songs were pared from the original. The musical numbers included 'Prologue: Take a Letter to Paramount Pictures' and 'Before the Picture Starts' (an opening scene in which a group of chorus girls sang the lines about the characters in the film being fictitious; one critic pointed out

BELOW: Nelson Eddy in the film *I Married an Angel* (1942).   RIGHT: King and Zorina on stage – *I Married an Angel* (1938).

Bud Abbott makes Lou Costello jealous in the second film version of *Rio Rita* (1942).

that this was probably a movie first – and last). Other numbers were: 'You're Lonely and I'm Lonely,' 'Louisiana Purchase,' 'It's a Lovely Day Tomorrow' and 'Dance With Me (at the Mardi Gras).'

Rodgers and Hart's *I Married an Angel* premiered on Broadway in 1938. The book was by Rodgers and Hart and was based on a Hungarian play by John Vaszary. The lyrics were by Hart, the music by Rodgers. Directed by Joshua Logan with choreography by George Balanchine, the show starred Vera Zorina, Dennis King, Vivienne Segal, Audrey Christie and Walter Slezak.

Rodgers and Hart had liked Vaszary's play, and when they learned that MGM had the rights to it, they tried to get the studio to make a musical film of it. MGM didn't want to do that, so Rodgers and Hart bought the rights and turned it into a stage musical. In the play, Count Willy Palaffi (King), a Budapest banker, is tired of women and says he will marry only an angel. An angel does appear, played by Zorina, and he marries her. The problem is that she is incapable of lying, and so gets her husband into some embarrassing situations. Finally she acquires some of the less desirable human traits, and the two live happily ever after.

Vera Zorina was a ballet dancer – a graduate of the Ballet Russe de Monte Carlo, and had been in the London cast of *On Your Toes* as well as in its screen version. Her most ambitious dance number in *I Married an Angel* was the 'Honeymoon Ballet' in the first act. Other numbers included 'I Married an Angel,' 'Spring Is Here,' 'Did You Ever Get Stung?' 'At the Roxie Music Hall' and two musical interludes: 'The Modiste' and 'Angel Without Wings.'

The film version of *I Married an Angel* (1942) changed the plot, added songs that were not so hot, turned the fun to stone and cut much of the score. Also cut were the satirical observations on love and marriage that were the core of the

stage production. Nelson Eddy played a middle-aged philanderer who falls asleep at his own birthday party and dreams that he has married an angel (Jeanette MacDonald) who deserts him when he becomes bored with her naiveté. He wakes up and finds that the angel is one of his party guests. Also in the cast were Edward Everett Horton, Binnie Barnes and Reginald Owen.

The movie kept some of the Rodgers and Hart songs: 'I Married an Angel,' 'I'll Tell the Man In the Street' and 'Spring Is Here,' plus 'At the Roxy Music Hall,' retitled 'Tira Lira La,' and 'A Twinkle in Your Eye' with new lyrics by Bob Wright and Chet Forrest. Other numbers included '*Caprice Viennoise*' by Fritz Kreisler, '*Chanson Bohème*' from Georges Bizet's *Carmen*, '*Anges Purs*' from Charles Gounod's *Faust*, '*Aloha Oe*' by Hawaiian Queen Liliuokalani and a group of songs by Herbert Stothart, Wright and Forrest: 'Hey Butcher,' 'There Comes a Time,' 'To Count Palaffi,' 'May I Present the Girl,' 'Now You've Met the Angel' and 'But What of Truth.'

Rio Rita was refilmed in 1942 with Bud Abbott and Lou Costello in the Bert Wheeler and Robert Woolsey roles. It was less faithful to the stage version than was the 1929 film with John Boles and Bebe Daniels, keeping only two songs from the stage musical – 'The Ranger's Song' and the title song. Kathryn Grayson, in her second film, and John Carroll composed the love interest. With the world at war, the screen writers Richard Connell and Gladys Lehman introduced fifth columnists and saboteurs. New songs included 'Long Before You Came Along' by E Y Harburg and Harold Arlen, 'Brazilian Dance' by Nilo Barnet and '*Ora o Conga*' by Lacerdo.

ABOVE: Treacher, Harrington, Merman, Hyers and Marshall in the Broadway *Panama Hattie* (1940).

RIGHT: Merman and Carroll in the 'Let's Be Buddies' number.

FAR RIGHT: Arthur Treacher and Betty Hutton on stage in *Panama Hattie*.

OPPOSITE: Blue, Skelton, Sothern and Ragland in the film *Panama Hattie* (1942).

Panama Hattie was first presented on Broadway in 1940, with a book by Buddy de Sylva and words and music by Cole Porter. Directed by Edgar MacGregor with dances by Robert Alton, it featured Ethel Merman, Rags Ragland, James Dunn, Joan Carroll, Betty Hutton and Arthur Treacher. One of Porter's more substantial hits, it ran for 501 performances – the first Porter musical to top 500 and, indeed, the first Broadway musical in 12 years to exceed 500 performances.

Hattie Maloney (Merman) runs the Tropical Shore Bar in the Panama Canal Zone. She is earthy and brassy and decides that she needs some social polish, probably because she has fallen in love with Nick Bullett (Dunn), a society man from Philadelphia, who is serving the United States Government in Panama. He has an eight-year-old daughter, Geraldine (Carroll), whom Hattie insists on having flown down to give her approval of the marriage. But Geraldine doesn't approve. Hattie overhears a plot to blow up the canal, and with three of her sailor friends she outwits the saboteurs. Geraldine gives her approval to the wedding.

The hit song of the show was 'Let's Be Buddies,' a duet with Carroll and Merman. It was a rather odd song, but Porter explained why it was written the way it was. 'There was a spot where Joan Carroll, who is eight years old, and Ethel Merman, who is more than sixteen, had to sing and dance a duet. The spot required it. The law forbade it. The spot also stipulated that the song – as Ethel sang it – must be boozily sentimental . . . and in rhythm that can be walked to, in order to compensate for Joan having been prevented by law from dancing, and with a patter in between so that Joan could recite instead of courting jail by singing. Also, I put in an A-natural for Ethel, because while all her notes are extraordinarily good, A-natural is her best. It worked. Brooks Atkinson of *The New York Times* said: 'Gruff old codgers are going to choke a little this winter when tot and temptress sing "Let's Be Buddies" and bring down the house.'

Merman carried the show. As John Mason Brown, the critic, put it: 'She is in her finest form, than which there is none finer. Ethel Merman sweeps triumphantly through *Panama Hattie* . . . The evening she dominates with all the strident precision which is hers is a happy example of our professional theater when it is functioning at its professional best.' *Panama Hattie* gave June Allyson her big break. She was in the chorus and acted as an understudy for Betty Hutton, who played Florry, a friend of Hattie's. One night in 1941 Hutton came down with measles. Merman later commented, 'June Allyson did a perfect job. I've never seen an understudy take over with such confidence.' Some other numbers from the stage musical were 'You Said It,' 'My

Mother Would Love You,' 'I've Still Got My Health' and 'Make It Another Old Fashioned Please.'

The film version of *Panama Hattie* (1942) starred Ann Sothern, Red Skelton, Rags Ragland, Lena Horne and Dan Dailey. Although it was a hit on the stage, it was a miss on the screen. The problem was that the play had been written for Ethel Merman. Ann Sothern just couldn't handle the job, and was also overwhelmed by the talents of Red Skelton, Dan Dailey and Lena Horne.

Some Porter songs survived in the movie – 'Let's Be Buddies,' 'Make It Another Old Fashioned Please' and, from his 1935 musical *Jubilee*, 'Just One Of Those Things.' But the rest of the score was written by other people: 'The Sping' by Phil Moore and J Le Gon, 'Did I Get Stinkin' at the Savoy' by E Y Harburg and Walter Donaldson, 'The Son of a Gun Who Picks on Uncle Sam' by Harburg and Burton Lane, 'Hattie From Panama' and 'Good Neighbors' by Roger Edens, 'Berry Me Not' by Moore, 'La Bumba Rhumba' by Alex Hyde and 'Hail, Hail, The Gang's All Here,' with lyrics by Theodore F Morse set to Sir Arthur Sullivan's music for the song 'Come Friends Who Plow the Sea' from *The Pirates of Penzance*.

Cabin in the Sky was a most unusual Broadway musical for 1940, since it had an all-black cast, something rarely seen in those days. It had a book by Lynn Root, lyrics by John La Touche and music by Vernon Duke, directed and choreographed by George Balanchine. It starred Ethel Waters, Todd Duncan, Rex Ingram and Katherine Duncan and lasted for 156 performances.

Cabin in the Sky told the story of parallel struggles – Lucifer Jr (Ingram) versus the Lawd's General (Duncan) for the soul of Little Joe (Dooley Wilson); and Joe's wife, Petunia (Waters), versus the scheming Georgia Brown (Dunham), who wants to steal Joe away from her. Joe shoots Petunia in a dance hall, but she forgives him so that he can go to Heaven.

The songs were magnificent. They included 'Cabin in the Sky,' 'Taking a Chance on Love,' 'Honey in the Honeycomb' and 'Love Me Tomorrow.' When *Cabin in the Sky* was revived off-Broadway in 1964, several new songs were added. 'We'll Live All Over Again' and 'My Old Virginia Home by the River' had been written for the original but not used. There was also a new song written by Vernon Duke, 'Living It Up,' plus another Duke song that came from his *Banjo Eyes* (1941), 'Not a Care in the World.'

When the film version of *Cabin in the Sky* appeared in 1943, critics accused it of perpetuating black stereotypes, but with more unsophisticated audiences, there wasn't a dry eye in the house. At least the movie allowed black artists to express themselves more than they would have otherwise been permitted to do in the segregation-conscious movies of the time.

Producer Arthur Freed had the good sense to assign Vincente Minnelli to his first directing job on the film. Rex Ingram and Ethel Waters re-created their original Broadway roles. Eddie 'Rochester' Anderson was Little Joe, Lena Horne was Georgia Brown and Kenneth Spencer was the messenger from Heaven. This time, Joe is shot and Spencer and Ingram battle for his soul. Others in the cast were Louis Armstrong, Mantan Moreland, Willie Best, Butterfly McQueen, Duke Ellington and his Orchestra and the Hall Johnson Choir.

The songs included from the stage musical were 'Taking a Chance on Love,' 'Honey in the Honeycomb,' 'Life's Full of Consequences,' 'Li'l Black Sheep' and 'In My Old Virginia Home.' Added to the film score were 'Going Up' by Duke Ellington, 'Things Ain't What They Used to Be' by Ted Pearsons and Mercer Ellington, 'Shine' by Lew Brown, Ford Dabney and Cecil Mack and the song that was to become the greatest hit of all, 'Happiness Is Just a Thing Called Joe,' by Harold Arlen and E Y Harburg.

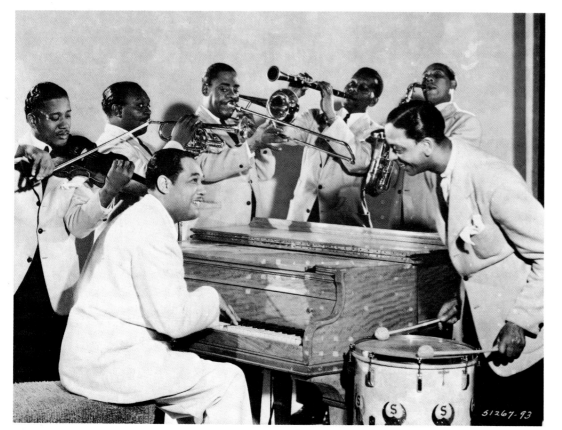

LEFT: Duke Ellington and some of the members of his orchestra in the film *Cabin in the Sky* (1943). Ellington also wrote one of the songs that was used in the film – 'Going Up.'

OPPOSITE TOP: Lena Horne makes herself pretty in order to try to seduce Joe in the movie version of *Cabin in the Sky* (1943).

OPPOSITE BOTTOM: The stars of the stage version of *Cabin in the Sky* (1940) – Dooley Wilson as Little Joe, Ethel Waters as Joe's wife, Petunia, and Todd Duncan as the Lawd's General.

Best Foot Forward was a rollicking campus musical that ran for 326 performances on Broadway beginning in 1941. It had a book by John Cecil Holm and lyrics and music by Hugh Martin and Ralph Blane. Directed by George Abbott with dances by Gene Kelly, it starred Rosemary Lane, Nancy Walker, June Allyson and Gil Stratton Jr.

The setting was the Winsocki School near Philadelphia, whence Bud Hooper (Stratton) has sent a wistful letter to fading movie-star sex queen Gale Joy (Lane), asking her to be his date for the junior prom. Joy's press agent (Marty May) realizes the publicity value of the trip and urges her to go to the dance. Bud ditches his own girl friend Helen (Maureen Cannon) for Joy. Helen is so frustrated that she tears Joy's sash off her dress at the prom, and the other girls tear her gown to pieces for souvenirs. But everything turns out all right. Joy leaves and Helen and Bud are reunited.

Some of the delightful songs were 'Buckle Down Winsocki,' 'Who Do You Think I Am?' 'Just a Little Joint with a Juke Box,' 'That's How I Love the Blues,' 'You're Lucky,' 'Wish I May,' 'Three Men on a Date,' 'Ev'ry Time,' 'The Three B's' and 'Alive and Kicking.' When Best Foot Forward was revived off-Broadway in 1963, Liza Minnelli was in the cast in her first stage appearance.

The film version of Best Foot Forward (1943) had Lucille Ball as the Hollywood star and Tommy Dix as Bud, with William Gaxton, Virginia Weidler, Gloria De Haven and Harry James and his orchestra. The producers had the good sense to bring in June Allyson and Nancy Walker to re-create their Broadway roles. Added to the score were 'The Flight of the Bumble Bee' by Nicolai Rimsky-Korsakov and 'Two O'Clock Jump' by Count Basie, Harry James and Benny Goodman.

Let's Face It (1941) was a Broadway musical with a book by Herbert and Dorothy Fields that had been based on a stage comedy, The Cradle Snatchers (1925) by Norma Mitchell and Russell G Medcraft. Directed by Edgar MacGregor, it had words and music by Cole Porter, dances by Charles Walters, and starred Danny Kaye, Eve Arden, Mary Jane Walsh and Ethel Meiser. It ran for 547 performances.

The Cradle Snatchers had been a Broadway sex comedy about three women who take revenge on their erring hus-

OPPOSITE TOP: Virginia Weidler, Tommy Dix, William Gaxton, Lucille Ball and Chill Wills in the film version of *Best Foot Forward* (1943).

OPPOSITE BELOW: Rosemary Lane loses her dress on stage in *Best Foot Forward* (1941).

ABOVE: Mary Jane Walsh, Danny Kaye, Ethel Meiser, Benny Baker, Jack Williams and Vivian Vance in the stage version of *Let's Face It* (1941).

TOP: Bob Hope and Betty Hutton took over the leads in the film *Let's Face It* (1943).

bands by hiring three gigolos for a weekend. The musical version took the bare bones of the story and turned it into a military musical. The three women, Nancy Collister (Vivian Vance, long before she became Ethel Mertz in the television series 'I Love Lucy'), Cornelia Abigail Pigeon (Meiser) and Maggie Watson (Arden) take on three inductees from a nearby Army camp – Jerry Walker (Kay), Frank Burns (Benny Baker) and Eddie Hilliard (Jack Williams). Not much hanky-panky goes on, and Jerry is eventually forgiven by his true love, Winnie Potter (Walsh). Nanette Fabray, who had begun her career at age three in vaudeville touring as 'Baby Nanette,' played Jean Blanchard, a minor role, but she sang one of the hit songs, 'Ace in the Hole.' Some of the other numbers were 'Melody in Four F' (a Danny Kaye speciality – a tongue-twister telling of being drafted) and 'A Modern Fairy Tale,' both with lyrics by Sylvia Fine, Kaye's wife. Other Porter songs were 'You Irritate Me So' and 'Ev'rything I Love.'

When the film *Let's Face It* appeared in 1943, Hollywood had done it to Porter again. Only two of his songs remained – 'Let's Not Talk About Love' and 'Let's Face It.' Among the other songs in the film by Jule Styne and Sammy Cahn was 'Who Did? I Did.'

Bob Hope took over the Danny Kaye part and Betty Hutton played his girl friend. The three women were Eve Arden, ZaSu Pitts and Phyllis Povah. A subplot was added in which Hope captures an enemy submarine by holding a mirror to the periscope and sending it aground in Long Island Sound.

BELOW: On Broadway in *Du Barry Was a Lady*, Bert Lahr was Louis Blore (Louis XV of France) and Ethel Merman was May Daley (Madame Du Barry).

Another triumph for Cole Porter was his Broadway musical *Du Barry Was a Lady* in 1939. The book was by Buddy de Sylva and Herbert Fields, with words and music by Porter. The director was Edgar MacGregor, the choreographer Robert Alton, and it featured Ethel Merman, Bert Lahr, Ronald Graham, Betty Grable and Benny Baker. It ran for 408 performances.

The whole thing started when Fields wrote a scenario for a film that was rejected by Paramount. But Field's agent thought that it would be a perfect vehicle for Lahr, and Lahr was fed up with Hollywood. So de Sylva and Fields rewrote the scenario to fit in with Lahr's personality. When the name Ethel Merman came up as a suggestion for the leading lady, it was rumored that Porter would be willing to write the score. And that's the way it turned out.

The story was simple. A night-club washroom attendant, Louis Blore (Lahr) is in love with the Club Petite's star entertainer, May Daley (Merman). He wins $75,000 in the sweepstakes and buys the club (things were cheaper then). He tries to slip a Mickey Finn to his rival for May's hand, Alex Barton (Graham), but drinks it himself. Lahr dreams that he is Louis XV of France and that May is Madame Du Barry. At this point the show became a typical bedroom farce.

Among Porter's songs were 'Ev'ry Day a Holiday,' 'Friendship,' 'Katie Went to Haiti,' 'Do I Love You?' and 'Well, Did You Evah?' The last song was little remembered until Porter dug it out of his trunk and used it in his smash film *High Society* (1956), where the inebriated Frank Sinatra and Bing Crosby made a duet of it.

For the second time in 1943 alone, Hollywood sabotaged Cole Porter again. In the belief that his lyrics were too risqué, all but three of his songs were yanked – 'Do I Love You?,' 'Katie Went to Haiti' and 'Friendship.' Apart from these, the film score had 'No Matter How You Slice It, It's Still Salome' and 'Ladies of the Bath' by Roger Edens, 'Du Barry Was a Lady' by Ralph Freed and Burton Lane, 'I Love an Esquire Girl' by Freed, Edens and Lew Brown, 'Madame, I Love Your Crepes Suzettes' by Freed, Lane and Brown and an instrumental rendition of 'I'm Getting Sentimental Over You' by Ned Washington and Ned Bassman.

Lucille Ball and Red Skelton played the Merman and Lahr roles, with Rags Ragland, Zero Mostel and Gene Kelly in support as a dancer in love with Ball. Kelly also played a revolutionary known as the Black Arrow in the dream sequences. Also in the cast were Virginia O'Brien and Tommy Dorsey and his Orchestra, featuring vocalists Dick Haymes and Jo Stafford.

Girl Crazy was remade as a film in 1943, this time starring Judy Garland and Mickey Rooney. And it was one of the few Hollywood musicals up to that time to use the score of the original show with few changes and few additions. Even the screenplay pretty much stuck to the characters and story of Gershwin's 1930 Broadway musical. In the score were 'Embraceable You,' 'Bidin' My Time,' 'But Not for Me,' 'Treat Me Rough,' 'I've Got Rhythm,' 'Could You Use Me?' 'Cactus Time in Arizona,' 'Bronco Buster' and one extra song, 'Happy Birthday Ginger,' by Roger Edens.

Another refilming of 1943 was *The Desert Song.* Starring Dennis Morgan, Irene Manning, Bruce Cabot, Gene Lockhart and Faye Emerson, the plot had been updated to reflect those wartime years. This time the Riffs are opposed by the Nazis in French Morocco in 1939. The Germans try to build a road from Dakar to the North African coast, but the Riffs are led by an American who had fought in the Spanish Civil War. Naturally, the road is never built. The Harbach, Hammerstein and Romberg contributions like 'The Riff Song,' 'Desert Song,' 'One Alone,' 'Romance,' 'French Military Marching Song' and 'One Flower' were supplemented by 'Fifi's Song' by Jack Scholl and Romberg, 'Gay Parisienne' by Scholl and Serge Walters and 'Long Live the Night' by Mario Silva and Romberg.

ABOVE: Rooney, Garland and Miller starred in Hollywood's *Girl Crazy* (1943).

BELOW: Cabot, Emerson and Morgan: *The Desert Song* (1943).

Richard Rogers and Lorenz Hart's minor success *Higher and Higher* opened on Broadway in 1940. The book by Joshua Logan and Gladys Hurlbut told of the domestic staff of a New York mansion who pool their resources to pass off a parlormaid as a débutante. There was also a subsidiary plot concerning a fortune hunter who is after the rich daughter of the man who owns the house. It starred Jack Haley and Marta Eggerth.

The film rights to the show were purchased by RKO to introduce the young Frank Sinatra to movie audiences. When the movie came out in 1944, only one song remained from the original score – 'Disgustingly Rich.' Still, the Jimmy McHugh-Harold Adamson songs were pleasant enough – 'This Is a Lovely Way to Spend an Evening,' 'I Saw You First,' 'Boccherini's Minuet in Boogie,' 'It's a Most Important Affair,' 'Today I'm a Débutante,' and 'You're on Your Own' – and Sinatra's songs stood out: 'The Music Stopped' and 'I Couldn't Sleep a Wink Last Night.'

Michele Morgan was the maid turned débutante, Jack Haley was the butler and Leon Errol was the rich man. Sinatra played the wealthy boy next door, whom Morgan spurns to go back to the butler. Although he didn't get the girl, Frank had the bobby-soxers screaming every time he opened his mouth.

OPPOSITE TOP AND BOTTOM:
Marta Eggerth, Jack Haley and
Leif Erickson in the Broadway
musical *Higher and Higher*
(1940); Frank Sinatra and
Michele Morgan in the movie
version (1944).

Gertrude Lawrence, as Liza
Elliott, has a session with
Donald Randolph, as her
psychiatrist, Dr Brooks, in the
Broadway hit *Lady in the Dark*
(1941).

Lady in the Dark opened on Broadway in 1941 with a book by Moss Hart, words by Ira Gershwin and music by Kurt Weill, who had escaped the Nazi regime in Germany. Directed by Hassard Short, with choreography by Albertina Rasch, it starred Gertrude Lawrence, Victor Mature, Danny Kaye and Bert Lytell, and ran for 388 performances.

The idea had come to Hart as a result of some experiences in psychoanalysis, but this was not the first musical to concern itself with the subject. Sigmund Romberg had included psychoanalysis in his operetta *May Wine* in 1935.

Liza Elliott (Lawrence), the editor of *Allure*, a fashion magazine, complains of fatigue, melancholia and psycho-somatic ailments. She sees Dr Brooks, a psychiatrist, who asks her to tell him of the first thing that pops into her head. She remembers a childhood song, 'My Ship,' which she sings, and the first of several dream sequences starts. She imagines herself as a siren whom 12 men, dressed in white tie and tails, are serenading with 'Oh, Fabulous One.' In the dream her chauffeur, Russel Paxton (Kaye), who is really the photographer for the magazine, drives her to Columbus Circle, where she enters an expensive night club. The head waiter is Kendall Nesbitt (Lytell), actually her lover – the publisher of *Allure.*

Later, back at the job, Liza meets Randy Curtis (Mature), a cowboy movie star being photographed for the magazine. Nesbitt comes in to tell her that his wife will give him a divorce and they can be married. This depresses Liza, who sings 'My Ship' again and has another dream. She is graduating from Mapleton High School and sees Nesbitt buying her

wedding ring. The jeweller brings him, not a ring, but a golden dagger. Randy enters to make love to Liza, but is enticed away by six attractive women. Liza sings about a princess who can be won only by the man who can solve a riddle. Now Liza and Nesbitt are being married, but the choir denounces her for marrying someone she doesn't love:

Next Liza is back in the doctor's office, telling him that she is about to break a date with Randy. The doctor tells her that she insists on looking plain because she thinks that she can't compete with other women. The next day Liza tells Nesbitt that she doesn't love him, then dresses up glamorously for her date with Randy.

At a conference at the magazine, a circus issue is being discussed when the whole circus scene becomes another dream with Paxton as the ringmaster. Suddenly Liza is in court being charged with inability to make up her mind. Paxton is her defense lawyer and he sings 'The Best Years of His Life,' which is followed by a patter song about Russian composers – 'Tschaikowsky' (Ira Gershwin's spelling of Tchaikovsky). Kaye – who was discovered by Moss Hart, who wrote a special part for him in the play – was able to rattle off the names of 49 Russian composers in 39 seconds. Years later he broke his own record in Madrid by singing it in 31 seconds. Liza defends herself in the song 'The Saga of Jenny,' and wins the court case.

The same day she returns to the doctor's office and tells him of a childhood experience in which she had been humiliated. Her mother had been so pretty that Liza decided not to care about boys and to purposely maintain her plainness.

A week later Randy proposes to her. It turns out that he admires her strength because he is weak. Liza realizes that the man she really loves is Charley Johnson (MacDonald Carey), one of her editorial associates. Charley comes into the office, she makes her feelings known, and all ends happily.

The film version of *Lady in the Dark* (1944) just didn't work very well. Part of the reason was probably Moss Hart's com-

LEFT: Ray Milland (Charley) as the ringmaster and Ginger Rogers (Liza) as Jenny, in the circus dream sequence from the motion picture *Lady in the Dark*, released in 1944.

OPPOSITE TOP: Walter Huston made a splendid Peter Stuyvesant in the Broadway musical *Knickerbocker Holiday* (1938).

OPPOSITE BOTTOM: Sam (Paul Bryant) polishes the silver decorations on the peg leg of Governor Stuyvesant (Charles Coburn), as they prepare to disembark at New Amsterdam – from the Hollywood version of *Knickerbocker Holiday* (1944).

plicated book. Another factor was the way the dream sequences were photographed and directed. The stage version used four concentric revolving stages and each dream was used as an extended operetta finale. The film version hacked the dreams into little bits. Finally, the producers didn't think the sophisticated Weill score could stand on its own feet.

Ginger Rogers played Liza in her first Technicolor film, and, although she was paid a whopping $122,500 for the job, she was no match for Gertrude Lawrence. Also in the cast were Ray Milland (Charley), Warner Baxter (Kendall) and Jon Hall (Curtis), with Mischa Auer playing the Danny Kaye role.

'My Ship' was eliminated, thus also eliminating the psychological point explained by the song. 'Tschaikowsky' was thrown out, too. Who else could sing it but Danny Kaye? The final dream sequence took place at the circus, and when 'The Saga of Jenny' was sung at the circus, it lost its point. In addition to 'Jenny,' about all that remained from the score were 'Girl of the Moment,' 'One Life to Live,' 'It Looks Like Liza' and 'This Is New.' Added were the inferior 'Suddenly It's Spring' by Johnny Burke and Jimmy Van Heusen, 'Dream Lover' by Clifford Grey and Victor Schertzinger and 'Artist's Waltz' by Robert Emmett Dolan.

Another Kurt Weill musical opened on Broadway in 1938. It was *Knickerbocker Holiday*, with book and lyrics by Maxwell Anderson. Directed by Joshua Logan with choreography by Carl Randall and Edwin Denby, it featured Walter Huston, Ray Middleton, Jeanne Madden and Clarence Nordstrom, and ran for 168 performances.

This was Anderson's first venture into musical comedy, but his book and lyrics fitted Weill's music like a glove. He used Washington Irving's *Father Knickerbocker's History of New York* and set it in New Amsterdam in 1647. In a way, it compared the political problems of those times with the ones current in 1938; both eras were marked by an invasion of Fascism and a suppression of liberty.

Originally, the part of Peter Stuyvesant was to have gone to Martyn Greene, the celebrated star of so many D'Oyly Carte Gilbert-and-Sullivan operettas. But he couldn't make it, and Walter Huston was given the role in one of the more fortuitous accidents in theater history.

Peter Stuyvesant was the governor-general of New Amsterdam – a peg-legged tyrant who sets up a semi-Fascist, semi-New Deal state, antagonizing the Dutch people there who hate confining systems. His councilmen exploit the people and Stuyvesant exploits the councilmen. Washington

Irving (Middleton) appears in the prologue and introduces Stuyvesant on his arrival in the New World. Then he introduces the hero of the musical comedy, Brom Broek, a knife-sharpener. Brom loves Mynheer Tienhoven's daughter Tina (Madden). Tienhoven is head of the Town Council, and it is hanging day. So, with nobody to hang, the Town Council elects Brom to be their victim, since he has not asked them for a permit to sharpen knives.

Brom claims that they are not qualified to pass judgment on him since they have sold brandy and firearms to the Indians. Stuyvesant arrives and saves his life. But Stuyvesant also issues laws putting himself in charge of illicit operations. Tienhoven decides he wants Stuyvesant to be Tina's

husband and Brom, naturally, objects and, equally naturally, is thrown into jail. When the wedding is interrupted by an Indian raid, Brom escapes and joins the settlers in the fight. But in escaping, he has defied Stuyvesant, who orders him to be hanged. Washington Irving reappears and warns Peter that he should change his ways in order to be remembered kindly in history. Stuyvesant agrees and Tina and Brom are wed.

Walter Huston was wonderful, giving an earthy, infectious portrayal of Stuyvesant, especially when singing 'September Song' in a half-recitative style, sitting alone on the stage and staring at the audience. Actually, Weill had written the music for this song with Huston's non-singing style in mind. Also in the score were 'How Can You Tell an American?,' 'It Was Never You,' 'There's Nowhere to Go But Up' and 'The One Indispensable Man.'

The film version of *Knickerbocker Holiday* (1944) put more emphasis on the romance than the politics, but the big crime, so usual in those days, was that all but three of the original songs were omitted, and others were stuck in. The movie kept 'September Song,' 'The One Indispensable Man' and 'There's Nowhere to Go But Up.' Other songs were 'Hear Ye,' 'Love Has Made This Such a Lovely Day,' 'Zuyder Zee' and 'One More Smile' by Jule Styne and Sammy Kahn; 'Holiday' by Theodore Paxton and Nelson Eddy; 'Jail Song' by Weill, Furman Brown and Eddy; and 'Sing Out' by Franz Steininger and Brown.

The film was tedious. Nelson Eddy played the lead, but this time he was a printer of subversive literature rather than a knife-sharpener. Constance Dowling played the love interest. As Peter Stuyvesant, Charles Coburn was no Walter Huston. The picture almost disappeared without a trace, and today is hardly ever seen, even on 'The Late, Late Show.'

Very Warm for May was, unquestionably, the biggest Broadway flop that the team of Jerome Kern and Oscar Hammerstein II ever had. It opened in 1939 and lasted a mere 59 performances, despite the classic song 'All the Things You Are,' and despite the talented cast, featuring Donald Brien, Jack Whiting (the father of Margaret Whiting, the popular singer of the 1940s and 1950s), a very young Eve Arden and, in the chorus line, the even younger June Allyson and Vera-Ellen. It was a simple romance – that's all.

MGM came out with their film version of *Very Warm for May* in 1944, calling it *Broadway Rhythm*, and everything disappeared except for 'All the Things You Are.' It told the story of a Broadway producer (George Murphy) and the problems he has with his musical show. It was little more than a showcase for some talented people – Lena Horne, Ginny Simms, Nancy Walker, Ben Blue, Hazel Scott, Gloria de Haven and Tommy Dorsey and his Orchestra.

The music was the thing, however. The score included 'Somebody Loves Me' by Buddy de Sylva, Ballard MacDonald and George Gershwin; 'Who's In Your Love Life?' 'Solid Pota-to Salad,' 'Irresistible You' and 'Milkman Keep those Bottle Quiet' by Don Raye and Gene De Paul; 'Manhattan Serenade' by Louis Alter; 'Pretty Baby' by Gus Kahn, Tony Jackson and Egbert Van Alstyne; 'Oh You Beautiful Doll' by A Seymour Brown and Nat Ayer; 'Amor' by Sunny Skylar, Gabriel Ruiz and Ricardo Lopez Mendez; 'National Emblem March' by E E Bagley; 'What Do You Think I Am?' by Hugh Martin and Ralph Blane; 'Waltz in D Flat, Opus 64, No 1' ('The Minute Waltz') by Frederic Chopin, 'Ida, Sweet As Apple Cider' by Eddie Leonard and Eddie Munson and 'A Frangesa' by P M Costa.

Something for the Boys, which opened on Broadway in 1943, was a war-time musical comedy in which three heirs to a house near an Air Corps Base turn it into a billet for airmen's wives. It starred Ethel Merman and Bill Johnson. The book was by Herbert and Dorothy Fields, the words and music were by Cole Porter, and it ran for 422 performances – a modest hit.

By the time the film version of *Something for the Boys* came out in 1944, it was to be expected that the only part of the Cole Porter score that remained was the title song. The

movie starred Carmen Miranda (who was then making some $200,000 a year), Vivian Blaine and Phil Silvers, and introduced Perry Como to movie audiences. In one of the smallest parts was Judy Holliday.

The rest of the score was by Harold Adamson and Jimmy McHugh, and some of the songs were 'I'm In the Middle of Nowhere,' 'Wouldn't It Be Nice,' 'Samba Boogie,' 'I Wish We Didn't Have to Say Goodnight' and 'Boom Brachee.'

The 1927 Broadway hit *Good News* was refilmed in 1947. In this version, Patricia Marshall had her eyes on the football hero (Peter Lawford), and demure little June Allyson eventually got him. A good deal of the stage score was used – 'Good News,' 'The Varsity Drag,' 'Just Imagine,' 'Lucky in Love,' 'He's a Ladies' Man' and 'The Best Things In Life Are Free,' all by Buddy de Sylva, Lew Brown and Ray Henderson. Added were 'Pass That Peace Pipe' by Roger Edens, Ralph Blane and Hugh Martin and 'The French Lesson' by Edens, Betty Comden and Adolph Green. As critic Clive Hirshhorn wrote, 'June Allyson was not the greatest singer on MGM's roster, and Peter Lawford's song-and-dance efforts would give Astaire no sleepless nights, but that didn't stop *Good News* . . . from being knockout entertainment.'

Are You With It? was a rather pleasant Broadway show of 1945 about a mathematics whiz who leaves his job and joins a carnival. The music was by Harry Revel and the lyrics by Arnold B Howitt. Unfortunately, it is now almost forgotten.

The movie version of *Are You With It?* is almost forgotten, too. It was released in 1948 and promptly disappeared. The stars were Donald O'Connor, Olga San Juan and Lew Parker, and except for a couple of superb dance numbers by O'Connor, the film pretty much concentrated on his mugging. Among the songs by Sidney Miller and Inez James, which replaced the original score, were 'Down At Ali Baba's Alley,' 'It Only Takes a Little Imagination,' 'What Do I Have to Do to Make You Love Me?' 'Daddy Surprise Me,' 'I'm Looking for a Prince of a Fellow' and 'Are You With It?'

Up in Central Park had its Broadway opening in 1945. It
was a musical comedy with a book by Herbert and Dorothy
Fields, lyrics by Dorothy Fields and music by Sigmund Romberg. Directed by John Kennedy with dances by Tamiris, it
featured Wilbur Evans, Betty Bruce, Maureen Cannon and
Noah Beery Sr. It ran for an astonishing 504 performances.

The musical was viewed as Romberg's first successful
attempt to get away from the European operetta style with
which he had made his reputation. It had a thoroughly
American subject – political corruption, focusing on Boss
William Marcy Tweed and his infamous reign in New York's
Tammany Hall. The idea of making a musical comedy about
Tweed came to producer Mike Todd after he read Dennis
Lynch's book *Boss Tweed and His Gang*. He talked it over
with Herbert and Dorothy Fields, who called in Romberg to
do the music. The Philadelphia critics were unanimous in
hating the show when it tried out there. But after the Broadway opening, the New York critics raved. They called it 'a
flawless production,' 'about as big as its namesake and just
as pretty to look at.' 'The overall effect is one of beauty and
charm,' was the verdict. During its long New York run, *Up in
Central Park* grossed $4 million, giving Todd a profit of over
$20,000 per week.

The play took place in the New York of the 1870s. Rosie
Moore (Cannon) is the daughter of one of Tweed's flunkies
and wants to become a theater star. Rosie falls in love with
John Matthews (Evans), not knowing that his job with *The
New York Times* is to expose Tweed's fraudulent deals in the
creation of Central Park. Tweed (Beery) tries to bribe Matthews and *The Times* (nineteenth-century payola) to no
avail. The Tweed Ring is smashed and Rosie's father is
ruined. Now Rosie is disgusted with Matthews and runs off
with Richard Connolly, the city comptroller. Connolly turns
out to be a bigamist, and Rosie is reunited with Matthews – at
the bandstand in Central Park, of course.

The show contained some of the most appealing songs
that Romberg ever wrote, such as 'Carousel in the Park,'
'Close As Pages in a Book,' 'It Doesn't Cost You Anything to
Dream,' 'When You Walk in the Room,' 'The Fireman's Bride,'
and 'Currier and Ives.'

The film version of *Up in Central Park* (1948) was a disaster. Only three of the songs remained, and for some reason,
'Pace, Pace Mio Dio' from Guiseppe Verdi's *La Forza del
Destino* was thrown in. Another problem was that the Rosie
in the film was Deanna Durbin, who was a much better singer
than she was an actress. As Matthews, crooner Dick Haymes
didn't have the lusty voice of Wilbur Evans, and Vincent
Price was too cultured to be the raucous Boss Tweed.

One Touch of Venus was one of Broadway's biggest hits of

ABOVE: Mary Martin and Kenny Baker on stage in *One Touch of Venus* (1943).

RIGHT: Robert Walker and Ava Gardner were in the film *One Touch of Venus* (1948).

wonders of suburban living, but this turns Venus off because it sounds too pedestrian and dull. She returns to her own realm and the statue reappears. Rodney goes back to the museum and runs into a young girl who looks exactly like Venus, and even comes from suburban Ozone Heights, which is, of course, his idea of heaven. When Rodney asks her if she likes it, she answers, 'Ozone Heights? I wouldn't think of living anywhere else.' Rodney escorts her out of the museum and we all know he has found his true love.

The songs were magnificent. Among them were 'How Much I Love You,' 'I'm a Stranger Here Myself,' 'Foolish Heart,' 'Way Out West in Jersey,' 'Venus in Ozone Heights,' 'Speak Low,' 'The Trouble With Women,' 'That's Him,' 'Very, Very, Very' and 'Wooden Wedding.'

The film version of *One Touch of Venus* (1948) was a stinker. It wasn't the change in the script that did it, although that was no help – Robert Walker was a window dresser who kisses a department-store dummy and brings her to life. Rather, it was because Walker as Rodney and Ava Gardner as Venus were terrible – he was a wimp, and she was no Mary Martin, even though her voice was dubbed by Eileen Wilson. Also, of the 16 Weill songs in the original, only a handful survived and only one had the original Nash lyrics – 'The Trouble with Women.' Dick Haymes, Eve Arden and Olga San Juan didn't further the action much, either.

A Connecticut Yankee hit Broadway in 1927 and stayed for 418 performances. The book by Herbert Fields was based on Mark Twain's *A Connecticut Yankee at King Arthur's Court*; the lyrics were by Lorenz Hart and the music by Richard Rodgers. Directed by Alexander Leftwich with dances by Busby Berkeley, it starred William Gaxton, Constance Carpenter, William Norris and June Cochrane.

Berkeley was not exactly a hot property at the time. He had just come from being a dance director for *Castles in the Air* and *Lady Do* – neither of them blockbusters – and, most recently, *Sweet Lady*, which collapsed out of town, although

1943; it would run for 567 performances. With its book by S J Perelman and Ogden Nash, lyrics by Nash and music by Kurt Weill, it had everything. Directed by Elia Kazan with dances by Agnes De Mille, it starred Kenny Baker, Mary Martin, John Boles and Paula Lawrence.

Rodney Hatch (Baker) is about to pop the question to his girl friend Gloria (Ruth Bond) when he stops in the Whitelaw Savory Foundation of Modern Art. There he sees a statue of Venus and, as a lark, puts Gloria's engagement ring on its finger. The goddess (Martin) comes to life and falls in love with Rodney at first sight. She follows him to his apartment, where he tells her he is in love with Gloria. But that doesn't stop her. Venus goes to a dress shop, takes the clothing from a dummy in the window and dresses herself in full view of the people on the sidewalk. Of course the police come, but she is rescued by millionaire Whitelaw Savory (Boles), who falls in love with her. Venus, however, still loves Rodney. Gloria comes in from New Jersey and demands the ring from Rodney and, naturally enough, she doesn't believe his story about a statue coming to life. Venus is irritated and sends Gloria to the North Pole. Complications set in – Rodney is suspected of stealing the statue, and he and Venus are accused of murdering the absent Gloria. They are sent to jail, but Venus opens the prison doors and the two escape to a hotel. Rodney falls in love with Venus and tells her of the

it featured a young English dancer named Archie Leach, who later changed his name to Cary Grant. In *Yankee*, Berkeley operated very largely on nerve; he had a reputation as a dance director, but he had never taken a dancing lesson. He worried about it:

The second act opened with Queen Guinevere's dancing class in the castle. I thought it would be a good ploy to start the scene with the Queen teaching the class the first five positions of dance. The trouble was I didn't know even the first position, let alone the others. So I walked around the stage rubbing my head and pretending I was thinking up something. I said to one of the girls, "I think I'll have the Queen start off by showing the first position." She said, "Oh, you mean this," and pointed her feet in a certain way. I looked out of the corner of my eye to see what she was doing and then pointed to another girl. "Second position," and so on. In this way, and without their knowing it, I learned the first five positions of dance.'

One New York critic wrote, 'A new dance director has been born on Broadway.'

The story did veer a little from Samuel Clemens. Alic Carter (Carpenter) is so angry with her flirting fiancé (Gaxton) that she hits him over the head with a bottle of champagne, knocking him unconscious. He turns up in King Arthur's Court, where he is so different that he is sentenced to be burned at the stake. Just before the pile of faggots is to be ignited, he remembers that there is to be an eclipse of the sun at that moment. He predicts the eclipse and is hailed as a wizard. He then assumes the management of the kingdom (being paid on a percentage basis).

The hit song from the musical, 'My Heart Stood Still,' was first presented in a London revue by Rodgers and Hart, *One Dam Thing After Another*, in 1927. It hadn't been a hit until the Prince of Wales (later to become Edward VII of England, who abdicated the throne to marry American-born divorcée Wallis Warfield Simpson) asked for it to be played at the Café de Paris in London. The band leader didn't know the tune, so the Prince whistled the melody and the band picked it up. The publicity made the song popular, and Rodgers and Hart bought back the rights from the revue producer and put it into *A Connecticut Yankee*. Some other songs in the score were 'Thou Swell,' 'On a Desert Island with Thee' and 'I Feel at Home with You.' The show was revived in 1943 with Dick Foran, Vivienne Segal, Vera-Ellen and Robert Chisholm. Six songs were added – among them 'To Keep My Love Alive.'

The first film version of the Mark Twain tale appeared in 1921, with William Fox, but this, of course, was a silent picture. The second time around was in 1931, with Will Rogers and Maureen O'Sullivan, but this was not a musical. Finally the musical version of *A Connecticut Yankee in King Arthur's Court* (1949) hit the screen. It starred Bing Crosby, Rhonda Fleming (who had beaten out Gail Russell for the part), Sir Cedric Hardwicke, William Bendix and Henry Wilcoxon. This time the hero was a blacksmith who had been knocked unconscious. The film was lovely to look at and pretty good to listen to, although none of the Rodgers and Hart tunes were used. It wasn't that Paramount didn't want to use them, but rather that MGM owned the rights, having bought them up when they made their film biography of Rodgers and Hart, *Words and Music* (1948). The score for the movie was written by Johnny Burke and Jimmy Van Heusen, and included 'Once and For Always,' 'Busy Doing Nothing,' 'If

William Gaxton moons over Constance Carpenter as a knight looks on, in the Broadway show *A Connecticut Yankee* (1927).

You Stub Your Toe on the Moon' and 'When Is Sometime?'

The musical comedy *On the Town* premiered on Broadway in 1944. It had a book and lyrics by Betty Comden and Adolph Green and music by Leonard Bernstein. Directed by George Abbott with choreography by Jerome Robbins, it featured Sono Osato, Betty Comden, Adolph Green, Nancy Walker, Chris Alexander, John Battles and Alice Pearce, and ran for 463 performances.

Comden and Green borrowed the basic plot for the musical from a ballet, *Fancy Free*, which had been choreographed by Robbins to music by Bernstein, but they had to teach Bernstein how to be a song writer, since this was his first musical comedy. It was a rousing success, and the Newspaper Guild of New York presented it with its Page One Award as the outstanding achievement in the theater in 1945. In 1959 it was revived in two off-Broadway theaters, and Walter Kerr, the critic, said of *Fancy Free* 'It still stands as one of the most original, inventive and irresistibly charming of all American musicals.'

In the show, three American sailors are on leave for just 24 hours. Gabey (Battles) is the romanticist, Ozzie (Green) is the carefree one and Chip (Alexander) is the serious one. In the subway Gabey sees a photograph of that month's 'Miss Turnstiles' (Osato) and wants to meet her. Chip meets Claire (Walker), a woman taxi driver. Ozzie finds Hildy (Comden) in the American Museum of Natural History. Gabey goes to a music studio in Carnegie Hall and finds 'Miss Turnstiles' taking singing lessons. The six protagonists explore New York, and at the end of the 24 hours, the three sailors return to their ship.

On the Town has been called a young people's frolic, with the average age of the producers, co-authors, stars and composer being about 25. The production moved at a breathless pace, causing critics to say 'It shoves dullness off the curbstone' and 'One of the freshest of musicals to come to town in a long time.' Among the wonderful numbers were 'I Get Carried Away,' 'I Can Cook, Too,' 'New York, New York,' 'Lucky to Be Me' and 'Lonely Town.' Robbins contributed a subway-ride fantasy and two choreographic conceptions,

'Miss Turnstiles' and 'Gabey in the Playground of the Rich.'

At MGM, Louis B Mayer really didn't want to buy the rights to the Broadway show; he called it 'smutty' and 'communistic' because of one scene in which a black girl danced with a white man. But Arthur Freed persuaded him, and five years later Freed started the movie version of On the Town. It was perfect for Gene Kelly – he not only starred in the picture but also directed it and, with Stanley Donen, did the choreography. Vera-Ellen was Miss Turnstiles, Frank Sinatra was the sailor chased by the lady cab driver, Brunhilde Esterhazy (Betty Garrett), and Jules Munshin captured the anthropologist (Ann Miller).

Great as it was as a ballet film, unfortunately, most of Bernstein's work was jettisoned. What remained included some ballet music – 'Miss Turnstiles,' 'Day in New York' and a few songs from the original – 'New York, New York,' 'I Feel Like I'm Not Out of Bed Yet' and 'Come Up to My Place.' The rest of the score was by Roger Edens, Comden and Green, including 'Prehistoric Man,' 'Main Street,' 'You're Awful,' 'On the Town,' 'You Can Count on Me,' 'Pearl of the Persian Sea' and 'That's All There Is, Folks.'

LEFT: Sono Osato being held aloft in the 'Miss Turnstiles' ballet in the stage version of On the Town (1944).

BELOW: Betty Garrett, Ann Miller, Gene Kelly, Jules Munshin, Frank Sinatra and Alice Pearce in 1949's film version.

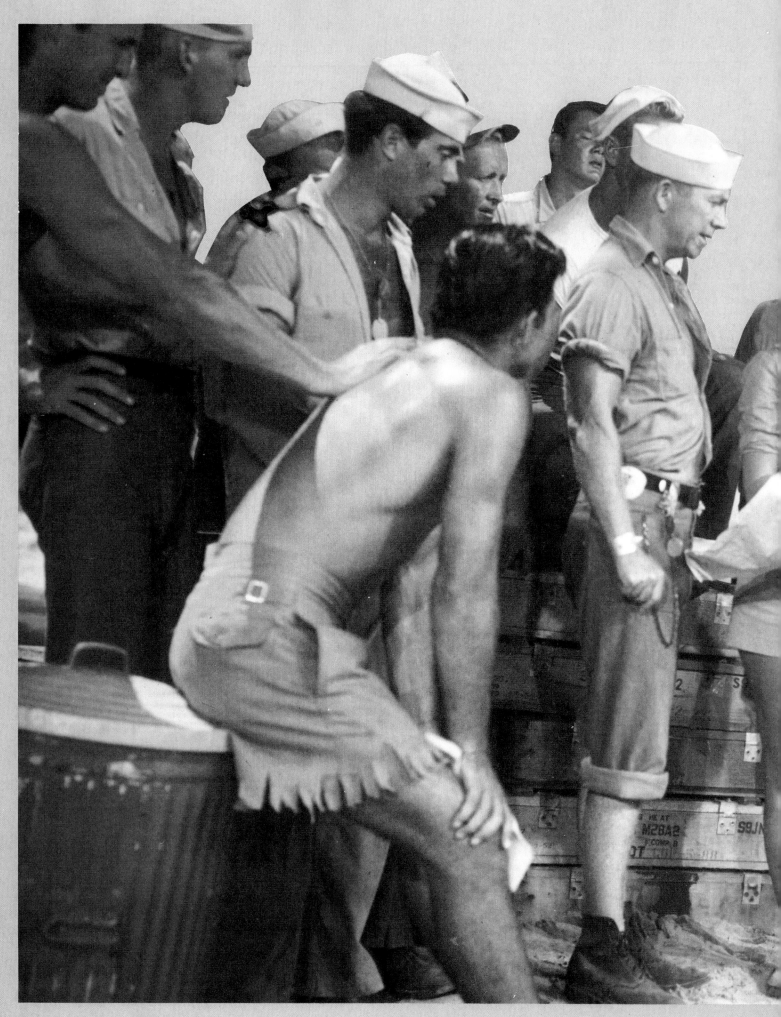

THE STAGE-STRUCK FIFTIES

Broadway hits were the source of almost all the great Hollywood musicals of the 1950s. The studios were reeling from the impact of television, and musical adaptations promised an audience pre-sold on the songs via juke-box, radio and TV. With box-office success almost guaranteed, Hollywood spent millions to turn lavish stage productions into even more opulent wide-screen spectacles that moviegoers flocked to see. Television – that upstart – had failed in its bid to supplant the movies entirely.

LEFT: Mitzi Gaynor, Ray Walston and sailors, in the film version of Rodgers and Hammerstein's *South Pacific* (1958).

BELOW: Gordon MacRae as Curly in the movie *Oklahoma!* (1955). 'The corn is as high as an elephant's eye.'

ABOVE: Ray Middleton as Frank Butler and Ethel Merman as Annie Oakley, in the Broadway production of *Annie Get Your Gun* (1946).

Howard Keel as Frank Butler and Betty Hutton as Annie Oakley, in the movie version of Irving Berlin's *Annie Get Your Gun* (1950).

als got much better during the 1950s.

Annie Get Your Gun opened on Broadway in 1946. It had a book by Herbert and Dorothy Fields, words and music by Irving Berlin and was produced by Richard Rodgers and Oscar Hammerstein II. It starred Ethel Merman and Ray Middleton and lasted a phenomenal 1147 performances on Broadway. There were 1304 performances in London (with Dolores Gray) and a national company (starring Mary Martin) that seemed to go on for years. Its revival in 1966 with Merman and Bruce Yarnell was also a hit, and Berlin added another song to the show – 'Old Fashioned Wedding.'

Originally, Rodgers and Hammerstein had wanted Jerome Kern to do the stage musical, but when Kern died they turned to Berlin. He was so enthusiastic that he wrote five songs for the show in a mere three days. The result was a musical that broke no new ground, tore down no barriers. It was just broad-humored fun and was probably the finest score in Irving Berlin's long list of hits.

The plot was simple. Annie Oakley (Merman), a backwoods girl, becomes the beautiful rifle-shooting star of Buffalo Bill's Wild West Show. The rival Pawnee Bill's Show has a male marksman – the handsome Frank Butler (Middleton). When the two shows play Cincinnati simultaneously, the two meet and Annie falls helplessly in love. Eventually, the two Wild-West shows merge, and after a lot of confrontations and rivalry, Annie decides to marry Frank and trade in shooting fame for domestic bliss.

Some of the hit songs were 'Colonel Buffalo Bill,' 'I've Got the Sun in the Morning,' 'You Can't Get a Man with a Gun,' 'They Say that Falling in Love Is Wonderful,' 'My Defenses Are Down,' 'There's No Business Like Show Business,' 'Doin' What Comes Naturally,' 'The Girl That I Marry,' 'Anything You Can Do,' 'Moonshine Lullaby,' 'Who Do you Love, I Hope' and 'I'm an Indian Too.'

MGM's film version of *Annie Get Your Gun* was released in 1950. Judy Garland had been signed to play Annie, but she was fired, probably for lack of professionalism, and it was Betty Hutton who finally appeared in the role. Recordings do exist, however, of Gatland singing some of the songs from the film – made before she was fired. Frank Butler was played by Howard Keel and Buffalo Bill by Louis Calhern. (Frank Morgan was the original choice to play Buffalo Bill, but he died before the shooting started.) Edward Arnold was Pawnee Bill and J Carroll Naish was Sitting Bull. The film was remarkably faithful to the original, with only a few numbers eliminated.

No, No Nanette came out of Hollywood once more in 1950, this time retitled *Tea For Two*. Starring Doris Day, Gordon MacRae and Gene Nelson, it was an unpretentious little gem. The plot had been changed, of course. Doris Day is forced to say 'No' to every proposition, offer or question in order to win a bet whose payoff would be enough money to finance and star in a Broadway show. Most of the original songs were eliminated, but a great number of golden oldies were substituted. Among the numbers were 'I Want to Be Happy' and 'Tea For Two' by Vincent Youmans and Irving Caesar; 'No, No Nanette' by Youmans and Otto Harbach; 'Oh Me, Oh My!' by Youmans and Ira Gershwin; 'I Know That You Know' by Youmans and Anne Caldwell; 'Do Do Do' by the Gershwins; 'Crazy Rhythm' by Caesar, Joseph Meyer and Roger Wolf Kahn; 'Charleston' by Cecil Mack and Jimmie Johnson; 'I Only Have Eyes for You' by Al Dubin and Harry Warren; and 'The Call of the Sea' by Youmans, Caesar and Harbach.

Beginning in 1950, the films made from Broadway musicals changed. Since about 1947 the specter of television had loomed large over film production, and the movie musical suffered a decline, both in quality and in quantity. Then things changed. Hollywood found that if it was more faithful to the original stage-musical books and scores, it could save a great deal of money by not hiring extra writers, composers and lyricists. Also, stage musicals had changed from vehicles that used songs as mere fillers when the action slowed or the dialogue faltered to modern comedies or dramas where the songs were integrated with the plot and moved the story line along. The result of this happy combination was that music-

The *Cotton Blossom* docks in Natchez in the 1951 remake of *Show Boat.* Ava Gardner (Julie) is standing on the gangplank.

Another revival of the early fifties was *Show Boat* (1951). This stunning Technicolor extravaganza starred Kathryn Grayson as Magnolia, Ava Gardner as Julie (MGM had wanted Judy Garland, but she couldn't make it, and Gardner's voice had to be dubbed by Eileen Wilson), Howard Keel as Ravenal, Joe E Brown as Cap'n Andy, William Warfield as Joe, Agnes Moorehead as Parthenia Hawks and Marge and Gower Champion as Ellie and Frank. Although the ending was slightly changed, most of the songs from the stage version remained, and the whole production was wonderful to see and hear.

A remake of *Roberta*, retitled *Lovely to Look At*, was released in 1952. This time the hero was an American comedian (Red Skelton) who inherits a half interest in a Parisian dress salon. Skelton and two friends (Howard Keel and Gower Champion) go to Paris in hope of selling his interest in the shop. But the salon is almost bankrupt, despite the efforts of the two women who run it (Kathryn Grayson and Marge Champion). Skelton takes over and turns it into a roaring success. Grayson and Keel, Skelton and Ann Miller, and Champion and Champion live happily ever after.

The show was filled with wonderful Jerome Kern melodies. Among them were (lyricists listed) 'Yesterdays,' 'The Touch of Your Hand' and 'Smoke Gets in Your Eyes' by Otto Harbach, 'LaFayette' by Dorothy Fields, 'Lovely to Look At' by Fields and Jimmie McHugh, 'The Most Exciting Night,' 'You're Devastating' and 'I Won't Dance' by Fields, McHugh, Harbach and Oscar Hammerstein II, 'I'll Be Hard to Handle' by Fields and Bernard Dougall, plus one song not by Kern – 'Opening Night' by Fields and McHugh.

The postwar Broadway audiences were ready for a musical farce, and they got it in *Where's Charley?* (1948). The book by George Abbott was based on an 1893 play by Brandon Thomas, *Charley's Aunt*, which almost immediately became a staple of amateur theaters and high-school dramatic societies. The lyrics and music were by Frank Loesser, Abbott was the director and starring in the production were Ray Bolger, Allyn McLerie, Doretta Morrow and Byron Palmer. It ran for 792 performances.

Cy Feuer, head of the music division of Republic Studios in Hollywood, along with Ernest Martin, had acquired the rights to the old play for a musical-comedy treatment; they tried to convince Loesser to do the score. Loesser, knowing that it had been around for years and that several films had been made of it (one starring Jack Benny), was convinced that it was too tired and hackneyed to make a successful musical. But he finally yielded to the blandishments of Feuer, who was a close friend.

Two Oxford students, Charles Wykeham (played by the then 44-year-old Bolger) and Jack Chesney (Palmer), want to invite their lady friends, Amy Spettigue (McLerie) and Kitty Verdun (Morrow) to the university with the intent of proposing marriage. But the guardian of the girls, Stephen Spettigue (Horace Cooper) insists that they have a chaperone for the visit. Charley is expecting a visit from his aunt, Donna Lucia D'Alvadores, a rich Brazilian widow, and he volunteers her as the chaperone. Meanwhile, Jack's father is in debt so deeply that he tells Jack to leave school and marry Donna Lucia. But Donna Lucia is delayed in Brazil, and Charley is forced to impersonate her in drag – black dress, gray wig, lace gloves and all. The widow does make an appearance at the end, but sizes up the situation and takes a false identity. The boys win the girls, Jack's father wins Donna Lucia and his financial problems are over.

Bolger was terrific. His female impersonation was never camp, his dancing was flawless and in his big hit song, 'Once In Love With Amy,' he was able to get audiences to participate in singing the chorus. Sometimes the routine stopped the show for 20 minutes. It was an accidental inspiration. Early in the run, Feuer's seven-year-old son was at a matinee sitting in the front row. He knew everything about the show, so when Bolger temporarily forgot some of the words and unself-consciously asked the audience, 'What were those lyrics, anyway?,' Feuer's son started singing them. The result was such a success that it was decided to keep the bit in the show.

LEFT: Ray Bolger as the tea-drinking Donna Lucia D'Alvadores in the film *Where's Charley?* (1952).

ABOVE: Bolger and MacLerie dance the Pernambuco in the hit *Where's Charley?*, which opened on Broadway in 1948.

Another song from the show, 'My Darling, My Darling,' was number one on the radio show 'Your Hit Parade' for weeks. Other numbers in the show were 'The New Ashmolean Marching Society and Student Conservatory Band,' 'Make a Miracle,' 'At the Red Rose Cotillion' and 'Better Get Out of Here.'

Bolger repeated his success in the film version of *Where's Charley?* (1952), as did Allyn McLerie. The Technicolor movie, choreographed by Michael Kidd, was shot on location in Oxford, England, and the Loesser songs survived quite nicely.

Yet another film version of *The Merry Widow* was released in 1952. But gone was the sense of fun of the 1934 Lubitsch version. Lana Turner (her singing voice dubbed by Trudy Erwin) was miscast as the widow, Fernando Lamas performed in a stereotyped operetta style, and the dances were uninspiring.

Another of Irving Berlin's long-running hits (644 performances), *Call Me Madam*, premiered on Broadway in 1950. With a book by the old masters Howard Lindsay and Russel Crouse, it featured Ethel Merman, Russell Nype, Galina Talva and Paul Lucas.

In the play, Merman played the fictional counterpart of the real-life Perle Mesta, the 'Hostess with the Mostest,' who was appointed to be the United States Ambassador to Luxembourg. Merman was Sally Adams, the American Ambassador to Lichtenberg, who is attracted to Prime Minister Cosmo Constantine (Lucas). There was a subplot involving the romance between the ambassador's assistant, Kenneth Gibson (Nype), and Princess Maria (Talva). Otherwise, there was no plot.

Merman dominated all the proceedings on the stage, and when the movie version of *Call Me Madam* came out in 1953, she dominated all the proceedings on the screen, too. Donald O'Connor had the Nype part, Vera-Ellen (with her voice dubbed by Carole Richards) had the Talva part and George Sanders played Merman's suitor.

OPPOSITE TOP: Ethel Merman as Ambassador Sally Adams and Paul Lucas as Prime Minister Cosmo Constantine, in the Broadway hit *Call Me Madam* (1950).

OPPOSITE BOTTOM: Donald O'Connor, Vera-Ellen, Ethel Merman, George Sanders and Billy De Wolfe were the stars of Hollywood's *Call Me Madam* (1953).

RIGHT: Lana Turner and Fernando Lamas played the widow and Count Danilo, respectively, in the filmed remake of *The Merry Widow* (1956).

But the music, on stage and on screen, was the thing. The movie added an old Berlin song, 'International Rag,' but otherwise stuck pretty closely to the original score. One song that never failed to stop the show was the rendition of 'You're Just in Love,' sung by Merman in counterpoint with Nype/O'Connor. This was added to the play at the last minute and was written in just two days. Then there were other hits, such as 'The Hostess with the Mostest,' 'Can You Use Any Money Today?,' 'Marrying for Love,' 'It's a Lovely Day Today,' 'Welcome to Lichtenberg,' 'Mrs Sally Adams,' 'The Ocarina,' 'What Chance Have I with Love?' 'Something to Dance About' and 'The Best Thing for You.'

It has been said that *Call Me Madam*, as well as two other Broadway musicals made into films in 1953, *Gentlemen Prefer Blondes* and *Kiss Me Kate*, sounded the death knell for original screen musicals. At least they helped to clear the path for one Broadway import after another.

Gentlemen Prefer Blondes made its debut on Broadway in 1949. It had a book by Anita Loos and Joseph Fields, which was based on Loos's stage play of 1926 of the same name, starring June Walker, Frank Morgan and Edna Hibbard. This in turn was based on Loos's best-selling book of the same name. The lyrics were by Leo Robin and the music was by

Jule Styne. Directed by John S Wilson with dances by Agnes De Mille, it featured Carol Channing, Yvonne Adair and Jack MacCauley, and ran an astonishing 740 performances.

The time was the raucous, jazz-mad, iconoclastic 1920s. Lorelei Lee (Channing) became the personification of that decade. The *Ile de France* is sailing from New York to France in 1924 with two girls on board – Lorelei and Dorothy Shaw (Adair). Not only do they want to escape Prohibition, they want rich husbands. In Paris, Dorothy meets and falls in love with Henry Spofford (Erich Brotherson), a Philadelphian. Lorelei borrows $5000 from Sir Francis Beekman in order to buy a diamond tiara from Sir Francis's wife. The wife sends lawyers to find Lorelei when she finds out where she got the money, but Lorelei's boy friend arrives in Paris, pays back the money, and all's well.

Some of the fine songs in the show were 'A Little Girl from Little Rock,' 'Diamonds Are a Girl's Best Friend,' 'Bye Bye Baby,' 'Just a Kiss Apart,' 'Mamie Is Mimi' and 'Keeping Cool with Coolidge.'

The movie version of *Gentlemen Prefer Blondes* (1953) starred Marilyn Monroe and Jane Russell as Lorelei and Dorothy, respectively, and both of them gave their best performances up to that time. Choreographer Jack Cole

devised superb dances, especially in 'Diamonds Are a Girl's Best Friend' and 'A [Two] Little Girl[s] from Little Rock.' Charles Coburn was delightful as the millionaire chased by Monroe, and Tommy Noonan was her American fiancé.

Unfortunately, the only songs kept from the original Styne-Robin score were 'Diamonds Are a Girl's Best Friend,' 'Bye Bye Baby' and 'A Little Girl from Little Rock.' But there were good substitutions, such as the Hoagy Carmichael-Harold Adamson 'Ain't There Anyone Here for Love,' where Russell and a dozen handsome weightlifters do a dance in the ship's gymnasium, ending up in the pool, and another Carmichael-Adamson number, 'When Love Goes Wrong.'

It could be argued that *Kiss Me Kate* (1948) was Cole Porter's Broadway masterpiece. Certainly it was his most popular show. It played in New York for a monumental 1077 performances, and the National Company toured for three years. It was translated into 18 languages, playing in, among other places, Berlin, Turkey, Japan, Czechoslovakia, Hungary, Poland (the first American musical ever seen there) and South America. Indeed, the *Volksoper* in Vienna premiered it in German in 1956, and it was the greatest box-office draw in the history of that opera house, retained in its repertory for nearly a decade.

The book was by Sam and Bella Spewack, based on Shakespeare's play *The Taming of the Shrew*. The words and music were by Porter, and it was directed by John C Wilson with choreography by Hanya Holm. Starring in it were Alfred Drake, Patricia Morison, Lisa Kirk and Harold Lang.

The musical opened with a touring theatrical company in Baltimore about to present *The Taming of the Shrew*. The four principals in the company are Fred Graham (Drake), his former wife, Lilli (Morison), Bill Calhoun (Lang) and his girl

LEFT: Alfred Drake, as Petruchio in *The Taming of the Shrew*, spanks Patricia Morison, as Kate, in this play-within-a-play scene from the Broadway hit *Kiss Me Kate* (1948).

OPPOSITE: Kathryn Grayson and Gordon MacRae were the stars of the 1953 Hollywood remake of *The Desert Song*.

BELOW: Howard Keel and Kathryn Grayson as Petruchio and the tamed shrew in the film version of *Kiss Me Kate* (1953). James Whitmore (top) and Keenan Wynn, as the two gangsters, keep watch on the principals from behind the screen at right.

friend Lois Lane (Kirk). Bill owes $10,000 to professional gamblers. Then the scene shifts to Shakespeare. The play within a play explains that Bianca (Kirk) cannot get married until her older sister, Kate (Morison), is married. Petruchio (Drake) has come to Padua to find a rich wife, and Katherine seems to be the most likely candidate, but she rejects him. The scene shifts to the present. Lilli threatens to leave the company, and the gangsters come for the money that Bill owes them. Then it's back to Shakespeare. Kate has now married Petruchio, but although she is a shrew, it turns out that she is tameable, so *that* part of the show ends up happily. It also turns out that a shake-up in the underworld has caused Bill's debt to be cancelled. Ultimately, Fred and Lilli are reconciled and Bill and Lois are engaged.

Since the story revolved around the lives of actors who were rehearsing Shakespeare, Porter had to write a score with both modern and Elizabethan rhythms. He was brilliant, and some of the 14 songs have become classics. Among them were 'Wunderbar,' 'Why Can't You Behave?' 'So In Love,' 'We Open in Venice,' 'Too Darned Hot,' 'I Hate Men,' 'Were Thine That Special Face,' 'Where Is the Life that Late I Led?' 'Always True to You in My Fashion,' 'I Am Ashamed that Women Are So Simple,' 'Brush Up Your Shakespeare,' 'Kiss Me Kate,' 'Tom, Dick and Harry' and 'I've Come to Wive It Wealthily in Padua.'

It took a long time – five years – for the movie version of *Kiss Me Kate* (1953) to appear. MGM had bought the film rights to the show, but there was a clause in the contract saying that the picture could not be released until the stage show had closed. That took quite a while.

The film starred Kathryn Grayson, Howard Keel, Ann Miller and Bobby Van as the four actors, and they got a lot of help from Keenan Wynn and James Whitmore as the gangsters. The result was a sensational film, although purists might quibble about some of the changes that were made in the original play. For some reason, a previous Porter hit, 'From This Moment On,' was stuck in as a ballet-and-tap-dance speciality number. The wonderful song 'I Am Ashamed That Women Are So Simple' was spoken by Grayson, rather than sung. The camera was concentrating on a backstage discussion while Grayson was on stage singing the clever 'I Hate Men,' and most of the lyrics were lost.

The film, oddly enough, was produced in both 3-D and flat versions. But by the time of its release, the 3-D fad was over, so only the flat version was seen in theaters.

The Desert Song came back in yet another film incarnation in 1953, this time with Gordon MacRae and Kathryn Grayson. Some changes had been made. This was at the height of the McCarthy Era, and the hero could no longer be referred to as the Red Shadow. This time he saves the French garrison from the evil Sheik Youssef (Raymond Massey) and wins the general's daughter. In addition to the Sigmund Romberg-Oscar Hammerstein II tunes like 'Desert Song,' 'Long Live the Night,' 'The Riff Song,' 'Romance,' 'One Alone' and 'One Flower,' a song by Jack Scholl and Serge Walter, 'Gay Parisienne,' was added.

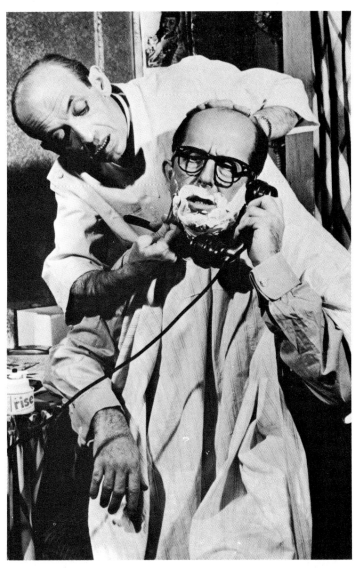

Top Banana opened on Broadway in 1951 and stayed for 350 performances. With its book by Hy Kraft, and music and lyrics by Johnny Mercer, it starred Phil Silvers and was a pleasant enough musical comedy with very deep roots in burlesque.

Silvers played a television comic, obviously patterned after Milton Berle, whose sponsors insist that there be more love interest in his scripts. So he hires a pair of youngsters to play the love interest and ends up falling in love with the ingénue. But by that time, the two kids have fallen in love with each other.

The film version of Top Banana (1954) stuck pretty closely to the original. Some of the numbers were 'A Word A Day,' 'If You Want to Be a Top Banana,' 'I Fought Every Step of the Way,' 'Sans Souci,' 'Only if You're in Love,' 'The Man of the Year This Week' and 'My Home Is in My Shoes.'

Still another film version of Rose Marie appeared in 1954, and it had several things going for it – Eastman Color, Bert Lahr and Howard Keel. But it had one disadvantage: Cinema-Scope – that distorting lens that created wide-open spaces not even Busby Berkeley could fill.

In this version, which starred Ann Blyth, Keel, Lahr, Fernando Lamas and Marjorie Main, Rose Marie is now a pretty little waif of the forest who falls in love with a trapper of dubious character, and the Mountie behaves in a brotherly fashion. The daughter of an Indian chief (Joan Taylor) falls in love with the trapper, too, and when her father (Chief Yowlahie) beats her for it, she knifes him to death, using the trapper's weapon. The trapper is accused of the deed, but is later cleared. A subplot concerned the wooing of Marjorie Main, the operator of a saloon-hotel, by Lahr, whose buffoon-like Mountie provided a lot of laughs, but must have offended the entire population of Canada.

Four of the original songs were kept – 'Rose Marie,' 'The Indian Love Call,' 'The Mounties' and 'Totem Tom-Tom,' all

ABOVE: Herbie Faye gives Phil Silvers a shave in the stage version of Top Banana (1951).

RIGHT: Hollywood remade Rose Marie yet again in 1954, starring Fernando Lamas, Ann Blyth and Bert Lahr.

with music by Rudolf Friml and words by Oscar Hammerstein II and Otto Harbach. Friml, then 72 years old, was hired to write some other melodies to which Paul Francis Webster added the lyrics – 'The Right Place to Be for a Girl,' 'Free to Be Free,' 'Love and Kisses' and 'I Have Love.' One more song, 'The Mountie Who Never Got His Man' by Hubert Baker and George Stoll, was sung as a lament by Bert Lahr.

The elaborate Indian ceremonial dance 'Totem Tom-Tom' was the show stopper. Staged by Busby Berkeley, it featured Joan Taylor and some 100 Indian braves. Berkeley later said about it:

We rehearsed this number for a month and it ended up costing $200,000. We used Stage 15 at MGM, then the largest sound stage in the world, and turned it into a mountain stronghold. We tried to make the number as dramatic and frenzied as possible, and at the climax I had one of the Indians grab Joan Taylor, lift her over his head, and throw her from a cliff 50 feet high into the outstretched arms of the Indians below, who then bound her to a great totem pole. It was an exciting routine to stage, and people seemed to be very impressed with it.

One of the most unusual Broadway musicals of 1943 was *Carmen Jones*, and it was a tour de force for Oscar Hammerstein II. He had written new lyrics for Georges Bizet's *Car-*

men, updated the opera to World-War-II times, changed the setting from early nineteenth-century Seville to a Southern town in the United States. The cigarette factory was changed to a parachute factory; Don José, the Spanish dragoon, became Joe, the American soldier; Escamillo, the toreador, became Husky Miller, the prize fighter, and the whole cast consisted of talented black singers. So taxing were the roles of Carmen and Joe that two performers alternated in each role – Muriel Smith and Muriel Rahn (Carmen) and Luther Saxon and Napoleon Reed (Joe). It ran for 502 performances.

Joe falls in love with Carmen, goes absent without leave and flees with her to Chicago. There she rejects him in favor of Husky Miller, and he kills her outside a boxing arena. The 'Habanera' aria became 'Dat's Love,' the 'Seguidilla' became 'Dere's a Café on de Corner,' the 'Gypsy Song' became 'Beat Out dat Rhythm on a Drum,' the 'Toreador Song' became 'Stan' Up and Fight,' The 'Flower Song' became 'Dis Flower' and 'Michaela's Air' became 'My Joe.' Some of the other songs were 'You Talk Just Like My Maw,' 'Card Song' and 'Whizzin' Away Along de Tracks.'

Bizet's opera probably holds the record for the number of films it has spawned – 14. The film version of *Carmen Jones* (1954) starred Harry Belafonte and Dorothy Dandridge (whose voices were dubbed by La Verne Hutchinson and Marilyn Horne) and Pearl Bailey. Unfortunately, the film contains a classic Hollywood boo-boo. The camera tracks with Dorothy Dandridge down a street full of shops, and the entire crew is seen reflected in the windows that she passes.

Brigadoon, which opened on Broadway in 1947, brought back fantasy to the musical stage. After World War II, audiences were more willing to suspend disbelief and to accept as real the story about a Scottish village that had disappeared in 1747 to reappear once each hundred years. With a book and lyrics by Alan J Lerner and music by Frederick Loewe, it was a charming sensation, running for 581 performances. Directed by Robert Lewis with choreography by Agnes De Mille, it featured David Brooks, Marion Bell and George Keane.

Loewe had mentioned to Lerner that faith could move mountains, and they decided to make faith the theme of a musical comedy. Tommy Albright (Brooks) and Jeff Douglas (Keane) are two Americans wandering through the Scottish countryside. They hear the strains of a song, 'Brigadoon,' from the distance, and the town comes into being for the first time in a century. Fiona MacLaren (Bell) and her sister Jean, who is married to Charlie Dalrymple (Lee Sullivan), are out gathering heather, and Tommy and Jeff help them. There are various subplots, but the main thing is that Tommy and Fiona fall in love. He can't bring himself to stay in Brigadoon, however, knowing that it will soon disappear for another 100 years, so he leaves. Later he changes his mind, returns to the empty field and, because of his faith in his love, the town reappears and he is reunited with Fiona.

Actually, with the exception of two songs, 'Come to Me, Bend to Me' and 'I'll Go Home with Bonnie Jean,' the music was not particularly Scottish-sounding. Still, *Brigadoon* was the first musical play to win the Drama Critics Circle Award as the best play of the year. Among the other songs were 'The Heather on the Hill,' 'Almost Like Being in Love,' 'Waitin' for My Dearie' and 'There But for You Go I.'

To put it mildly, the film version of *Brigadoon* (1954) left much to be desired. To begin with, MGM's studio boss, Dore Schary, decided to shoot it on a sound stage rather than outdoors on location. Gene Kelly (Tommy) tended to overact; Van Johnson (Jeff) was no dancer and Cyd Charisse (Fiona), although her dancing was flawless, acted listlessly.

OPPOSITE TOP: Gene Kelly and Van Johnson being chased by Scotsman Eddie Quillan in the movie *Brigadoon* (1954).

OPPOSITE BOTTOM: On Broadway, David Brooks was Tommy Albright and Marion Bell was Fiona MacLaren in *Brigadoon* (1947).

TOP RIGHT: Howard Marsh and Ilse Marenga in the original stage production of *The Student Prince*, which premiered on Broadway in 1924.

RIGHT: Ann Blyth as the barmaid and Edmund Purdom (using Mario Lanza's singing voice) as the prince, in the Hollywood version of *The Student Prince* (1954).

The Student Prince opened on Broadway in 1924. With music by Sigmund Romberg and lyrics by Dorothy Donnelly, it starred Howard Marsh and Ilse Marenga. It was revived on Broadway in 1943, starring Jan Keipura and Marta Eggerth.

It told the story of the heir to a European throne, Prince Karl, who is sent to the University of Heidelberg for one last fling; there he falls in love with a barmaid, Kathie. *The Student Prince* was first filmed as a silent by Ernst Lubitsch in 1927 and starred Ramon Novarro and Norma Schearer.

The sound version of *The Student Prince* (1954) starred Ann Blyth, Edmund Purdom and Louis Calhern. Mario Lanza had been scheduled to play the role of the prince: his temper tantrums and increasing obesity caused him to be fired, but not until after he had recorded the songs. The result was that Edmund Purdom stepped in with his wooden acting technique and mouthed the lyrics that Lanza had taped. The songs were still thrilling, among them 'Deep in My Heart,' 'Golden Days,' 'The Drinking Song' and 'Serenade.' Added were three new songs by Nicholas Brodszky and Paul Francis Webster: 'Beloved,' 'Summer in Heidelberg' and 'I'll Walk with God.'

The 1955 Hollywood remake of *Hit the Deck*: Powell and Damone, Miller and Martin and Reynolds and Tamblyn.

A remake of *Hit the Deck* was released in 1955, featuring Kay Arman, Jane Powell, Vic Damone, Tony Martin, Ann Miller, Debbie Reynolds, Walter Pidgeon, J Carrol Naish and Russ Tamblyn. It told the tale of three sailors on leave (sound familiar?) who find love. The pairings were: Miller and Martin, Damone and Powell and Reynolds and Tamblyn.

The plot was dull, but the music was far more interesting. The score included 'Hallelujah,' 'Join the Navoo-Loo,' 'Lucky Bird' and 'Why Oh Why' by Vincent Youmans, Clifford Grey and Leo Robin; 'The Lady from the Bayou' and 'A Kiss or Two' by Youmans and Robin; 'Sometimes I'm Happy' by Youmans, Grey and Irving Caesar; 'I Know That You Know' by Youmans and Anne Caldwell; 'More Than You Know' by Youmans, Billy Rose and Edward Eliscu; 'Keepin' Myself for You' by Youmans and Sidney Clare; and 'Ciribiribee' by A Pestalozza.

There is no doubt that the biggest musical hit on Broadway in 1950 was *Guys and Dolls*. The book was by Jo Swerling and Abe Burrows, and was based on characters and a short story 'The Idylls of Sarah Brown,' By Damon Runyon. The words and music were by Frank Loesser. Directed by George S Kaufman with dances by Michael Kidd, it featured Isabell Bigley, Sam Levene, Robert Alda, Vivian Blaine and Pat Rooney. This musical triumph ran for 1200 performances.

The plot was simple. A Broadway gambler, who later falls in love with a Save-A-Soul Mission lassie, wins a bet by taking her to Havana and later brings in all his fellow gamblers to save the mission. The show involved two love stories, that between Sky Masterson, the gambler (Alda), and missionary Sarah Brown (Bigley), and the one between gambler Nathan Detroit (Levene) and night-club entertainer Miss Adelaide (Blaine). Nathan and Adelaide have been engaged for 14 years, but their marriage is always postponed by a crap game.

Robert Alda, who had been rejected by Hollywood despite his fine performance as George Gershwin in *Rhapsody in Blue* (1945), was perfect as Sky Masterson. Vivian Blaine as Miss Adelaide was the archetypal dumb chanteuse. Adding to the color of the show were various Broadway types – Benny Southstreet (Johnny Silver), Laverne (Veda Ann Borg), Lieutenant Brannigan (Robert Keith), Big Jule (B S Pully), Louie (John Indrisano), Rusty Charlie (Dan Dayton), Society Max (George E Stone) and Nicely-Nicely Johnson (Stubby Kaye), whose rendition of 'Sit Down, You're Rockin' the Boat' was a thrilling show-stopper.

Other songs from the show included 'Fugue for Tinhorns' ('I've Got the Horse Right Here'), 'I'll Know,' 'A Bushel and a Peck,' 'Take Back Your Mink,' 'Adelaide's Lament,' 'If I Were a Bell,' 'I've Never Been in Love Before,' 'The Oldest Established Permanent Floating Crap Game in New York,' 'Follow the Fold,' 'Guys and Dolls' and 'Luck Be a Lady.'

Samuel Goldwyn paid $1,000,000 for the screen rights to

LEFT: Jack Prince, Carl Eberle and Al Nesor sing the 'Fugue for Tinhorns' ('I've Got the Horse Right Here') in the 1953 Broadway revival of *Guys and Dolls*.

BELOW: Jean Simmons was Sarah Brown of the Save-a-Soul Mission and Marlon Brando was Sky Masterson, the gambler, in the movie version of *Guys and Dolls* (1955).

153

RIGHT: Doretta Morrow singing 'Baubles, Bangles and Beads' in the Broadway production of *Kismet* (1953).

BELOW: In the Hollywood film version of *Kismet* (1955), Howard Keel was Hajj, Dolores Gray was Lalume, Ann Blyth was Marsina and Vic Damone was the caliph.

the 1955 movie *Guys and Dolls*, and another $4,500,000 on the production of the film. Gene Kelly was wanted for the role of Sky Masterson, but MGM wouldn't release him. So a huge chunk of money was spent to get Marlon Brando, who couldn't sing and turned in a wooden performance. Frank Sinatra, as Nathan Detroit, was at the peak of his vocal powers. Jean Simmons, as Sarah Brown, was properly beautiful and virginal. Enhancing the splendid movie version were some alumni of the original Broadway cast – Vivian Blaine, Stubby Kaye, B S Pully and Johnny Silver. Add to this the spirited choreography of Michael Kidd, and the two-hour-and-38-minute running time of the picture just flew by.

Two of the stage musical songs were removed – 'A Bushel and a Peck' and 'I've Never Been in Love Before.' On the other hand, three more Loesser songs were added – 'Adelaide,' 'A Woman in Love' and 'Pet Me Poppa.'

The play *Kismet*, by Edward Knoblock, was an old-fashioned drama that became a standard role for Otis Skinner beginning in 1912. But by the time that the musical version of *Kismet* opened on Broadway in 1953, the play had, fortunately, been forgotten. With its book by Charles Lederer and Luther Davis, its lyrics by Robert Wright and George 'Chet' Forrest and its wonderful melodies from the music of Alexander Borodin, it was a delight from beginning to end. Directed by Albert Marre with choreography by Jack Cole, *Kismet* starred Alfred Drake, Richard Kiley, Doretta Morrow and Joan Denier; it ran for 583 performances on Broadway and 648 in London.

Described in the program as 'A Musical Arabian Nights,' *Kismet* had a simple plot. A poor public poet of ancient Baghdad, Hajj (Drake), decides to become a beggar to make more money. He wants his daughter Marsinah (Morrow) to marry a handsome caliph (Kiley). Hajj's fortunes rise when the wicked wazir thinks he is a magician. After much wheeling and dealing, the caliph wins the daughter and Hajj kills the wazir and runs off with his seductive wife (Denier).

Some of the wonderful melodies from Borodin were made into the following songs: 'Stranger in Paradise' and 'He's in Love' from the Polovitsian Dances in the opera *Prince Igor*; 'And This Is My Beloved' from the Nocturne of his Quartette in D Major; 'Sands of Time' from 'On the Steppes of Central Asia'; 'Night of My Nights' from the piano piece 'Serenade'; and 'Baubles, Bangles and Beads' from a string quartette. Other songs were 'Fate,' 'The Olive Tree,' 'Not Since Nineveh,' 'Bored,' 'Rahadlakum,' 'Rhymes Have I,' 'Gesticulate,' 'Was I Wazir,' 'Zubbediya' and 'Dance of the Three Princesses of Ababu.'

The film version of *Kismet* (1955) was a picture you loved or hated – either an eye-filling bore or a total sensory experience. At any rate, it stuck to the original book and score. Unfortunately, it was filmed in Eastmancolor, and when viewed today looks remarkably washed out.

Howard Keel (giving an uncharacteristically hammy performance) was Hajj, Ann Blyth was his daughter, Vic Damone (in a role that reminded filmgoers what a great voice he had) was the caliph, Sebastian Cabot was the wazir and Dolores Gray was Lalume. Also in the cast were Monty Woolley, Jay C Flippen, Mike Mazurki, Jack Elam, Ted De Corsia and Julie Robinson.

For some reason, the Hollywood brass decided not to have Hajj knife the wazir, and thus eliminated a wonderful scene where Hajj talks his way out of the caliph's execution orders. He merely holds him under water until he confesses. So the wazir is still alive at the end of the film, and Hajj can't run off to the desert with Lalume. Pity.

The year 1943 was one of the most important in all theater history, for it was that year that *Oklahoma!* made its debut on Broadway. Not only was this, hands down, one of the most successful musical comedies of all time, it was also the first time that Richard Rodgers and Oscar Hammerstein II, the most dominant words-and-music team in theatrical history, had collaborated. Any day of the year, somewhere in the world, an audience will be found applauding a Rodgers and Hammerstein musical. The play is most likely to be *Oklahoma!*, the first, the favored work, and the players are apt to be amateurs on high-school stages – youngsters born after death had ended that wondrous Broadway collaboration.

Alfred Drake was Curly (right) and Howard da Silva was Jud Fry in the Broadway production of *Oklahoma!* (1943). Here they sing 'Pore Jud Is Daid.'

155

Professionals, too, are still presenting Rodgers and Hammerstein shows everywhere. In 1984 *South Pacific* (1949) began a national tour in revival in the United States and still remains a favorite in Japan (even though the Japanese are the unseen, omnipresent foe in the musical). Also in 1984, Yul Brynner continued to tour in *The King and I* (1951), and *The Sound of Music* (1959) finished a successful two-year run in Swedish in Stockholm. In 1983, by actual count, two new productions of *Oklahoma!* were staged every day in the year, on average.

Lynn Riggs had written a straight play – a real turkey – called *Green Grow the Lilacs*. Starring Franchot Tone and June Walker, it opened on Broadway in 1931 and ran for a pathetic total of 64 performances. For some reason, both Rodgers and Hammerstein, completely independently, thought that this flop might make a good musical comedy. Hammerstein asked his old partner, Jerome Kern, to collaborate with him on the project, but Kern wasn't interested. Rodgers talked with Teresa Helburn of the Theatre Guild about it, and she was eager to get a Rodgers-Lorenz Hart musical. But Hart was sick and said that he didn't want to do it. Rodgers was not too disappointed with this, because Hart's alcoholism and homosexuality had become, as Rodgers said, 'a source of permanent irritation,' and he asked Ira

Gershwin to come in on the project. When Gershwin, too, turned him down, he went to Hammerstein, with whom he had written college songs in 1919 when they were both students at Columbia.

The resulting musical, directed by Rouben Mamoulian with dances by Agnes De Mille, starred Alfred Drake, Joan Roberts, Celeste Holm, Betty Garde, Joan McCracken, Bambi Lynn, Howard da Silva, Joseph Buloff, Marc Platt (later to become the ballet master of Radio City Music Hall in New York City) and Lee Dixon. It told the story of a cowboy named Curly (Drake) who is in love with a ranch owner named Laurie (Roberts), and that was about it. It had 13 basic numbers, and, as usual, Hammerstein was the slow worker and Rodgers the speedy one. For example, the lyrics to 'Oh What a Beautiful Morning,' the opening song, took three weeks on Hammerstein's part for a melody that had been written in ten minutes.

Oklahoma! had everything going against it. First of all, there was no reason to believe that the public would be interested in a folksy, country-type musical show. Hammerstein's track record as a lyricist had been one failure after another for a decade, what with his operetta and old-style musical-comedy background. Agnes De Mille created highbrow ballets that furthered the plot, which was a Broadway

first, but a chancy thing to do. Besides, this meant that there was no chorus line. The show had no stars and little humor, and there was a killing in it (Curly is forced to kill his rival, the misanthropic Jud Fry, in a knife fight), which at the time was a muical-comedy no-no. It didn't open with a big production number, but rather with Curly coming onstage and singing 'Oh What a Beautiful Morning' as a solo. Finally, Mamoulian had never directed a musical comedy.

But a hit it was. Rodgers and Hammerstein had created a score in which even the smallest number became a standard song. These were songs that furthered the action, yet could be taken out of context by, for example, a night-club singer, with no loss of appeal. De Mille, in addition to her unusual ballet sequences – which got rave reviews – created such zesty Broadway-type dance routines as 'The Farmer and the Cowman' and 'Everything's Up to Date in Kansas City.'

Oklahoma! ran a phenomenal 2212 performances on Broadway and 1543 in London, where Howard Keel was Curly. The National Company toured for 10 years (at one time starring John Raitt as Curly), playing 250 cities. There were companies playing in Sweden, Denmark, Australia, and one that toured the Pacific to entertain troops. After World War II, other companies sprang up throughout Europe. And it made a mint for the investors. The original cost had been $83,000. The New York company grossed $7 million and the National Company grossed about $20 million. Over the years the show earned more than $100 million.

The film version of *Oklahoma!* was released in 1955, and was shot in Todd-AO. It was almost as entertaining as the stage musical had been, and it grossed more than $10 million in the United States alone. It starred Gordon MacRae and Shirley Jones, with Charlotte Greenwood, Gene Nelson, Gloria Grahame, Rod Steiger and Eddie Albert.

Among the songs from the original show were 'Oklahoma!' (which became the official song of the Sooner State), 'Oh What a Beautiful Morning,' 'Surrey with the Fringe on Top,' 'People Will Say We're in Love,' 'I Cain't Say No,' 'Many a New Day,' 'Pore Jud Is Daid,' 'All or Nothin',' 'The Farmer and the Cowman,' 'Out of My Dreams' and 'Everything's Up to Date in Kansas City.'

Carousel, Rodgers and Hammerstein's second collaboration, premiered on Broadway in 1945. The book was written by Hammerstein, based on a play, *Liliom*, by the Hungarian dramatist Ferenc Molnár. (The play's first Broadway appearance was in 1921, when it starred Joseph Schildkraut, Eva Le Gallienne and Evelyn Chard.) Hammerstein, of course, also wrote the lyrics and Rodgers the music. They were reunited with Rouben Mamoulian, the director, and Agnes De Mille, the choreographer. Starring were John Raitt, Jan Clayton, Christine Johnson, Murvyn Vye, Bambi Lynn and Jean Darling. The show ran for 890 performances.

The setting of the musical couldn't be Hungary, of course. That was too foreign, and besides, when the show was being written, the Hungarians were still the enemy. So Hammerstein selected New England as the setting, with its fishermen, mill girls and sailors. The plot was about a carnival barker, Billy Bigelow (Raitt), who marries a cotton-mill girl, Julie Jordan (Clayton). When he finds out that she is pregnant, he realizes that he must get some money together, and is killed while committing a robbery. Years later, he is permitted to return to earth from the afterlife in order to commit one good act and redeem himself.

OPPOSITE: Gene Nelson dances in the film version of *Oklahoma!*(1955).

ABOVE: John Raitt and Bambi Lynn in the stage *Carousel* (1945).

The scene in which he is granted his reprieve was one of the most difficult to stage. In the play, Billy is sent to Purgatory, but Hammerstein would have none of that, in the belief that 'There must be some feminine principle in God.' So he had Billy sent to an afterlife presided over by a man and woman called 'He' and 'She,' who live in a heaven that looked like a New England farmhouse parlor. 'He' sentences Billy while 'She' plays the harmonium. This didn't work, and Rodgers knew it, so he was stern with his collaborator. 'We've got to get God out of that parlor,' he said. He didn't mention 'Mrs God,' but he had Her in mind, too.

Hammerstein agreed. 'I know. But where am I going to put Him?' Rodgers replied, 'I don't care where you put Him! Put Him up on a ladder for all I care, but get Him out of that parlor!'

It took 10 days for Hammerstein to come up with an alternative, but finally he had decided on the back yard of heaven. 'She' was gone and 'He' became the Starkeeper, standing on a ladder and hanging stars from a clothesline.

The ending of *Carousel* on opening night left a cheering, applauding and weeping audience. Hammerstein, sitting in his box, listened with satisfaction and pride to this reaction. Suddenly he looked up and saw Molnár standing over him with tears in his eyes. The Hungaran cried, 'My Son! My Son!'

Some of the songs became classics. In the score were 'Carousel Waltz,' 'You're a Queer One, Julie Jordan,' 'When I Marry Mr Snow,' 'If I Loved You,' 'June Is Bustin' Out All Over,'

The 'June Is Bustin' Out All Over' ballet in the film version of *Carousel* (1956).

RIGHT: Gordon MacRae, as the carousel barker Billy Bigelow, romances Shirley Jones, as Julie Jordan, in Hollywood's *Carousel*.

'When the Children Are Asleep,' 'This Was a Real Nice Clambake,' 'What's the Use of Wondrin',' 'You'll Never Walk Alone,' 'Stonecutters Cut it on Stone' and 'Soliloquy.' The last-named number was a real risk. It was a complicated song for which it took Hammerstein three weeks to write the lyrics. It had eight different melodic fragments, and the worry was whether or not the audience wouuld sit still for a seven-minute number. But when Billy sang to himself about Julie's pregnancy and wondered how he would react to his child, there wasn't a dry eye in the house.

The film version of *Carousel* (1956) starred Gordon MacRae, Shirley Jones, Cameron Mitchell and Claramae Turner. It was one of the better transferrals from Broadway to Hollywood. The photography was beautiful, there was energetic choreography by Rod Alexander and even the studio orchestra sounded wonderful.

The King and I opened on Broadway in 1951, with book and lyrics by Oscar Hammerstein II and music by Richard Rodgers. The book was based on Margaret Landon's book *Anna and the King of Siam*, which had previously been made, with the same title, as a non-musical movie starring Irene Dunne and Rex Harrison in 1946. The Broadway production was directed by John Van Druten and had choreography by Jerome Robbins. The stars were Yul Brynner, Gertrude Lawrence, Dorothy Sarnoff, and Doretta Morrow. This was a welcome debut for Brynner, and, as it turned out, a sad farewell to Lawrence. It ran for 1246 performances.

Gertrude Lawrence had liked the non-musical film and saw herself in a musical version, playing Anna. She asked her lawyer to buy the stage-musical rights, which he did. Rodgers and Hammerstein were a little dubious about their ability to pull off the project. Hammerstein had to prepare a text, as he said, 'with an Eastern sense of dignity and pageantry, and none of this business of girls dressed in Oriental costumes and dancing out onto the stage and singing "Ching-a-ling-a-ling" with their fingers in the air.' Rodgers said, 'I never heard the music of the Far East and I couldn't write an authentic Far Eastern melody if my life depended on it.' But the result was a magnificent combination of English culture and Oriental elegance.

The King and I was an unusual musical for several reasons. In the huge cast there were only four Anglo-Saxons, and only Anna had a major role. The part of her son was a minor one, and the other two were mere walk-ons. Besides, none of the four were Americans. Also, there was no love interest between the two central characters. Finally, the hero dies at the end.

There was a real-life tragedy connected with *The King and I*. During the show's run, Gertrude Lawrence died of hepatitis. Her part was taken over by Constance Carpenter – whom Lawrence had requested when she became ill.

Many of the numbers have become standards. Among them were 'The Little House of Uncle Thomas,' 'My Lord and Master,' 'Shall I Tell You What I Think of You?' 'Western

Anna (Gertrude Lawrence) tries to protect one of the wives of the King of Siam (Yul Brynner) from his wrath in the Broadway production of *The King and I* (1951).

People Funny,' 'I Have Dreamed,' 'I Whistle a Happy Tune,' 'Hello Young Lovers,' 'March of the Siamese Children,' 'A Puzzlement,' 'Getting to Know You,' 'We Kiss in a Shadow,' 'Something Wonderful,' 'Song of the King' and 'Shall We Dance?'

The film version of *The King and I* (1956) starred Yul Brynner as the king who had imported the English widow, Anna Leonowens, played by Deborah Kerr using Marni Nixon's voice, to teach his many children. It was the pictorial magnificence of the appropriately regal production that distinguished the film and made it a lasting classic that is still seen often on television. One thing to notice – when Brynner sings 'It's a Puzzlement,' he is wearing an earring in some shots and not in others. Brynner won an Oscar for his work in the film.

The Vagabond King reached the screen yet again in 1956. It starred a young tenor from Malta, Oreste Kirkop (who was billed merely as Oreste) as François Villon, and his co-star was Kathryn Grayson. Also in the cast were Rita Moreno,

Walter Hampden, Sir Cedric Hardwicke and Leslie Nielson. Some of the songs were from the original Friml score: 'Only a Rose,' 'Song of the Vagabonds,' 'Some Day, 'Vive Le You' and 'Valse Huguette.' Other numbers were added to the film with music by Friml and lyrics by Johnny Burke. They included 'Watch Out for the Devil,' 'Bon Jour' and 'This Same Heart.'

Still another Hollywood remake of 1956 was *Anything Goes*. The old book was thrown out, but the new one by Sidney Sheldon wasn't much of an improvement. Donald O'Connor and Bing Crosby were two big-name actors who set out on a round-the-world cruise to look for a leading lady for their next show. Zizi Jeanmaire and Mitzi Gaynor enter their lives, and that's about all there was to it.

But the music was the point of the whole thing. From Cole Porter came 'You're the Top,' 'All Through the Night,' 'I Get a Kick out of You,' 'Its Delovely,' 'Blow, Gabriel, Blow,' plus three new songs by Sammy Kahn and Jimmy Van Heusen – 'You Can Bounce Right Back,' 'You Gotta Give the People Hoke' and 'A Second-Hand Turban and a Crystal Ball.'

OPPOSITE: Yul Brynner and Gertrude Lawrence on stage in *The King and I* (1951): 'Shall We Dance?'.

OPPOSITE INSET: In the film *The King and I* (1956), Brynner costarred with Deborah Kerr. Here they are about to go into their dance.

RIGHT: Another film version of *The Vagabond King* was released in 1956, starring Oreste [Kirkop] and Kathryn Grayson.

Funny Face hit Broadway in 1927, with a book by Gerard Smith and Fred Thompson. The music was by George Gershwin and the lyrics by Ira Gershwin. Directed by Edgar Mac-Gregor with dances by Bobby Connolly, it starred the toasts of Broadway – Fred and Adele Astaire – along with Victor Moore and Allan Kearns. It ran for 244 performances.

Jimmy Reeve (Fred) is the guardian of Frankie (Adele) and insists on keeping her pearls in a safe. This upsets Frankie and she gets her boy friend, Peter (Kearnes), to get the pearls for her. But two thugs, Dugsie Gibbs (William Kent) and Herbert (Moore), are also after the treasure. Finally, Frankie gets her man and her pearls.

It had wonderful songs, although the great 'How Long Has This Been Going On?' was cut before the play opened. Among the other numbers were 'The Babbit and the Bromide,' 'S'Wonderful,' 'Funny Face,' 'Let's Kiss and Make Up,' 'He Loves and She Loves' and 'My One and Only.'

It took Hollywood 30 years to come out with the film version of *Funny Face* (1957). There were two schools of thought about the movie. Some said that the stage musical had been butchered. Others thought that this was the first time the Gershwins had been given fair treatment on the screen. The book was certainly unrecognizable, but at least there were some Gershwin songs and 'How Long Has This Been Going On?' was reinstated.

It was a fun picture, starring Fred Astaire, Audrey Hepburn and Kay Thompson. It told the tale of a gamin-like Greenwich Village bookseller (Hepburn) who is found by a fashion photographer (Astaire) and taken to Paris where, with the help of a fashion magazine editor (Thompson), she is turned into a top model.

Fred was a little over-age for the part, but he still had that old magic. And Audrey was, as usual, impeccable.

Among the Gershwin songs in the film, in addition to 'How

BELOW: Audrey Hepburn, as the shy bookseller, proved to be a good dancing partner for Fred Astaire in the film *Funny Face* (1957).

RIGHT: Hepburn in *Funny Face*, after her metamorphosis into a high-fashion model.

Long Has This Been Going On?,' were 'He Loves and She Loves,' 'Let's Kiss and Make Up,' 'Clap Yo' Hands' and 'S'Wonderful.' Other numbers were added by Leonard Gershe and Roger Edens, such as 'Think Pink,' 'Basal Metabolism,' 'Bonjour Paris,' 'On How to Be Lovely' and 'Marche Funebre.'

The opening of *Silk Stockings* on Broadway in 1955 marked Cole Porter's 25th score for a stage musical; during its run he marked his 40th anniversary as a composer for the theater. It had a book by George S Kaufman, Leueen McGrath and Abe Burrows based on the Greta Garbo movie of 1939, *Ninotchka*. Directed by Cy Feuer with dances by Eugene Loring, it featured Don Ameche, Hildegard Neff (formerly Kneff) and Gretchen Wyler, and ran for 478 performances.

The critics raved. Brooks Atkinson of *The New York Times* said it was 'One of Gotham's memorable shows, on the level of *Guys and Dolls* and with some of the wittiest dialogue in years.' To John Chapman it was 'Everything a musical should be ... handsome, slick, brisk, intelligent, witty and delightfully acted, and whenever the plot shows the merest sign of trying to take over more than its share, Cole Porter shoulders it aside with some of his best melodies, lyrics and rhythms.'

But it was a sad triumph. This was to be Porter's last score for the Broadway stage. Fittingly enough, both his first two musical comedies, *Paris* and *Fifty Million Frenchmen*, and his last two, *Can-Can* and *Silk Stockings*, were set in Paris, the city he loved the most.

A Soviet composer, Peter Boroff (Philip Sterling), is in Paris to write the score for a Russian-made film adaptation of *War and Peace*, but while there he meets an American theatrical agent, Steve Canfield (Ameche), who wants him as a client. Boroff is delighted to remain in Paris to take on more assignments, and the Soviets send the disciplined Ninotchka (Neff) to get him back to the Motherland. But both Paris and Steve overwhelm her, and she begins to love her freedom.

ABOVE: Gretchen Wyler in one of her sizzling dances in the Broadway production of *Silk Stockings* (1955).

LEFT: Fred Astaire as Steve Canfield confronts Cyd Charisse as Ninotchka in the film version of *Silk Stockings* (1957). Looking on are the three Soviet agents: Peter Lorre, Jules Munshin and Joseph Buloff.

In the film *Silk Stockings* (1957), Cyd Charisse proved that she was Fred Astaire's best dancing partner since Ginger Rogers.

OPPOSITE TOP: Gene Kelly, as Joey, dances with Shirley Paige in the Broadway production of *Pal Joey* (1940).

OPPOSITE BOTTOM: June Havoc as Gladys, the chorus girl, Jack Durant as the manager, Gene Kelly as Joey and Vivienne Segal as the wealthy Vera Simson on stage in *Pal Joey*.

Meanwhile, film star Janice Dayton (Wyler) arrives from America to produce a film in Paris – it turns out to be *War and Peace* – and she wants to put a striptease into the picture. Three Russian agents arrive to keep track of Ninotchka. They take her back home, but Steve goes to the USSR and smuggles her out again.

The main songs were 'Siberia,' 'Too Bad,' 'Josephine,' 'Stereophonic Sound,' 'All of You,' 'As on Through the Seasons We Sail' and 'Paris Loves Lovers.'

In the film vesion of *Silk Stockings* (1957), Cyd Charisse once again proved that she was Fred Astaire's best dancing partner since Ginger Rogers; this was also the last decent

musical film that Astaire made. Charisse was Ninotchka, and in the movie she was sent to check on the three Russian agents who had been dispatched to bring back the composer. With her vocals dubbed by Carole Richards, Charisse gave the performance of her life. Producer Astaire is preparing a musical about Napoleon and Josephine for the American movie star, played by Janice Paige. Also in the cast were Peter Lorre, Jules Munshin and Joseph Buloff as the agents. The big news was that virtually the entire stage score was used in the film, and Porter wrote another song especially for the picture, 'Fated to Be Mated.'

The musical comedy *Pal Joey* opened on Broadway in

1940. It had a book by John O'Hara, based on his stories, lyrics by Lorenz Hart and music by Richard Rodgers. Directed by George Abbott with dances by Robert Alton, it starred Gene Kelly, June Havoc, Vivienne Segal and Leila Ernst, and ran for 374 performances.

Pal Joey originated as a series of letters in story form by John O'Hara, published in *The New Yorker*. Joey was a rotten apple who started out as a night-club singer-dancer and ended up running a night club himself. It was O'Hara who suggested to Rodgers and Hart that they make a musical of the stories, and they were delighted to do it. And a strange musical it was – perhaps the first adult musical comedy of all time – combining blackmail, illicit love affairs, hypocrisy, skulduggery and crass opportunism. Truly, Joey was the first anti-hero in an American musical comedy, and he made Macheath in *The Threepenny Opera* look like a piker. Some people were shocked. Even the venerable critic of *The New York Times*, Brooks Atkinson, asked 'Can you draw sweet water from a foul well?'.

The milieu of *Pal Joey* was the small-time night-club world of Chicago, a rough, tawdry world of con men and crooks. Joey (Kelly) has a way with him and lands a job in a night club, where two girls become interested in him: Gladys (Havoc) from the chorus and Linda (Ernst), who works in a pet shop. Linda goes to see Joey perform and is ignored because Joey has set his sights on one of the customers – the wealthy Vera Simson (Segal). But Vera is put off by Joey's brazenness and leaves the club; the manager threatens to fire Joey because he has insulted one of the customers.

However, Vera, on thinking it over, becomes fascinated by Joey and begins to shower him with gifts – one of them being a night club of his own, 'Chez Joey.' An agent and a singer plot to blackmail Vera by threatening to tell her husband about her affair with Joey, but she is not frightened by them and calls the police. The blackmailers run off, Vera breaks with Joey and he drifts back to the penny-ante life that suits him so well.

The run was not all that long because people were shocked at the show, especially the women in the audiences. Kelly later reflected: 'The character of Joey made a lot of women dislike the show – mature women. They thought Joey was mean and immoral. Joey's living with an older woman and kept by her. . . . He's also making love with a young girl at the same time and having affairs with every member of the chorus. He was completely self-centered, brought up in an era in America where whatever you could do to get ahead, you did.' To illustrate how times change, when *Pal Joey* was revived on Broadway in 1952 starring Segal and Harold Lang, it ran twice as long – 542 performances – the longest run of any musical-comedy revival in the history of the American theater.

The big hit of the score was 'Bewitched, Bothered and Bewildered,' which in the beginning suffered because the American Society of Composers, Authors and Publishers (ASCAP) was having a dispute with the radio networks and had banned the music of its members from the airwaves. So the song wasn't heard on the radio until the dispute ended and didn't catch on until the late 1940s. Meantime, it was the rage in Paris under the title of '*Perdu dans un rêve immense d'amour.*' Other numbers in the show included 'I Could Write a Book,' 'What Is a Man?,' 'In Our Little Den of Iniquity,' 'Take Him,' 'That Terrific Rainbow' and 'Zip.'

The film rights for *Pal Joey* were bought by Columbia Pictures studio head Harry Cohn in 1944. He was determined that Gene Kelly should play Joey, and when MGM's Louis B Mayer, who had Kelly under contract, asked for too much money, the project was shelved.

Seventeen years after *Pal Joey* had opened on Broadway, the film version (1957) came out. It starred Frank Sinatra as Joey, Rita Hayworth as the wealthy matron (voice dubbed by Jo Ann Greer) and Kim Novak as a chorus girl (voice dubbed by Trudy Erwin). Some things were changed. The dialogue was bowdlerized, the setting was shifted to San Francisco, the character of Joey was sweetened up and, probably because Hollywood was not ready for gross infidelity, the society woman was recast as a widow. Naturally, few songs survived from the original – only 'Zip,' 'Bewitched, Bothered and Bewildered,' 'I Could Write a Book' and 'That Terrific Rainbow.'

But the picture had more plusses than minuses going for it. The three stars turned in excellent performances. The direction, choreography and photography were outstanding. And, even though original songs were dropped, other wonderful numbers by Rodgers and Hart were added, including 'My Funny Valentine' and 'The Lady Is a Tramp' (from *Babes in Arms*), 'There's a Small Hotel' (from *On Your Toes*) and 'I Didn't Know What Time It Was' (from *Too Many Girls*).

The Pajama Game opened on Broadway in 1954, with a book by George Abbott and Richard Bissell, based on Bissell's novel *Seven and a Half Cents*. The score was by Richard Adler and Jerry Ross. Directed by George Abbott and Jerome Robbins with choreography by Bob Fosse, it starred John Raitt, Eddie Foy Jr, Carol Haney and Janice Paige. The show ran a triumphant 1063 performances.

The Pajama Game used the raw talents of a lot of wonderful newcomers. It was the first complete musical-comedy score for Adler and Ross. Of the three producers, Frederick Brisson, Robert Griffith and Harold Prince, only Brisson had produced on Broadway before. Bob Fosse and Carol Haney were making their debuts. And in the chorus, appearing for the first time, was a dancer called Shirley MacLaine. (When Haney became ill during the run, Fosse had MacLaine fill in for her. Hollywood producer Hal Wallis was in the audience and signed her to her first film contract.)

The plot about union problems in a pajama-manufacturing plant was not the sort of stuff from which musical comedies are made. Besides, with much of the action happening in the factory and in the union headquarters, the sets had to be drab. But the show knocked out the critics. One of them called it 'About the best-natured musical you may have ever seen ... young and funny and earthy and fast.' Another rave called it 'a royal flush and grand slam all rolled into one.'

The scene is the Sleep-Time Pajama Factory in Cedar Rapids, Iowa. The factory's manager and efficiency expert, Hines (Foy), steps up operations in the plant striving for higher levels of production. But the union is trying to get

OPPOSITE: Frank Sinatra, as Joey, serenades the rich widow, Rita Hayworth, in the film version of *Pal Joey* (1957).

ABOVE RIGHT: Janice Paige was Babe and John Raitt was Sid in the Broadway production of *The Pajama Game* (1954).

RIGHT: Doris Day (center) as Babe and the chorus at the factory picnic, in the Hollywood version of *The Pajama Game* (1957).

wage increases of 7½ cents an hour. Babe Williams (Paige) is head of the union's grievance committee and presents the demands to the factory superintendent, Sid Sorokin (Raitt). Sid asks Babe for a date, but she tells him that they are on opposite sides of the fight and turns him down. Sid keeps at it, stealing a kiss at the annual factory picnic, and calling at Babe's house. The raise is turned down by the factory's owner, and the workers decide to sabotage production by being careless and slowing down their pace. When Sid says that if things don't improve he will fire everyone, Babe kicks the machinery so hard that the plant breaks down and Sid fires her. But Sid is suspicious that the factory is making more than the owner lets on, and that he could afford the raise. To get evidence, he romances Gladys the bookkeeper (Haney), who is Hines's girl, in order to get at the books. Sid gets Gladys drunk and steals the keys to the office safe. He reads the locked-up ledgers, gets his proof, the workers get their raise and Sid and Babe are reunited.

Some of the songs were 'Hey, There,' 'Hernando's Hideaway,' 'There Once Was a Man,' 'Once a Year Day,' 'I'll Never Be Jealous Again,' 'Steam Heat,' 'Jealousy Ballet,' 'Think of the Time I Save,' 'The Pajama Game,' 'I'm Not at All in Love,' 'Racing With the Clock' and 'Seven and a Half Cents.'

The film version of *The Pajama Game* (1957) proved that it was possible to transfer a stage musical to the screen without losing the zest of the play or making a stagey movie. Coming from the Broadway production were Raitt, Foy, Haney and Reta Shaw. Doris Day was a good choice for Babe, since she gave her most enchanting performance ever, managing to look both sexy and wholesome at the same time.

New York audiences put up the money for the largest advance sale in theatrical history for *South Pacific*, which opened on Broadway in 1949. It was a musical play with a book by Oscar Hammerstein II based on James A Michener's first book, *Tales of the South Pacific*. Hammerstein wrote the lyrics and Richard Rodgers wrote the music. Directed by Joshua Logan, the cast included Mary Martin, Ezio Pinza, William Tabbert, Myron McCormick, Juanita Hall and Betta St John, and the show ran for an amazing 1925 performances.

It started at a dinner party in 1947. Kenneth MacKenna, the story editor at MGM, mentioned to Jo Mielziner and Joshua Logan, the Broadway producers, that he had just turned down an intriguing book of World War II short stories, but that he thought it might make a good stage play. Logan was, at the time, the producer of *Mister Roberts* on Broadway. He read the book and was so enthusiastic that he and his

RIGHT: Emile de Becque (Ezio Pinza) embraces his true love, Nellie Forbush (Mary Martin) in the Broadway production of *South Pacific* (1949).

OPPOSITE: Liat (Betta St John) and Lieutenant Cable (William Tabbert) – 'Happy Talk.'

co-producer of *Mister Roberts*, Leland Hayward, bought the stage rights. Logan thought it would make a better musical than a straight play, and talked with Richard Rodgers about it. Rodgers liked the idea and convinced Hammerstein. When the book won the Pulitzer Prize for fiction, they knew that it was a great idea.

Rodgers and Hammerstein could use only two of the stories from the book – 'Our Heroine,' about the love between a French planter and a United States Navy nurse, and 'Fo' Dolla,' about an American Marine Corps lieutenant and his love for a native girl. Then came the job of casting the two main roles – Emile de Becque (the planter) and Nellie Forbush (the nurse).

Casting Ezio Pinza as Emile was a chancy undertaking. For one thing, he was 57 years old at the time. For another, although he was the reigning basso on the opera stage, he had never appeared on the Broadway stage. But Pinza became a matinee idol immediately. Mary Martin was another risk. She was an established star, having made her debut stealing the show from William Gaxton, Victor Moore and

Sophie Tucker by singing, in a bit role, 'My Heart Belongs to Daddy' in Cole Porter's *Leave It to Me* (1938). But she was 36 years old and was being asked to play an innocent Nellie Forbush – a girl in her early twenties. Hammerstein, however, had seen her in an innocent role before – Venus, in *One Touch of Venus* – and had said to his wife, 'This is the real Mary Martin, a corn-fed girl from Texas – and that's the kind of part she should play.'

Another risk that Rodgers and Hammerstein took was with the subplot: the romance between the Anglo-Saxon Marine Lieutenant Cable and the native girl Liat. They wanted to make it a plea for racial tolerance, and they succeeded. But it took courage to have Cable killed off in the last act.

The beginning of *South Pacific* is set in de Becque's house on a Pacific island during World War II. He is the dinner host of Ensign Nellie Forbush, and immediately falls in love with her. Across the bay is the island of Bali Ha'i, off-limits to American troops. One of the inhabitants of Bali Ha'i is Bloody Mary, a Tonkinese (Juanita Hall), who wants her 17-year-old daughter, Liat (St John), to marry Cable (Tabbert). But Cable

is more interested in his mission: to establish a coast-watch on a nearby Japanese-held island. Meanwhile, Nelly has decided not to fall in love with de Becque because of their differences in age, experience and background. But she gives in anyway. Cable has requested that de Becque go with him on the coast-watch; however now that Nellie has consented to marry him, de Becque turns down the assignment and the mission is postponed. Cable returns to Bali Ha'i, where he meets Liat and falls in love. Nellie discovers that de Becque has had a Polynesian girl as a mistress and that she has Eurasian children. This shocks her and she leaves him. Cable has come to believe that marriage between people of two different races is unthinkable, but when he hears of de Becque begging Nellie to marry him, despite his children of mixed races, he changes his mind. The two men go off on the mission. It is successful, but Cable is killed. De Becque survives and makes his way back to his plantation, where he

finds Nellie playing with his children. They resolve to marry.

The songs were all show-stoppers. They were tender, as in 'Younger Than Springtime.' They were joyful, as in 'I'm in Love With a Wonderful Guy.' They were robust, as in 'There Is Nothing Like a Dame.' They were poignant, as in 'Carefully Taught.' The latter was one of the sensations of the show, with its approach to bigotry: 'You've got to be taught before its too late / Before you are six or seven or eight / To hate all the people your relatives hate.' In tryouts, the lyrics stunned the Boston audience, but the song was kept in the show.

Among the other numbers were 'Dites-moi,' 'A Cockeyed Optimist,' 'Bloody Mary,' 'I'm Gonna Wash that Man Right Out of My Hair,' 'Bali Ha'i,' 'Happy Talk,' 'Some Enchanted Evening,' 'Honey Bun' and 'This Nearly Was Mine.'

South Pacific created theatrical history. It had the second-longest run of any musical on Broadway – just 323 fewer performances than Oklahoma!, and was seen in New York

alone by 3,500,000 people. A national company toured for several years. It turned in a profit of $5 million before the film rights had been sold. Sheet-music sales ran more than two million and the original-cast record album sold one million. There were 'South Pacific' dolls, cosmetics, dresses, lingerie, and so on. It won the Pulitzer Prize for drama, and the Drama Critics, Antoinette Perry (Tony) and Donaldson Awards as the year's best musical.

By the time the film was released in 1958, Ezio Pinza was dead and Mary Martin was too old to play Nellie, and that was a pity. Things were not improved by the use of color filters in the musical numbers (which resulted in a peculiarly washed-out look) and the heavy-handed direction by Joshua Logan. Still, Rossano Brazzi (with voice dubbed by Giorgio Tozzi) as de Becque and Mitzi Gaynor as Nellie Forbush were fine, as were John Kerr (voice dubbed by Bill Lee) as Cable and France Nuyen as Liat. Oddly enough, Juanita Hall was the only import from the original Broadway cast, but her singing on the sound track didn't suit Rodgers, and he dubbed in the voice of Muriel Smith. Rodgers and Hammerstein added a new song to the movie: 'My Girl Back Home.'

Damn Yankees premiered on Broadway in 1955 with a book by Douglas Wallop and George Abbott, based on the Wallop novel *The Year the Yankees Lost the Pennant*. The score was by Richard Adler and Jerry Ross. Directed by Abbott with dances by Bob Fosse, it starred Stephen Douglass, Gwen Verdon and Ray Walston and ran for 1019 performances.

ABOVE: The nurses of the chorus help Mitzi Gaynor wash that man right out of her hair in the movie *South Pacific* (1958).

RIGHT: In the film *South Pacific*, Mitzi Gaynor was Ensign Nellie Forbush and Rossano Brazzi was the planter Emile de Becque.

The story concerned a middle-aged Washington Senator baseball fan who is turned into superstar Joe Hardy and wins the pennant for the Senators. Of course, he had signed a pact with the Devil. Douglass was Hardy and Ray Walston was the Devil, *aka* Mr Applegate. Gwen Verdon, as the sexy Lola, played the temptress sent by Applegate to keep Joe in line. She had stolen every scene in which she had appeared since her minor role in *Can-Can* in 1953.

Some of the songs were 'You've Got to Have Heart,' 'Whatever Lola Wants,' 'Two Lost Souls,' 'Those Were the Good Old Days,' 'The Game,' 'Goodbye Old Girl' and 'Shoeless Joe from Hannibal, Mo.'

The film version of *Damn Yankees* (1958) made only one mistake. Tab Hunter was cast as Joe Hardy, and he seemed to do nothing more than stand around with his mouth open, as if marveling at the talents that surrounded him. Apart from Hunter, all the main people involved – actors, choreographers and writers – were recruited from the original stage musical, making this a most perfect marriage between Broadway and Hollywood. Verdon and Walston were great, and remember that Adler, Ross, Abbott and Fosse made up the team that had also given audiences *The Pajama Game*.

ABOVE: Steven Douglas, as Joe Hardy, listens as Gwen Verdon, playing Lola, tempts him with 'Whatever Lola Wants (Lola Gets)' in the Broadway hit *Damn Yankees* (1955).

LEFT: The same scene from the film version of *Damn Yankees* (1958). This time, Verdon sings to Tab Hunter.

OPPOSITE: The Broadway version of *Porgy and Bess* (1935) began with a crap game. At center, Bess (Anne Brown) drapes her leg over the shoulder of her lover, Crown (Warren Coleman). Sportin' Life (John Bubbles) is in the derby and Porgy (Todd Duncan) is in white shirt at right.

Porgy and Bess opened on Broadway in 1935, and was immediately a controversial production. Actually, it was not a musical comedy, but rather an opera. It had a book, or, perhaps, rather a libretto by DuBose Heyward based on the novel *Porgy* by Dorothy and DuBose Heyward. Lyrics were by DuBose Heyward and Ira Gershwin, with music by George Gershwin. Directed by Rouben Mamoulian, it featured Todd Duncan, Anne Brown, John W Bubbles, J Rosamond Johnson and the Eva Jessye Choir. It ran a mere 124 performances.

The idea for the work came to George Gershwin years before he began to write the music. He had read the novel *Porgy* and written to the authors telling them how much he liked it. He and DuBose Heyward decided that they would collaborate on an opera, but both men were busy for a time. Trouble loomed in 1933, when Heyward found out that the Theatre Guild was planning to turn the play into a musical comedy that would star Al Jolson. He told Gershwin, 'I want you to tell me if you really want to write our opera. If you do, I'm going to turn the Guild down definitely.' Gershwin started writing immediately.

The project took Gershwin about 20 months to write and orchestrate – some of it spent in South Carolina learning about the way of life of the black people there. The original cast was mostly black, and some of them were new to show business. Todd Duncan (Porgy) was a music teacher at Howard University in Washington, DC. Anne Brown (Bess) was without professional experience. John W Bubbles (Sportin' Life) had been a vaudeville entertainer as part of the Buck and Bubbles team.

The story takes place in a black ghetto, Catfish Row, in Charleston, South Carolina. A crap game is going on and in a resulting argument, a man is killed by Crown (Warren Coleman). Crown gets away, but leaves his girl, Bess, behind. Sportin' Life tries to get Bess to go with him to New York, but she prefers to stay with the crippled Porgy, who loves her. Bess learns to love Porgy, too. Later he and Bess go to a lodge picnic on Kittiwah Island. But Crown is hiding on the island; he grabs Bess and takes her into the woods. Bess returns to Catfish Row a few days later. She is sick and is nursed by Porgy. Then Crown returns and is strangled by Porgy, who is taken in for questioning. While Porgy is away, Sportin' Life also returns to plague Bess, giving her some narcotics and taking her to New York. When Porgy gets back, he finds out where Bess is heading and gets into his goat cart to follow her as the curtain falls.

Many of the songs, or arias, have become classics. Among them were 'Summertime,' 'A Woman Is a Sometime Thing,' 'My Man's Gone Now,' 'Oh, the Train Is at the Station,' 'I Got Plenty of Nuttin',' 'Bess, You Is My Woman Now,' 'It Aint Necessarily So,' 'I Loves You, Porgy,' 'A Red-Headed Woman Makes a Choochoo Jump Its Tracks,' 'There's a Boat Dat's Leavin' Soon for New York,' 'Oh, Lawd, I'm on My Way,' 'What You Want Wid Bess,' 'Oh, I Can't Sit Down,' 'It Take a Long Pull to Get There,' 'Bess, Oh Where's My Bess?' and 'The Buzzard Song.'

The Boston critics liked *Porgy and Bess* in the tryouts, but the New York papers were not so kind. Apparently, they couldn't understand the combination of classical, jazz and

said 'It was worth waiting 17 years for "Porgy".' An Israeli newspaper raved that it was 'an artistic event of first-class importance.' When it played the opera house in Milan, La Scala, the newspaper *L'Unità* placed the work 'among the masterworks of the lyric theater.'

Many European opera companies have since mounted their own productions, including Vienna (the Volksoper), Bulgaria, Turkey, France and East and West Germany.

The film version of *Porgy and Bess* was released in 1959, starring Sidney Poitier as Porgy (the part was originally offered to Harry Belafonte) and Dorothy Dandridge as Bess. Also in the cast were Sammy Davis Jr as Sportin' Life, Diahann Caroll and Pearl Bailey. It was Samuel Goldwyn's last film, and he spent $6,500,000 on the Todd-AO Technicolor production. It was good, but not as good as it should have been. The singing was all right, with Poitier's voice dubbed by Robert McFerrin and Dandridge's by Adele Addison. But the direction was heavy-handed. Mamoulian had originally been signed on to repeat his Broadway triumph, but he and Goldwyn had many differences of opinion and Otto Preminger was brought in. In a way, Poitier and Dandridge, although they were good actors, were miscast. Their good looks just didn't seem to fit in with the squalor and seediness of Catfish Row. Actually, Davis and Brock Peters, who played Crown, stole the show.

Li'l Abner was a splendid musical romp on Broadway in 1956. The show had a book by Norman Panama and Melvin Frank, based on the characters created by Al Capp in his comic strip of the same name. The lyrics were by Johnny Mercer and the music by Gene de Paul. Directed and choreographed by Michael Kidd, it starred Edith (later Edie) Adams, Peter Palmer, Stubby Kaye and Tina Louise. It had a run of 693 performances.

Daisy Mae (Adams) is bent on catching Li'l Abner (Palmer), but she doesn't manage this until the final scene when she slips him a love potion. Appassionata von Climax (Louise) is her rival for Abner in the annual Sadie Hawkins Day Race in which unmarried women chase the bachelors of their dreams. In a subplot of this musical comedy that managed to mock big business, the US defense establishment and modern science, their little community of Dogpatch has been chosen as a testing ground for an atomic bomb. All the other Dogpatch characters were appealing – Mammy Yokum (Charlotte Rae), Pappy Yokum (Joe E Marks), Marryin' Sam (Kaye), General Bullmoose, Senator Phogbound and Evil Eye Fleagle.

The songs were beautiful or funny, but above all, entertaining. Among them were 'Jubilation T Cornpone,' 'The Country's in the Very Best of Hands,' 'Oh, Happy Day,' 'Progress Is the Root of All Evil,' 'Namely You,' 'If I Had My Druthers,' 'Don't That Take the Rag Off'n the Bush,' 'A Typical Day,' 'Unnecessary Town,' 'I'm Past My Prime' and 'Put 'Em Back the Way They Was.'

Palmer (who not only filled the bill with his physical resemblance to Li'l Abner, but could also sing), Kaye and Marks repeated their Broadway roles in the film version of *Li'l Abner* (1959). Unfortunately, the delightful Edie Adams had been replaced by Leslie Parrish as Daisy Mae, and Stella Stevens was Appassionata von Climax. Norman Panama was the producer, which ensured that the screen version was as close to the original as possible. It was joyful, hilarious, loud, brassy, and corny, and it deserved more exposure than it got.

Sidney Poitier was Porgy and Dorothy Dandridge was Bess, in the film adaptation of Gershwin's *Porgy and Bess* (1959).

popular music. Gershwin didn't live to see his faith in the work justified, but when it was revived in 1942, it ran for eight months and became the longest-running revival of a musical up to that time.

In the 1950s it was taken on a world tour with Laverne Hutchinson and William Warfield alternating as Porgy and Leontyne Price as Bess, with Cab Calloway as Sportin' Life. It toured through Europe, the Near East, the Soviet Union and other countries behind the Iron Curtain, South America and Mexico. One Viennese critic said that no new foreign opera had been so well received in Vienna since the Austrian premiere of *Cavalleria Rusticana* in 1902. A London paper

RIGHT: Edie Adams was Daisy Mae, Peter Palmer was Li'l Abner and Tina Louise was Appassionata von Climax in the Broadway production of *Li'l Abner* (1956).

BELOW: The girls chase the boys on Sadie Hawkins' Day in Dogpatch. In this scene from the movie *Li'l Abner* (1959), it is obvious that they didn't always play fair.

RIGHT: Rex Harrison and Audrey Hepburn dance 'The Rain in Spain' number in the film *My Fair Lady* (1964).

BELOW: Maria (Julie Andrews) lines up the Trapp children in the movie version of *The Sound of Music* (1965).

THE STAR-CENTERED
SIXTIES

During the 1960s the camera was skillfully used to maximize energy and movement in such diverse stage originals as *West Side Story* and *The Sound of Music*. Hollywood producers shied away from screen unknowns like Julie Andrews, despite her success in Broadway's *My Fair Lady*, but Andrews showed them in the enormously popular *Sound of Music*. Elvis Presley, Frank Sinatra, Natalie Wood, Shirley MacLaine, all had their day in the sun. And Barbra Streisand originated the marathon, high-budget, one-woman show (with one memorable song) in *Hello Dolly!*

The decade of the sixties began where the fifties had left off: Hollywood musicals continued to lean heavily on Broadway shows.

Can-Can opened on Broadway in 1953 with a book by Abe Burrows and music and lyrics by Cole Porter. Burrows was the director, and it had dances by Michael Kidd and starred Lilo, Peter Cookson, Hans Conreid, Erik Rhodes and Gwen Verdon. This musical, which was the last of the Porter works that represented his life-long love affair with Paris, ran for 892 performances.

The setting was the Bohemian Paris of 1893, where the Can-Can is being danced at the Montmartre café of La Mome Pistache (Lilo). Aristide Forestier (Cookson), a lawyer, undertakes an investigation forced upon him by the bluenoses of the town, but finds that the dance is legal and not pornographic. Incidentally, he falls in love with Pistache. There is a subplot in which Claudine (Verdon) loves both a Bulgarian sculptor (Conreid) and an art critic (Rhodes).

The plot was terrible, but the music was vintage Porter. Among the songs were '*C'est Magnifique*,' 'I Love Paris,' 'The Apaches,' 'The Garden of Eden,' 'Can-Can,' '*Allez-vous En*' and 'It's All Right with Me.'

The film version of *Can-Can* was released in 1960 and starred Frank Sinatra, Shirley MacLaine, Maurice Chevalier and Louis Jourdan. MacLaine owned the bar and Sinatra and Jourdan were both after her. It was a real bore, but the picture was stolen by Juliet Prowse in the Verdon role; her

ABOVE: Gwen Verdon (center) was the star of the original stage production of Cole Porter's *Can-Can* (1953).

RIGHT: When *Can-Can* was made into a movie in 1960, Shirley MacLaine had the Verdon role and her co-stars were Frank Sinatra (left) and Maurice Chevalier. Here she surrenders her garter to her admirer, Sinatra.

dancing, choreographed by Hermes Pan, had class. Several of Porter's original songs were replaced with what could only be termed 'safe' Porter songs: 'Just One of Those Things,' 'Let's Do It' and 'You Do Something to Me.' Other numbers in the film were '*C'est Magnifique*,' 'Maidens Typical of France,' 'Come Along with Me,' 'Live and Let Live,' 'Adam and Eve Ballet,' 'Montmartre,' 'Snake Dance' and 'Apache Dance.'

The *Can-Can* movie had political overtones – not in the script, but in real life. While they were filming the musical, Nikita Khrushchev, then the premier of the USSR, was touring the studio and was shocked at the capitalistic decadence

of the can-can dance. So much for history.

Bells Are Ringing, which opened on Broadway in 1956, had a book and lyrics by Betty Comden and Adolph Green and lyrics by Jule Styne. Directed by Jerome Robbins, with dances by Robbins and Bob Fosse, it starred Judy Holliday, Sydney Chaplin and Eddie Lawrence for 924 performances.

This delightful musical comedy – a real showcase for Holliday, that talented comedienne whose early death ended a notable career – told the story of 'Susanswerphone,' a telephone-answering service run by Sue (Jean Stapleton long before she became Edith Bunker on televison) with the help of Ella Peterson (Holliday), a girl so addled and strait-

LEFT: Eddie Lawrence, Judy Holliday and Jean Stapleton in the Broadway production of *Bells Are Ringing* (1956).

OPPOSITE: Judy Holliday seems surprised at Jean Stapleton's woebegone expression in the film version of *Bells Are Ringing* (1960), but Ruth Storey and Eddie Foy Jr (in background) are unperturbed.

BELOW: Sydney Chaplin (the son of Charlie Chaplin) played the playwright Jeff Moss – who eventually wins Ella Peterson (Judy Holliday) in the stage production of *Bells Are Ringing*.

laced that she puts on lipstick before answering the phone. One of the clients, Jeff Moss (Chaplin), a playwright who is having problems with his play, faces an invasion by Ella, who comes to his apartment and helps him get rid of his writer's block. Meanwhile, Sue has fallen in love with Sandor (Lawrence), who heads Titanic Records, he says. He gets Sue to let him use her office for his business, turning it into a front for a gambling den that takes bets on horses. Everything turns out all right, and Ella wins Jeff.

The show was a reunion for Holliday, Comden and Green. They had appeared together in 1938 in a night-club act called 'The Revuers,' for which Comden and Green had written all the material. And a triumphant reunion it was, featuring such songs as 'Long Before I Knew You,' 'Just in Time,' 'The Party's Over,' 'It's a Simple Little System,' 'Drop that Name,' 'I'm Goin' Back (to the Bonjour Tristesse Brassiere Company),' 'Bells Are Ringing,' 'It's a Perfect Relationship,' 'I Met a Girl,' 'The Midas Touch' and 'Mu-Cha-Cha.'

The film version of *Bells Are Ringing* (1960) was another triumph for Judy Holliday, but five numbers were dropped from the original and two new ones, 'Better Than a Dream' and 'Do It Yourself,' were added. Dean Martin gave a more than creditable performance as the playwright, and Eddie Foy Jr as the bookmaker would have stolen the show except that no one could have stolen the show from Holliday. Jean

Stapleton was back, and others in the cast were Hal Linden (before *Fiddler on the Roof* on stage and 'Barney Miller' on the television screen) and Frank Gorshin (who imitated Marlon Brando).

West Side Story, one of the crowning masterworks of the American musical theater, premiered on Broadway in 1957. The book, an updating of William Shakespeare's *Romeo and Juliet* set in modern Manhattan, was by Arthur Laurents, and was based on an idea of Jerome Robbins, who wanted to call it *East Side Story* to feature the conflict between a Jewish gang and a Catholic gang. (One wag said, 'Can you imagine the hit song being "Rebeccah, I've Just Met a Girl Named Rebeccah"?') The lyrics were by Stephen Sondheim and the music by Leonard Bernstein. Directed and choreographed by Jerome Robbins, the cast included Carole Lawrence, Larry Kert and Chita Rivera. It ran for 734 performances in New York and many more on the road.

An interesting thing happened out of town. Musical shows that are so strictly New York do not often fare well away from Gotham. One such was the magnificent stage musical *Fiorello!*, the biography of Mayor Fiorello LaGuardia of New York, which ran on Broadway for 796 performances. It came close to being a bomb in Chicago and London because it was so parochial. Indeed, charming as it was, it was never made into a movie. But *West Side Story* was more than a New York

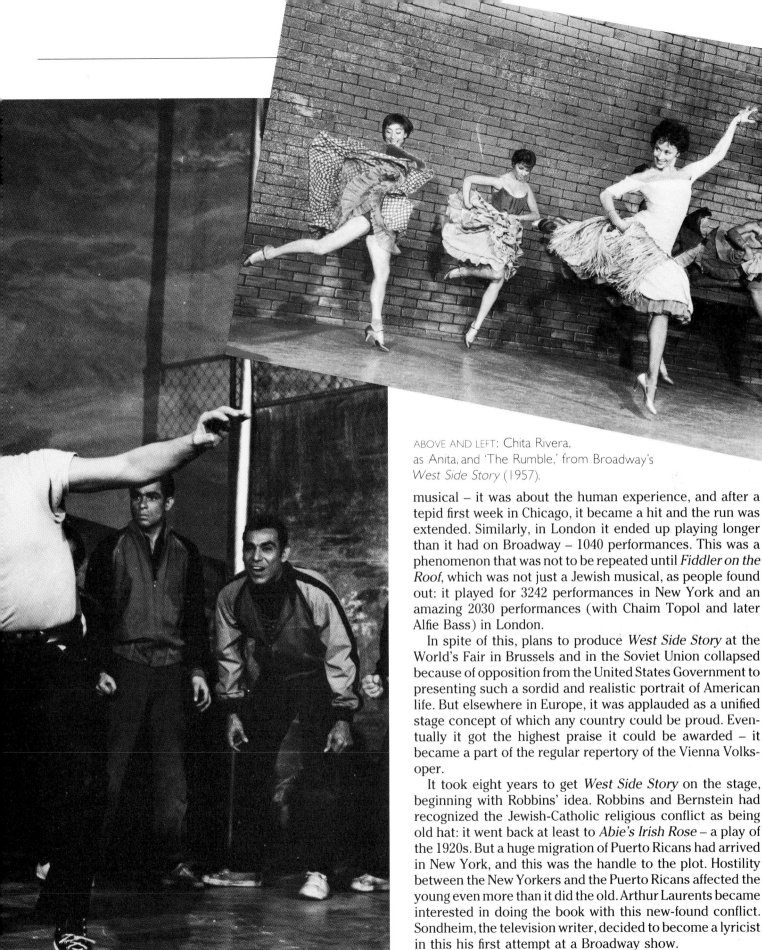

ABOVE AND LEFT: Chita Rivera, as Anita, and 'The Rumble,' from Broadway's *West Side Story* (1957).

musical – it was about the human experience, and after a tepid first week in Chicago, it became a hit and the run was extended. Similarly, in London it ended up playing longer than it had on Broadway – 1040 performances. This was a phenomenon that was not to be repeated until *Fiddler on the Roof*, which was not just a Jewish musical, as people found out: it played for 3242 performances in New York and an amazing 2030 performances (with Chaim Topol and later Alfie Bass) in London.

In spite of this, plans to produce *West Side Story* at the World's Fair in Brussels and in the Soviet Union collapsed because of opposition from the United States Government to presenting such a sordid and realistic portrait of American life. But elsewhere in Europe, it was applauded as a unified stage concept of which any country could be proud. Eventually it got the highest praise it could be awarded – it became a part of the regular repertory of the Vienna Volksoper.

It took eight years to get *West Side Story* on the stage, beginning with Robbins' idea. Robbins and Bernstein had recognized the Jewish-Catholic religious conflict as being old hat: it went back at least to *Abie's Irish Rose* – a play of the 1920s. But a huge migration of Puerto Ricans had arrived in New York, and this was the handle to the plot. Hostility between the New Yorkers and the Puerto Ricans affected the young even more than it did the old. Arthur Laurents became interested in doing the book with this new-found conflict. Sondheim, the television writer, decided to become a lyricist in this his first attempt at a Broadway show.

Italy's Verona became the extreme west side of Manhattan, where the Puerto Ricans had settled. The Montagues and the Capulets became two feuding gangs – the Jets and the Sharks. Romeo became a city boy named Tony, Juliet, a Puerto Rican girl, Maria. The balcony scene became a tryst on a fire escape. And, as in Shakespeare, there was a tragic ending.

Riff, the leader of the American boys' gang, the Jets, hates

the Puerto Rican gang, the Sharks. He enlists the aid of the former leader of the Jets, Tony (Kert). The two gangs meet at a dance at the gym, where their violent hostility becomes manifest. But Tony meets Maria (Lawrence), who is the sister of the leader of the Sharks, Bernardo (Ken Le Roy). She has just arrived from Puerto Rico to marry Chino, a member of the Sharks. It is love at first sight for Maria and Tony. Meanwhile, the two gangs leave for the drugstore to plan the final rumble that will establish control of the neighborhood. Tony engineers a plan to have a single fight between the champions of each gang. But Bernardo finds out that Tony and Maria are in love, and the rumble begins between the two gangs. Riff is killed and Tony murders Bernardo with Riff's knife in retaliation. Chino shoots and kills Tony.

The music was glorious. Bernstein confessed that he had the most trouble with the ballet sequences, especially the 'Rumble' number. 'If it had been too balletic, we would have fallen off on one side – all you'd have is just another ballet. And if it had been too realistic, we would have fallen off on the other side – and there would have been no poetry to it, no art.' But the dancing was a success. As critic John Martin said, the theatrical substance of the play was 'not in talked plot but in moving bodies.'

The musical score was one of the powerful assets of this

LEFT: Tony (Larry Kert) and Maria (Carol Lawrence) find true love in the Broadway production of *West Side Story* (1957) and sing 'Tonight.'

The dance at the gym number from *West Side Story*. After the gaiety seen here comes the confrontation between the Jets and the Sharks.

grim tragedy. The numbers included 'Prologue,' 'Jet Song,' 'Something's Coming,' 'Tonight,' 'Dance at the Gym,' 'Maria,' 'America,' 'Gee, Officer Krupke,' 'I Feel Pretty,' 'One Hand, One Heart,' 'Quintet,' 'Rumble,' 'Cool,' 'A Boy Like That,' 'I Have a Love,' 'Somewhere' and 'Roof Dance.'

The film version of *West Side Story* (1961) more than did justice to the Broadway version. For once, Hollywood had the courage to keep the intent of the original, with its emphasis on the dance. This could be explained by the fact that Robbins went to Hollywood to become the co-director with Robert Wise, and stayed to be the picture's choreographer. It starred Richard Beymer (whose voice was dubbed by Jim Bryant) as Tony, George Chakiris (who was a former dancer himself) as Bernardo, Rita Moreno (voice courtesy of Betty Wand) as Bernardo's girl friend Anita, and Natalie Wood (voice dubbed by Marnie Nixon) as Maria. The film hauled in the Academy Awards. It was selected best picture of the year. Robert Wise and Robbins got Oscars, as did Boris Leven (art direction), Chakiris (best supporting actor) and Moreno (best supporting actress).

The critics went wild. *The New York Times* reported, 'What they have done with *West Side Story* in knocking it down and moving it from stage to screen is to reconstruct its fine material into nothing short of a cinema masterpiece.' They raved about the songs, but what seemed to surprise critics most was Natalie Wood. They had known her as a child star, as in her sickly-sweet role in *Miracle on 34th Street* (1947). They knew her as a teenager in such films as *Rebel Without a Cause* (1955). But here she was in a musical, doing a wonderful job with real dancing and artificial singing, full of luster and charm.

ABOVE: 'The Rumble,' from the 1961 film *West Side Story*.

BELOW: Tommy Sands and Annette Funicello in *Toyland*

Babes in Toyland was resurrected once again by Hollywood in 1961. It was a Walt Disney flick, characterized as being 'a really dismal experience for anyone over the age of five.' For some reason, that effervescent Ray Bolger was cast as the villain, with Tommy Sands and Annette Funicello, those veterans of beach-blanket films, as the youthful hero and heroine. Ed Wynn was the toymaker, and Henry Calvin and Gene Sheldon played the Laurel and Hardy roles. It should never have been released.

Most of the songs were by Victor Herbert with lyrics by Glenn MacDonough, including 'I Can't Do That Sum,' 'Just a Toy,' 'Floretta,' 'We Won't Be Happy Till We Get It,' 'Lemonade,' 'Just a Whisper Away,' 'March of the Toys' and 'Toyland.' Additional songs were by George Bruns and Mel Leven. Among them were 'Slowly He Sank Into the Sea,' 'The Workshop Song' and 'The Forest of No Return.'

Richard Rodgers and Oscar Hammerstein II made their second foray into Oriental music with *Flower Drum Song* in 1958. The book was by Hammerstein and Joseph Fields, based on a novel by C Y Lee. The lyrics were by Hammerstein, the music by Rodgers and the choreography by Carol Haney, late of *The Pajama Game*. It starred Pat Suzuki, Miyoshi Umeki, Larry Blyden, Juanita Hall and Keye Luke (the former Number One Son of Charlie Chan and later to become the blind teacher of David Carradine on the 'Kung Fu' television series). *Flower Drum Song* ran for 600 performances.

This was more of a musical comedy than had been *Oklahoma!*, *South Pacific* and *Carousel*, with its striptease in a night-club and its buck-and-wing dance. The setting was San Francisco's Chinatown. Sammy Fong (Blyden), a Chinese American, tries to arrange a match between Wang Ta (Ed Kenney) and Mei Li (Umeki), an innocent girl from China. Wang Ta's father approves the match, but the girl's father has already signed a contract for her to marry Sammy. The result is a complicated plot about who will marry whom.

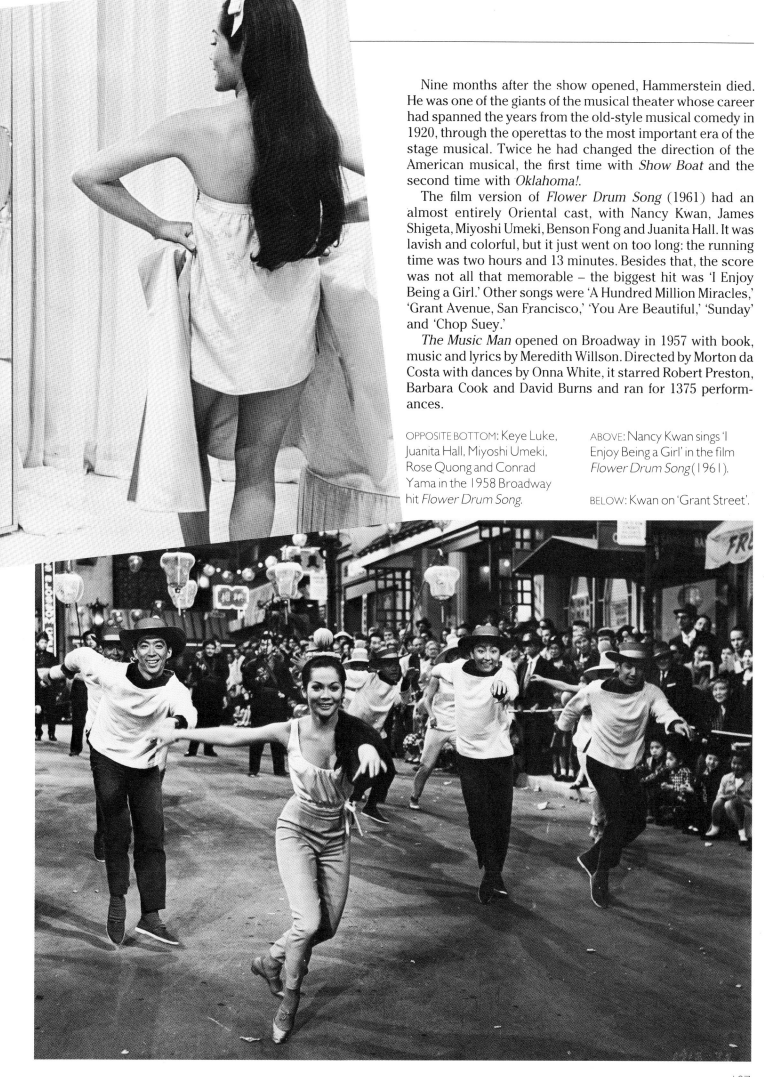

Nine months after the show opened, Hammerstein died. He was one of the giants of the musical theater whose career had spanned the years from the old-style musical comedy in 1920, through the operettas to the most important era of the stage musical. Twice he had changed the direction of the American musical, the first time with *Show Boat* and the second time with *Oklahoma!*.

The film version of *Flower Drum Song* (1961) had an almost entirely Oriental cast, with Nancy Kwan, James Shigeta, Miyoshi Umeki, Benson Fong and Juanita Hall. It was lavish and colorful, but it just went on too long: the running time was two hours and 13 minutes. Besides that, the score was not all that memorable – the biggest hit was 'I Enjoy Being a Girl.' Other songs were 'A Hundred Million Miracles,' 'Grant Avenue, San Francisco,' 'You Are Beautiful,' 'Sunday' and 'Chop Suey.'

The Music Man opened on Broadway in 1957 with book, music and lyrics by Meredith Willson. Directed by Morton da Costa with dances by Onna White, it starred Robert Preston, Barbara Cook and David Burns and ran for 1375 performances.

OPPOSITE BOTTOM: Keye Luke, Juanita Hall, Miyoshi Umeki, Rose Quong and Conrad Yama in the 1958 Broadway hit *Flower Drum Song*.

ABOVE: Nancy Kwan sings 'I Enjoy Being a Girl' in the film *Flower Drum Song* (1961).

BELOW: Kwan on 'Grant Street'.

Preston and Cook in Broadway's *The Music Man* (1957).

It was a happy, summer-day sort of musical about Professor Harold Hill (Preston), who arrives in River City, Iowa, to organize a boys' band, and, incidentally, to sell instruments and uniforms to all the kids. There he meets and falls in love with Marian, the librarian (Cook), who reforms him.

From the startling opening, in which the audience felt that an old steam locomotive was going to charge off the stage into the orchestra, to the ending, where Hill turns honest, it had irresistible charms. The play wore its heart on its sleeve, but no one minded that sentiment often turned to sentimentality or that the comedy occasionally turned to corn.

This was Preston's first musical, and he sang as if he had been doing it all his life and had dance steps that would have won first place in an old-fashioned dance contest. In short, he was superb, giving a lusty, vibrant virtuoso performance, and making one of the most sensational comebacks in theater history.

The Music Man was also Meredith Willson's first-ever stage show, and he composed it at the age of 55. His tunes were made for whistling, among them 'Seventy-Six Trombones,' 'Trouble,' 'My White Knight,' 'Marian the Librarian,' 'Lida Rose,' 'The Wells Fargo Wagon,' 'Gary, Indiana,' and 'Pick a Little, Talk a Little.'

The film version of *The Music Man* (1962) also starred Preston (after the role had been turned down by Cary Grant), and it was every bit as much fun as had been the stage version, probably partly because Morton da Costa was brought to Hollywood to direct it. The fine cast included Shirley Jones (replacing Barbara Cook), Hermione Gingold, Buddy Hackett and Paul Ford. For some reason, the beautiful 'My White Knight' was eliminated and a new song, 'Being in Love,' was substituted.

Gypsy made its Broadway premiere in 1959, bringing together the old team from *West Side Story*, Arthur Laurents, who wrote the book; Stephen Sondheim, who wrote the lyrics; and Jerome Robbins, who did the choreography. The music was by Jule Styne. Robbins directed this adaptation based on Gypsy Rose Lee's autobiography. Starring the earth-shaking Ethel Merman as Rose, the loud-mouthed, fast-talking and domineering stage mother, the show also featured Sandra Church and Jack Klugman, and ran for 702 performances.

It was a Cook's tour of auditions, backstage activities and dingy hotel rooms. *Gypsy* begins with a vaudeville act, 'Baby Jane and Her Newsboys,' managed by Herbie (Klugman), but actually controlled by Rose. Of course, Louise (later stripper Gypsy Rose Lee) is in the chorus of newboys while her sister June stars. Meanwhile, Rose has changed the act to 'Madame Rose's Toreadorables.' Herbie finds that he is in love with Rose and proposes, but she feels that she is much too busy for marriage. Vaudeville is fading, and Louise is faced with the necessity of becoming a burlesque stripper. She is a sensation, and the ugly duckling now has the nerve to quarrel with her mother. The show ends with their reconciliation.

After her performance as Maria in *West Side Story*, Natalie Wood was a natural for the part of Louise in the film version of *Gypsy* (1962). She turned in a fine performance in what

ABOVE: Sandra Church, Ethel Merman and Jack Klugman onstage in *Gypsy* (1959).

BELOW: Preston leads '76 Trombones' in the movie *The Music Man* (1962).

189

was probably the best stage-to-film effort up to that time. There were a couple of casting mistakes. Karl Malden was no Jack Klugman. But worst of all, Rosalind Russell (voice dubbed by Lisa Kirk) did not have the same kind of pizzazz as did the Broadway Rose, Ethel Merman. Russell wasn't bad, actually she was even good, but as one critic said, 'Where Merman had been volcanic, Rosalind Russell . . . was merely dynamic.'

Except for the deletion of the wonderful 'Together, Wherever We Go,' the film kept the score intact. Among the songs were 'Rose's Turn,' 'Some People,' 'Everything's Coming Up Roses,' 'Broadway, Broadway,' 'If Mama Was Married,' 'Let Me Entertain You,' 'Small World,' 'Baby June and Her Newsboys,' 'Mr Goldstone, I Love You,' 'Little Lamb,' 'All I Need Is the Girl,' 'Dainty June and Her Farmboys,' 'Cow Song' and 'You'll Never Get Away from Me.'

The last fling for New York's huge Hippodrome Theater occurred in 1935. The musical was *Jumbo*, produced by Billy Rose. Rose tore out the insides of the theater and put the

OPPOSITE: Natalie Wood played the grown-up Louise Hovick in the film version of *Gypsy* (1962).

RIGHT: Paul Whiteman in Broadway's *Jumbo* (1935). BELOW: Day, Jumbo and Durante in *Billy Rose's Jumbo* (1962).

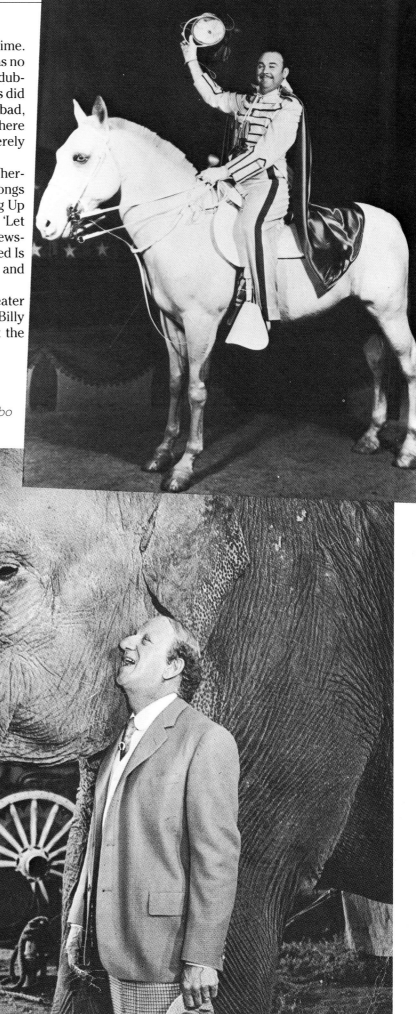

ABOVE: The chorus of kids and their 'Telephone Hour' from the Broadway show *Bye Bye Birdie* (1960). The sets were as imaginative as the score.

RIGHT: Dick Gautier as Conrad Birdie is flanked by Chita Rivera as Rose Grant and Dick Van Dyke as Albert Peterson, while he is interviewed by the press in the stage version of *Bye Bye Birdie*.

OPPOSITE: Jesse Pearson (Conrad Birdie) and his adoring fans in the film version of *Bye Bye Birdie* (1963). Behind him on the steps are Janet Leigh, as Rosie, and Dick Van Dyke repeating his Broadway role as Albert.

stage in the middle to make it look like a circus ring. The show included daredevil acts, jugglers, trapeze acts, clowns, contortionists, wire-walkers, bareback riders and 100 animals, including the elephant that played the title role.

The book was by Ben Hecht and Charles MacArthur, the lyrics by Lorenz Hart and the music by Richard Rodgers. Directed by George Abbott with dances by Alan K Foster, it starred Jimmy Durante, Gloria Grafton, Donald Novis and Paul Whiteman and his Orchestra. It ran for 233 performances.

Durante made his entrance on the elephant, and Whiteman entered on a white horse. What story there was concerned the rivalry of two circus proprietors – John A Considine (Arthur Sinclair) and Matthew Mulligan (W J McCarthy). Matt Mulligan Jr (Novis) falls in love with Considine's daughter Mickey (Grafton). The Considine Circus goes bankrupt, but in an effort to save it, Considine's press agent, Claudius B Powers (Durante), burns down his employer's house and collects the insurance. The feud is settled and the lovers marry.

Three of the numbers from *Jumbo* have become classics: 'Little Girl Blue,' 'The Most Beautiful Girl in the World' and 'My Romance.'

When the show was made into a film, it was retitled *Billy Rose's Jumbo* (1962), and the picture was the last that Busby Berkeley, as second unit director, ever worked on. Durante was in the film as Pop Wonder, the owner of a circus and father of Doris Day. Dean Jagger was the other circus owner, and his son was Stephen Boyd. A couple of old Rodgers and Hart songs were added: 'Why Can't I?' from *Spring Is Here*

and 'This Can't Be Love' from *The Boys from Syracuse*. The finale, 'Sawdust, Spangles and Dreams' was contributed by Roger Edens. The film was undistinguished and suffered mightily by comparison with Cecil B DeMille's *The Greatest Show on Earth* (1952).

Capitalizing on the popularity of Elvis Presley, *Bye Bye Birdie* opened on Broadway in 1960. It had a book by Michael Stewart, lyrics by Lee Adams and music by Charles Strouse. Directed and choreographed by Gower Champion, it starred Dick Van Dyke, Chita Rivera, Paul Lynde and Dick Gautier, and ran for 607 performances.

Conrad Birdie (Gautier). a rock singer, is going into the Army. Albert Peterson (Van Dyke), a songwriter, is a sort of mother's boy who wants to marry Rose Grant (Rivera), but his mother (Kay Medford) objects. Rose suggests that he cut the apron strings by composing a hit song – 'One Last Kiss' – for Birdie, who will introduce it as he kisses one of his fans goodbye. The song could be promoted on the Ed Sullivan television show, and Kim McAfee (Susan Watson), a teenager from Sweet Apple, Ohio, is chosen as the kissee. Rose, Albert and Birdie go to Sweet Apple and stay at Kim's house. Of course, she falls in love with Birdie, which angers her boy friend (Michael J Pollard), but everything comes out all right.

The whole thing looked quite unpromising. The show had an unknown producer, Edward Padula. It was the first musical book that Stewart had written and also the first time out for Adams and Strouse. Gautier and Van Dyke had never been in a Broadway musical, and Rivera was certainly not a household name at the time. But the show received the Antoinette Perry and the Outer Circle Awards as the year's best musical.

The musical numbers were fun. Among them were 'The Telephone Hour,' 'Sultan's Ballet,' 'How Lovely to Be a Woman,' 'Put on a Happy Face,' 'Bye Bye Birdie,' 'Honestly Sincere,' 'One Boy (Girl),' 'Kids,' 'Rosie,' 'A Lot of Livin' to Do.' 'One Last Kiss,' 'We Love You Conrad' and 'Hymn for a Sunday Evening.'

The film version of *Bye Bye Birdie* (1963) was as frenetic as the show. The producers even got Ed Sullivan to play himself in the movie. Van Dyke and Lynde repeated their Broadway roles as Albert and Kim's father, respectively. Janet Leigh (who got top billing) was Rosie, and Ann-Margret stole the show as Kim. Maureen Stapleton was Albert's mother and Jesse Pearson was Conrad Birdie.

If one takes a poll of one's friends and asks them 'What was the greatest musical of all time?' the answer is likely to be *My Fair Lady*. This was the musical that opened on Broadway in 1956 and was based on George Bernard Shaw's play *Pygmalion*. The play itself had an unusual history. Most people think that the original Eliza Doolittle, the heroine, was Mrs Patrick Campbell, the great English actress who, after appearing in *Pygmalion*, formed a life-long friendship with Shaw. Actually, the first performance of the play was in Vienna in 1913, in German, and Lili Marberg was Eliza. Mrs Pat didn't open in London in the English-language version until 1914. In addition, there are arguments against the idea that she was the greatest Eliza, since many people vote

LEFT: Eliza Doolittle (Julie Andrews), the guttersnipe, applies to Professor Henry Higgins (Rex Harrison) for speech lessons, in the Broadway musical *My Fair Lady*, which premiered in 1956.

OPPOSITE: In the film version of *My Fair Lady* (1964), Audrey Hepburn was Eliza. Here she has left Higgins' house and is planning to run away with Freddy Eynsford-Hill; the song is 'Show Me.'

either for Diana Rigg in a 1976 production or Wendy Hiller in the 1933 film version. There are a few who even lean toward Margot Kidder in the 1984 Canadian production, which also starred the overacting Peter O'Toole.

By now the whole world must know that *My Fair Lady* was a musical version of Shaw's *Pygmalion*, in which Professor Henry Higgins turns a guttersnipe, Eliza Doolittle, into a regal, proper, English-speaking lady to win a bet. At any rate, the book and lyrics were written by Alan Jay Lerner, with music by Frederick Loewe. Directed by Moss Hart and choreographed by Hanya Holm, it starred Rex Harrison, Julie Andrews and Stanley Holloway. It ran 2717 performances on Broadway and 2281 in London.

Rex Harrison was unique. He was the first non-singing actor to appear as the star of a Broadway musical since Walter Huston in *Knickerbocker Holiday*, and his rhythmical talking of the lyrics, his *Sprechgesang*, was sensational. Julie Andrews had been a star on the London stage at the age of 12, and here she was the toast of Broadway at the age of 21. In the beginning, Lerner had wanted Mary Martin to play Eliza, but she wasn't available, so the role went to Andrews, who had made but one Broadway appearance in 1954, in *The Boy Friend.*

Many producers had wanted to make a musical of *Pygmalion*, but Shaw had said no. 'After my experience with *The Chocolate Soldier*, nothing will ever induce me to allow any other play of mine to be degraded into an operetta and set to any music except my own. . . . Hands off.' But when the 1933 movie of *Pygmalion*, produced by Gabriel Pascal and starring Wendy Hiller and Leslie Howard, appeared, he rather liked it. Of course he hated the ending. In the play, Eliza runs off to marry Freddy Eynsford-Hill and never returns to Higgins's Wimpole Street house. In the film she comes back to Higgins, and all he can say is 'Eliza, where the devil are my slippers?'

After Shaw's death in 1950, Pascal asked Rodgers and Hammerstein if they were interested in turning the play into a musical, but they declined. So Pascal went to Theresa Helburn of the Theatre Guild, and she liked the idea. Helburn then talked, in turn, to Cole Porter, Leonard Bernstein, Gian-Carlo Menotti, Betty Comden and Adolph Green, and Lerner and Loewe about it and they all declined. Lerner later said, 'We had decided that *Pygmalion* could not be made into a musical because we just don't know how to enlarge the play into a big musical without hurting the content. But when we went through the play again . . . we had a big surprise. We realized we didn't have to enlarge the plot at all. We just had to add what Shaw had happening offstage.'

The result was unbelievable. In addition to the New York and London Companies, the National Company with Brian Aherne and Sally Ann Howes seemed to tour forever. *My Fair Lady* was produced in 22 countries in 11 translations. The stage productions grossed more than $80 million, and the original-cast record album sold more than 5 million. There were 50 other recordings of the score in many translations. The film rights went for $5.5 million plus a percentage of the gross.

The public had to wait eight years for *My Fair Lady* to appear on the screen in 1964. It had been in the news even when it was in production. Henry Higgins was played by Rex Harrison, although the part had first been offered to Cary Grant. Grant, ever the gentleman, turned down the role, as he

OPPOSITE: Stanley Holloway confounds Robert Coote and Harrison in the stage *My Fair Lady* (1956).

ABOVE: Eliza (Julie Andrews) dances with Higgins (Harrison), on stage in *My Fair Lady*.

had done before with the role of Harold Hill in *The Music Man*, saying that not only would he not play the part, he would not even see the picture if Rex Harrison were not Henry Higgins.

Hollywood was suspicious of the charming newcomer Julie Andrews, and instead they cast Audrey Hepburn in the role of Eliza, with her singing voice supplied by the redoubtable Marni Nixon. Of course, Julie showed them two years later when she won the Academy Award for best actress for her work in *Mary Poppins* (1964), another musical.

Harrison won the Academy Award as best actor for his work in *My Fair Lady*. The sets and costumes were resplendent. The movie was sumptuously filmed. But the credit should go to the Alan Jay Lerner-Frederick Loewe score, with such memorable numbers as 'Get Me to the Church on Time,' 'Ascot Gavotte,' 'The Rain in Spain,' 'With a Little Bit of Luck,' 'Show Me,' 'I Could Have Danced All Night,' 'Just You Wait 'Enry 'Iggins,' 'Wouldn't It Be Loverly,' 'Embassy Waltz,' 'On the Street Where You Live,' 'You Did It,' 'Servants' Chorus,' and Harrison's splendid soliloquies, 'Hymn to Him,' 'I've Grown Accustomed to Her Face,' 'Why Can't the English

Teach Their Children How to Speak?' and 'I'm an Ordinary Man.'

Stanley Holloway was great as Alfred P Doolittle, Eliza's father, the dustman, but he almost didn't get to re-create his Broadway role. The studio wanted James Cagney. The best surprise, however, was Audrey Hepburn. Audiences had been prepared to resent her, but she gave one of the greatest performances of her life. She justified the decision of the producer, Jack L Warner, to get her to play the title role that Julie Andrews had so charmingly and popularly originated on the stage. It was her brilliance that gave the extra touch of subtle magic and individuality to the film. One critic said, 'It is true that Marni Nixon provides the lyric voice that seems to emerge from Miss Hepburn, but it is an excellent voice, expertly synchronized. And everything Miss Hepburn mimes to it is in sensitive tune with the melodies and words.'

There was an interesting censorship problem while the film was in production. In the stage version, at the end of the Ascot Race sequence, the ladylike Eliza loses her sense of decorum in the excitement of the race, and, in her loudest and best Cockney, shouts at the horse, 'Move your bloomin' arse!' This was almost deleted from the film, but calmer heads prevailed and the shout remained. Had it been deleted, it would have seemed like history repeating itself. In the original non-musical film version of *Pygmalion*, another line had been deleted by the censors of the day – 'Not bloody likely!'

An interesting sidelight to these movies of the early 1960s was that the superspectacular musical had replaced the superspectacular Biblical film as the bonanza picture of the times. Because so much money was being spent, studio bigwigs felt that under current market conditions, a multi-million dollar picture must command a worldwide audience to turn a profit. It could not, therefore, reflect facets of national life that would not be understood in foreign countries. But there were two exceptions to the rule – *West Side Story*, about juvenile gangs in the streets of New York, and *My Fair Lady*, a story built around English class distinctions. Both of them did very well indeed around the world. Perhaps it was because they shared with other popular musicals a fairy-tale approach to their subjects. The musical form, after all, has always depended strongly on fantasy and artificiality.

The Unsinkable Molly Brown was Meredith Willson's second Broadway musical; it opened in 1960. The book was

not by Willson this time, but by Richard Morris. The score was by Willson and the director was Dore Schary. The dances were by Peter Gennaro and the show starred Tammy Grimes and Harve Presnell. It ran for 532 performances.

After *The Music Man*, Willson had been approached to do a musical version of Eugene O'Neill's *Ah, Wilderness*, which he turned down. It was eventually done by Robert Merrill with the title *Take Me Along* (1959), which did nothing for the career of Jackie Gleason. Then Willson was approached by Morris, who had heard stories about a fabulous female named Molly Brown who had become a legend in the mining towns of Colorado. Of course, Willson loved this sort of Americana; he later said, 'I saw in it things I believed fit my kind of interest – period Americana, and the love story of two characters I could like.'

Molly Tobin (Grimes), a turn-of-the-century human dynamo who wants to be a rich and powerful grand lady, travels from Hannibal, Missouri, to Leadville, Colorado, where she gets a singing job in the Saddle Rock Saloon. She falls in love with a young miner, Johnny Brown (Presnell). They marry, but Johnny disappears on their wedding night. He comes back in a week with $300,000 that he made by selling his claim. Molly accidentally burns the money, but Johnny finds another claim and they become rich. Wealthy as they are, they are snubbed by Denver society. The two go off to Europe, and Molly becomes the darling of the Continent. Then she takes some of her distinguished European friends to Denver, where she throws a lavish party. All Denver's 'Who's Who' attend, but so do some of Leadville's less desirables, and the party is a disaster. Molly goes back to Europe and Johnny goes back to Leadville. Molly misses Johnny and sails back to the States on the *Titanic*, which, of course, hits the iceberg. Molly, however, is unsinkable and goes home to Johnny.

The critics raved. Whitney Bolton said Willson 'writes Americana into his music the way Betsy Ross sewed a flag.' He went on to say that the songs were 'dyed, dunked, dimpled and dappled with the true and genuine richness of Americana. ... It is star-spangled, Yankee Doodle music, home-brewed and home-bottled.'

Among the songs were 'Belly Up to the Bar Boys,' 'I'll Never Say No,' 'I Ain't Down Yet,' 'Colorado My Home,' 'Soliloquy' and 'Up Where the People Are.'

The film version of *The Unsinkable Molly Brown* appeared in 1964, starring Debbie Reynolds as the Colorado mining-camp hellion, and Harve Presnell repeated his stage role as her gold-prospecting husband. Debbie was fine in her best role since *Singin' In the Rain* (1952), especially when she sang 'I Ain't Down Yet.'

One of the most popular musicals of the century opened on Broadway in 1959 – *The Sound of Music*. The book was by Howard Lindsay and Russel Crouse, based on the biography *The Trapp Family Singers* by Maria Augusta Trapp. The lyrics were by Oscar Hammerstein II and the music by Richard Rodgers. Directed by Vincent J Donehue with dances by Joe Layton, it featured Mary Martin, Patricia Neway, Kurt Kaszner and Theodore Bikel, and ran for 1443 performances in New York and an astonishing 2385 in London.

The show won six Antoinette Perry Awards, including the one for best musical of the season. The touring company kept moving for two-and-one-half years. The original-cast record album sold three million copies, and the original-cast album of the film version sold eight million – the largest in recording history. It was truly a blockbuster.

As almost everyone knows, it was the musical story of Maria von Trapp, who was born aboard a train as her mother hurried to the hospital. She was orphaned at age six and became the ward of a left-leaning anti-Catholic. As if to make amends, she converted to Catholicism at age 18 and decided to become a nun. It was at this point that the musical story began.

Because of her independent, tomboyish nature, Maria (Martin) became the black sheep of the convent. Nine months before she was to take her formal vows, she was assigned to work as governess to the family of Baron Georg von Trapp (Bikel), a World-War-I naval hero. She was torn when the widowed baron proposed marriage, but married him with the Mother Superior's (Neway) blessing in 1927. The family lost its wealth in the worldwide Depression of the 1930s, and their home was turned into a hostel for traveling students and clergy. One of their guests, the Reverend Franz Wasner, heard the family singing together and appointed himself their manager. At the urging of Wasner and the operatic soprano Lotte Lehmann, they entered the 1936 Salzburg Festival, where they won top honors. The family fled Austria after the 1938 Nazi takeover.

The music was wonderful – 'The Sound of Music,' 'Praeludium,' 'Morning Hymn and Alleluia,' 'Maria,' 'Sixteen Going on Seventeen,' 'Climb Every Mountain,' 'Lonely Goatherd,' 'Do-Re-Mi,' 'Edelweiss,' 'My Favorite Things,' 'So Long, Farewell,' 'How Can Love Survive?' and 'No Way to Stop It,' among others.

Mary Martin had seen a German movie of the story of the Trapp Family Singers, fell in love with it, and decided she

LEFT: Maria (Mary Martin) and her charges – the Trapp children – sing 'My Favorite Things' in the Broadway version of *The Sound of Music*, which opened in 1959.

OPPOSITE LEFT: Mary Martin, as Maria, arrives at the Trapp mansion. She has left the convent to become a governess – *The Sound of Music*.

OPPOSITE RIGHT: Baron von Trapp (Theodore Bikel) realizes that he loves Maria (Martin) in Broadway's *The Sound of Music*.

a single Nazi in uniform appear on the stage lest the show become too melodramatic.

There was no question that the biggest Broadway-to-Hollywood musical of 1965 was *The Sound of Music*. Indeed, it was referred to in some quarters as 'The Sound of Money.' The film made almost $80 million, which made it the biggest money-maker in the history of movie musicals. In terms of 1984 dollars, that would come to more than $200 million. Of course, it was so sweet that certain other unnamed people called it 'The Sound of Mucus.' Call it corn if you like, but the fact is that this blockbuster pleased more people than practically any other movie in history. A certain Myra Franklin of

wanted to play Maria von Trapp in a musical. It took her eight months to find Maria, who was finally located in a hospital in Innsbruck, Austria, recovering from, of all things, malaria. Only when Maria was convinced that it would mean huge sums of money that she could use for her missionary work did she agree.

Howard Lindsay, one of the writers of the musical book, was a little worried. 'We're in operetta country with this show. The minute you say "Vienna," everybody thinks of a chorus of boys in short pants, and the minute you have a waltz, you're sunk. We had to work to keep the story convincing and believable, not letting it get into the never-never-land operetta lives in.' The writers were also careful not to let

Cardiff, Wales, for example, claimed to have sat through the film 940 times in its first 10 years.

Mary Martin had played Maria on the stage, of course, but in the film it was Julie Andrews who starred – the sweet, wholesome, ebullient Julie Andrews. Maria von Trapp later admitted that she thought that Martin came closer to hitting the mark, but added that she had finally developed an affection for the movie, which she once considered almost unbearably syrupy.

The baron was played by Christopher Plummer, with a singing voice supplied by Bill Lee. And Marni Nixon, the woman who was the voice for Margaret O'Brien in *The Big City* (1948), for Deborah Kerr in *The King and I* (1956), for Natalie Wood in *West Side Story* (1961) and for Audrey Hepburn in *My Fair Lady* (1964), finally appeared on the screen – in a bit part as a nun.

The film used almost all of the original score, eliminating only 'How Can Love Survive?' and 'No Way to Stop It' as too stagey. The simple story, the happy ending and the sumptuous Austrian locales marked a public desire for less sophisticated fare. The movie won Academy Awards for best picture, best direction (Robert Wise), best editing (William Reynolds), best sound recording (Jane Corcoran) and best photography (Ted McCord).

Girl Crazy had yet another incarnation in movies in 1966. This time called *When the Boys Meet the Girls*, it starred Connie Francis and Harve Presnell. The only good thing about it was that five of the songs from the original George and Ira Gershwin score were retained: 'But Not for Me,' 'I Got Rhythm,' 'Bidin' My Time,' 'Embraceable You' and 'Treat Me Rough.'

This time out, the lead couple runs a dude ranch for divorcées, and the picture was dreadful. Catering to the young in the audience were Sam the Sham and the Pharaohs, and Herman's Hermits, two rock groups. And so as not to drive away the older set, Louis Armstrong and Liberace were also in the film.

The new music left much to be desired. There were such songs as 'When the Boys Meet The Girls' by Jack Keller and Howard Greenfield; 'Mail Call' by Fred Karger, Ben Weisman and Sid Wayne; 'Monkey See, Monkey Do' by Johnny Farrow; 'Listen People' by Graham Gouldman; and 'Throw It Out of Your Mind' by Louis Armstrong and Bill Kayle.

A Funny Thing Happened on the Way to the Forum burst upon the Broadway scene in 1962. It was a burlesque treatment of some of the plays of Plautus, with a book by Burt Shevelove and Larry Gelbart (who went on to become the guiding spirit behind the television series 'M*A*S*H'). The

OPPOSITE: Baron Von Trapp (Christopher Plummer) declares his love to Maria (Julie Andrews) in the film version of *The Sound of Music* (1965).

RIGHT: Zero Mostel, as Pseudolus the slave (with dancing girl on his lap), has a conference with Phil Silvers (in black toga) in the film *A Funny Thing Happened on the Way to the Forum* (1966).

BELOW: Jerry Lester, Edward Everett Horton and Arnold Stang in a stage presentation of *A Funny Thing Happened on the Way to the Forum*.

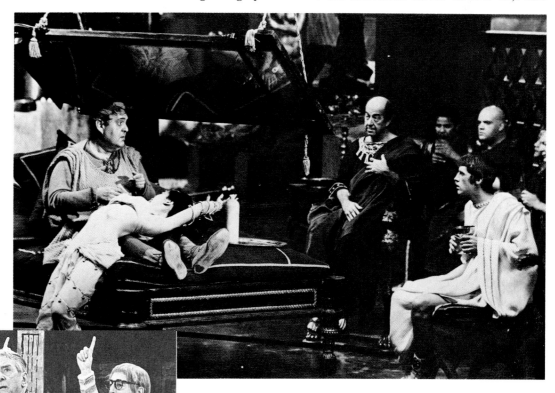

music and lyrics were by Stephen Sondheim, the director was George Abbott and the choreographer was Jack Cole. It starred a carload of zanies – Zero Mostel, Jack Gilford, David Burns, Raymond Walburn and John Carradine, and had a run of 964 performances in New York and a surprising 762 in London.

There were lechers and courtesans all over the place, and a slew of such double entendres as 'Carry my bust with pride' – a matron's order to a slave who is toting a statue. Pseudolus (Mostel), a slave, wants his freedom from Hero (Brian Davies). He tries to get Philia (Preshy Marker), a courtesan, for Hero from a brothel. But Milos Gloriosus (Ronald Hogate) buys her from Lycus (Carradine). Hero's father, Senex

(Burns), wants Philia, too, and Pseudolus tells Gloriosus that Philia has contracted the plague and died. Hysterium (Gilford) dresses up and plays the corpse. And so it goes.

The film version of *A Funny Thing Happened on the Way to the Forum* (1966) starred Mostel and Gilford, repeating their stage roles; Phil Silvers and Buster Keaton were two other comics. The songs that remained from the stage musical were 'Everybody Ought to Have a Maid (Sweeping Out, Sleeping In),' 'Comedy Tonight,' 'Lovely,' 'Bring Me My Bride' and 'The Dirge.'

How to Succeed in Business Without Really Trying opened on Broadway in 1961. The book was by the old master, Abe Burrows, with Jack Weinstock and Willie Gilbert, and was based on the novel of the same title by Shepherd Mead. Music and lyrics were by Frank Loesser. Directed by George Abbott with choreography by Hugh Lamber and musical staging by Bob Fosse, it starred Robert Morse, Virginia Martin, Bonnie Scott and Rudy Vallee. It ran for 1417 performances in New York and, surprisingly, since it was such a New York type business musical, 520 performances in London.

How to Succeed was a roaring success. It won the Pulitzer Prize for drama, the Tony for best musical (plus six other Antoinette Perry Awards), the New York Drama Critics Circle Award and the Theater Club Award for the best play of the season.

The show was a satire on business and the role that ambition, perseverence, self-confidence, brashness, opportunism and ruthlessness play in making a man a success. Finch (Morse) has them all. He is a window cleaner who is studying a success guide. Rule one is to get a job with a big company. So he joins the staff in the mail room of World Wide Wickets. Rosemary (Scott) is a secretary with the company, and she finds that she likes Finch. Mr Twimble is Finch's boss, and when Twimble is promoted, Finch is set to succeed him. But Finch turns the job down, for Rule Number Two is not to remain too long in the department in which one is employed. Of course, he says that he is turning it down for the sake of the team. This gesture catches the eye of the president of the firm, J B Biggley (Vallee), and Finch rises in the company. He finds he likes Hedy, who has flaming sex appeal, and she becomes his secretary. But Finch makes a pass at Hedy and realizes that he really likes Rosemary. All's well that ends well.

This was Loesser's last musical. He died of cancer at the age of 59 shortly after the show opened.

Some of the great numbers were 'Happy to Keep His Dinner Warm,' 'The Company Way,' 'Cinderella Darling,' 'Love from a Heart of Gold,' 'Pirate Ballet,' 'Paris Original,' 'Grand Old Ivy,' 'Brotherhood of Man,' 'How to Succeed,' 'Coffee Break,' 'A Secretary Is Not a Toy,' 'Been a Long Day,' 'Finch's Frolic,' 'Rosemary' and 'I Believe In You' (which Finch sings to his reflection in the mirror while shaving).

The film version of *How to Succeed in Business Without Really Trying* was released in 1967, and it had been lovingly done. Of course, some numbers were dropped – 'Cinderella Darling,' 'Love from a Heart of Gold,' 'Happy to Keep His Dinner Warm' and 'Pirate Ballet' – and 'Paris Original' was heard only in the background. But otherwise, the movie was true to the stage musical. Vallee and Morse repeated their Broadway roles, and Michelle Lee was wonderful as Rosemary. Even the choreography by Dale Moreda was faithful to Bob Fosse's concepts.

LEFT: Finch (Robert Morse) kisses Rosemary (Bonnie Scott), as J B Biggley (Rudy Vallee) looks on, in the Broadway musical *How to Succeed in Business Without Really Trying*, which opened in 1961.

OPPOSITE TOP: Finch, the window cleaner (Robert Morse), uses an open window to learn about the world of business in the film *How to Succeed in Business Without Really Trying* (1967).

OPPOSITE BOTTOM: The secretaries' chorus in the movie *How to Succeed . . .*

ABOVE: The film *Camelot*.
LEFT: Goulet, Andrews, Burton:
Broadway's *Camelot* (1960).

Camelot had its premiere on Broadway in 1960. The book and lyrics were by Alan Jay Lerner, the music by Frederick Loewe. Directed by Moss Hart with choreography by Hanya Holm, it starred Richard Burton, Julie Andrews, Roddy McDowall and Robert Goulet. It ran 873 performances.

The run was a fair one, but it had a three-and-one-half-million-dollar box office advance because of the success of *My Fair Lady*, Lerner and Loewe's smash collaboration. Like *My Fair Lady*, it featured Julie Andrews and Robert Coote. Other alumni were Hart, the director; Oliver Smith, the stage designer; Holm, the choreographer; Robert Russell Bennet, the orchestrator and Franz Allers, the conductor.

How could it miss? One problem was that it was based on T H White's *The Once and Future King*, a delightful trilogy which covered almost the whole life of King Arthur. And that was hard to cram into an evening's performance. So the text was not cohesive, the plot was not always clear, and the humor was pretty weak. In short, it was delightful to the eye and ear, but it lacked the unity and magic of *My Fair Lady*.

Julie Andrews was wonderful as Guenevere; Burton did the Rex Harrison form of non-singing to a fare-thee-well and turned in a moving performance in the bargain. Goulet was a virile Lancelot, MacDowell was a sinister Mordred and Coote was a winsome King Pellinore.

The songs were most pleasant, but one felt that there were too few to fill up the time. The numbers included: 'If Ever I would Leave You,' 'Then You May Take Me to the Fair,' '*C'est Moi*,' 'How to Handle a Woman,' 'The Lusty Month of May,' 'Guenevere,' 'What Do the Simple Folk Do?,' 'I Wonder What the King Is Doing Tonight,' 'Follow Me,' 'I Loved You Once in Silence,' 'Wedding Ceremony' and 'The Simple Joys of Maidenhood.'

The film version of *Camelot* was released in 1967. One critic called it 'an appalling film version with only good orchestrations to recommend it.' Part of the problem was that the original cast was not in the movie. Instead of Richard Burton there was Richard Harris; instead of Julie Andrews, Vanessa Redgrave; instead of Robert Goulet, Franco Nero. Besides that, it was too long – one minute short of three hours. It also had too little of the wit of *The Once and Future King*. The result was that Harris and Redgrave were probably the last non-singers to be entrusted with major singing roles.

There were those, however, who thought that the picture had strong dramatic action, vivid characterizations and an intensification of the romantic interest that made it superior to the stage musical. Then, too, it cost a whopping $15 million to make, and the wonderful photography and settings showed it. Still, it was a costly flop, recouping less than half its costs.

Redgrave wore one of the strangest costumes ever designed in one scene in the picture – a gown completely covered with pumpkin seeds stitched into the fabric. And the film contained one classic mistake. King Pellinore, played by Lionel Jeffries, first meets King Arthur about an hour into the movie, but 20 minutes before he was plainly visible at the King's wedding.

Funny Girl opened on Broadway in 1964. The book was by Isobel Lennart, the lyrics by Bob Merrill and the music by Jule Styne. Directed by Garson Kanin and Jerome Robbins, it had dances by Carol Haney and starred Barbara Streisand, Kay Medford, Danny Meehan and Sydney Chaplin. It ran for 1348 performances in New York, but was a relative flop in London where it lasted a mere 109 performances.

The musical told the story of Fanny Brice, a musical-comedy star who was warmly and fondly remembered, so a musical comedy about her could not have missed in the United States. The production was a triumph for Streisand. David Merrick, the Broadway producer, had taken her out of the Blue Angel Nightclub and signed her to play Miss Marmelstein in *I Can Get It For You Wholesale* (1962). She had but one song – 'Miss Marmelstein' – but she stole the show and became a star. *Funny Girl* had an advance ticket sale of one million dollars.

The show, telling its tale of Brice's romance with the gambler Nicky Arnstein, had wonderful songs. Among them were 'I'm the Greatest Star,' 'Cornet Man,' 'Bridal Finale,' 'Sadie, Sadie,' 'The Music that Makes Me Dance,' 'People' and 'Don't Rain on My Parade.'

Funny Girl hit the screen in 1968, with Streisand making her film debut, and, incidentally, winning the Academy Award as best actress for her trouble. She was simply fabulous – brassy and vulnerable – and as able to toss off such lines as (indicating her nose) 'Do you think beautiful girls are going to stay in style forever?' And what she did with the Merrill-Styne songs was perfection, especially with 'People' and 'Don't Rain on My Parade.'

She dominated the film, and, in addition, proved that she was actress enough to get blood out of a turnip – in this case, the badly cast Omar Sharif as Nicky Arnstein.

In addition to the Merrill-Styne songs, there were some additions: 'I'd Rather Be Blue' by Billy Rose and Fred Fisher, 'My Man' by Maurice Yvain and Channing Pollock and 'Second Hand Rose' by Grant Clarke and James Hanley.

One of Broadway's most whimsical and charming plays, *Finian's Rainbow*, premiered on Broadway in 1947, oddly enough the same year that an equally charming fantasy, *Brigadoon*, opened. The book for *Finian's Rainbow* was by E Y 'Yip' Harburg, Fred Saidy, with lyrics by Harburg and music by Burton Lane. Directed by Bretaigne Windust with choreography by Michael Kidd, it starred Ella Logan, David

LEFT: Sydney Chaplin (Nickie Arnstein) romances Barbra Streisand (Fanny Brice) in a scene from the Broadway production of *Funny Girl* (1964).

OPPOSITE TOP: Ella Logan (Sharon McLonergan) marries Donald Richards (Woody Mahoney), as her father, Albert Sharpe (Finian McLonergan), looks on in the Broadway production of *Finian's Rainbow* (1947).

OPPOSITE BOTTOM: In the movie version of *Funny Girl* (1968), Omar Sharif played Nickie Arnstein. Here Streisand looks longingly at her lover.

Wayne and Donald Richards. The musical had a run of 725 performances.

Finian's Rainbow was an odd marriage of an Irish-type fantasy with a tale of social-conscience conflicts. It involved sharecroppers, labor exploitation, racial prejudice, poll taxes, right-wing reaction and greed for gold. The setting was Rainbow Valley, Missitucky, where Finian McLonergan (Albert Sharpe) has brought his daughter, Sharon (Logan). Finian plants a pot of gold that he had stolen from a leprechaun in Ireland there, because he thinks the land near Fort Knox might make the pot grow even more gold. Og, the leprechaun (Wayne), wants the gold back, so he grants three wishes. The first transforms the bigoted Senator Billboard Rawkins into a black evangelist so that he will find out what it means to be black in the South. Og falls in love with Susan Mahoney (Anita Alvarez), a deaf-mute who speaks only through her dancing, and the second wish restores her speech and hearing. The third wish secures Sharon's happiness with her boy friend, Woody Mahoney (Richards). Finally, Og becomes a human being and wins Susan.

The score was excellent. Among the numbers were 'How Are Things in Glocca Morra?,' 'That Great Come-and-Get-It

ABOVE: Fred Astaire played Finian in the movie adaptation of *Finian's Rainbow* (1968).

RIGHT: In the stage version of *Finian's Rainbow* (1947), David Wayne played Og, the leprechaun, and Anita Alvarez, was his true love, the deaf-mute Susan Mahoney.

Day,' 'Look to the Rainbow,' 'Old Devil Moon,' 'When the Idle Poor Become the Idle Rich,' 'The Begat,' 'Necessity,' 'When I'm Not Near the Girl I Love,' 'Something Sort of Grandish' and 'This Time of the Year.'

Director Francis Ford Coppola was still pretty much of a neophyte when his filmed version of *Finian's Rainbow* was released in 1968. It was a self-indulgent movie, and he later learned that camera tricks are no substitute for expertise. The picture was grandiose, and one never knew whether it was a romantic tale or a political and social satire. The best things about the film were the choreography by Hermes Pan and Fred Astaire, and Astaire's dancing. But, to be fair, the fault was not exclusively Coppola's. It had taken 21 years for the play to reach the screen, and social-consciousness fantasies were not exactly a burning issue at the time of the picture's release. Also, Astaire, good as he was as Finian, would have been much better 10 or 15 years before.

BELOW: The effervescent Gwen Verdon in the title role of the Broadway hit *Sweet Charity*.

RIGHT: Gwen Verdon, Helen Gallagher and Thelma Oliver on stage in *Sweet Charity*.

Sweet Charity was one of the hits of Broadway in 1966. It had a book by Neil Simon that was based on the Italian motion picture *Nights of Cabiria* (*Notti di Cabiria*) of 1957, which had been written by Federico Fellini, Tullio Pinelli and Ennio Flaiano – a story of a prostitute with a heart of gold. The lyrics were by Dorothy Fields and the music by Cy Coleman. Directed and choreographed by Bob Fosse, it starred Gwen Verdon (Fosse's wife at the time), John McMartin and Helen Galagher, and ran for 608 performances in New York and 484 in London.

The whole thing started when Fosse and Verdon took in a revival showing of the Fellini movie, and both of them thought it would make a good musical. They called in Simon, who voted for changing the lusty Roman streetwalker into a more demure, but still dynamic, American dance-hall hostess.

Charity Hope Valentine (Verdon) is a simple girl looking for the romance of her life. She is a dance hostess at the Fandango Ballroom (a 'musical snakepit'), where she says that the girls 'have to defend themselves to music.' She meets Vittorio Vitale (James Luisi), the Italian movie idol, just after he has argued with his girl friend. She ends up in his apartment, but the other woman storms back in and Charity has to spend the night hiding in a closet. Later, to improve her mind, she goes to a lecture at the 92nd Street Young Men's Hebrew Association and meets Oscar (McMartin), who has claustrophobia, and the two of them get stuck in an elevator. They are rescued, Oscar calms down, and they go to Coney Island and get stuck halfway down on the para-

ABOVE: Shirley MacLaine (on table) and the other girls sing 'Big Spender' in the film *Sweet Charity* (1969).

RIGHT: James Barton and Olga San Juan in the Broadway production of *Paint Your Wagon* (1951).

chute ride. This frightens Charity. Oscar decides that he cannot marry a dance-hall hostess, but at the end, Charity still hopes for the best.

The score and the book were good, the choreography was excellent, but Verdon stole the show. Singing, dancing, acting and cracking jokes, she really *was* the show.

Some of the numbers were 'The Rich Man's Frug.' 'Rhythm of Life,' 'Big Spender,' 'If They Could See Me Now,' 'Where Am I Going?,' 'I'm a Brass Band,' 'There's Gotta Be Something Better Than This,' 'Baby, Dream Your Dream,' 'The Hustle,' 'My Personal Property,' 'It's a Nice Face' and 'I Love to Cry at Weddings.'

When *Sweet Charity* was transferred to the screen in 1969, some of the bloom had gone off the rose. Shirley MacLaine was wonderful in the title role, but Bob Fosse directed with too much flash, as if he distrusted the impact of the material, and some of the production numbers were really overproduced. For example, MacLaine sang the 'I'm a Brass Band' number on a rooftop dressed in a drum majorette's uniform. But the Coleman-Fields score made up for much of this directorial overkill. MacLaine deserved better.

Paint Your Wagon first hit Broadway in 1951, with book and lyrics by Alan J Lerner and music by Frederick Loewe. Directed by Daniel Mann with dances by Agnes De Mille, it featured James Barton, Olga San Juan and Tony Bavaar, and ran for 289 performances.

It came as close to being a bomb as any Lerner-Loewe

musical could come, and the critics panned it. Walter Kerr wrote the kindest review, but even he said, 'Writing an integrated musical comedy – where people are believable and the songs are logically introduced – is no excuse for not being funny from time to time. But the librettist of *Paint Your Wagon* seems to be more interested in the authenticity of his background than in the joy of the audience.'

The story was inane – all about life in a California boom town during the gold rush of the 1840s. But there were some good numbers in the show: 'Hand Me Down That Can o' Beans,' 'Whoop-Ti-Ay,' 'Wandrin' Star,' 'They Call the Wind Maria,' 'Another Autumn,' 'I Talk To the Trees,' 'I Still See Elisa,' 'There's a Coach Comin' In' and 'Paint Your Wagon.'

There are those who say that the film version of *Paint Your Wagon* was the worst adaptation in history. The plot of the Broadway musical didn't have much going for it in the first place, but at least the stage version had real singers for the only two songs that anyone remembers – 'They Call the Wind Maria' and 'I Talk to the Trees.' Harve Presnell did a fine job with the former in the film, but letting Clint Eastwood sing the latter was a disaster. And Lee Marvin's singing left much to be desired, even though a film in which Marvin plays a drunk can't be completely awful. The scenery was beautiful. The picture ran for almost three hours, and as one critic said, 'A boring, dated Broadway musical of the late 40s has been turned into an enormously expensive [$20 million], stupe-

BELOW: One of the rowdier scenes from the movie *Paint Your Wagon* (1969).

RIGHT: Lee Marvin in the film *Paint Your Wagon*.

fyingly boring movie musical . . . a clinker. Let this wagon roll by without you.'

The movie kept 'Wandrin' Star,' 'They Call the Wind Maria,' 'There's a Coach Comin' In' and 'I Talk to the Trees.' Added were five new songs – none of them memorable – by Alan Jay Lerner and André Previn: 'Gold Fever,' 'The First Thing You Know,' 'A Million Miles Away from the Door,' 'Gospel of No Name City' and 'Best Things.'

Hello Dolly! opened on Broadway in 1964. The book was by Michael Stewart based on the Thornton Wilder play *The Matchmaker*, whose plot Wilder had borrowed himself. The music and lyrics were by Jerry Herman. Directed and choreographed by Gower Champion, it starred Carol Channing, David Burns, Eileen Brennan, Sondra Lee and Charles Nelson Reilly. The musical ran for a phenomenal 2844 performances on Broadway and 794 in London.

The show had run on Broadway for three years and ten months when producer David Merrick had the inspiration to mount a second, all-black cast starring Pearl Bailey and Cab Calloway. After five years, *Hello Dolly!* had earned an $8-million profit on its original cost of $350,000. It had also played on tour in the United States and in West Germany, Czechoslovakia, England, Israel and Spain.

The year was 1898. Dolly Levi (Channing) was a widowed marriage broker who tries to find a second wife for Horace Vandergelder (Burns), a shopkeeper from Yonkers, New York, but is actually trying to win him for herself. Her rival is Mrs Molloy (Brennan), the owner of a ladies' shop in New

James Barton in the Broadway *Paint Your Wagon* (1951).

BELOW: Carol Channing, as Dolly Levi, and David Burns, as Horace Vandergelder, in Broadway's 1964 *Hello Dolly!*

LEFT: The same scene from the all-black-cast Broadway version of *Hello Dolly!* (1968), with Pearl Bailey and Cab Calloway.

York City. Vandergelder's two store clerks decide to take the day off when Horace is in New York, and they also go to the big city. The clerks, Cornelius (Reilly) and Barnaby (Jerry Dodge), go to Molloy's shop, but Horace arrives and the boys hide. Vandergelder is angry when he suspects that men are hiding in the shop, but he doesn't know who they are. The scene shifts to the Harmonia Gardens, a lavish restaurant. Cornelius and Mrs Molloy and Barnaby and Mrs Molloy's clerk, Minnie Fay (Lee), arrive. But so does Vandergelder, who first fires the boys and then is arrested for disturbing the

OPPOSITE: The magnetic, lovable Carol Channing – the original Broadway Dolly in *Hello Dolly!*, which opened in 1964.

ABOVE: The wonderful dance sequence titled 'Put on Your Sunday Clothes,' from the Hollywood version of *Hello Dolly!* (1969).

peace. Later he goes back to the shop, but Dolly enters and he realizes that he loves her.

Very few of the songs were blockbusters. The numbers included 'It Takes a Woman,' 'Hello Dolly!' 'So Long, Dearie,' 'Before the Parade Passes By,' 'Put on Your Sunday Clothes,' 'Ribbons Down My Back,' 'Dancing,' 'Motherhood,' 'Elegance,' 'I Put My Hand In,' 'The Waiter's Gavotte' and 'It Only Takes a Moment.' They were good, but not sensational.

The one thing that the producers knew in the beginning was that this show needed a star – someone whom audiences could root for. So they went after the best – Ethel Merman – who turned them down. (She eventually did do the show in 1970, when some of the songs that were written for her were put back in.) But Carol Channing filled the bill admirably. Over the years, other strong stage personalities have played the role – among them Ginger Rogers, Betty Grable, Mary Martin and Martha Raye.

However, Channing was considered too weird for the movies at the time that the film version of *Hello Dolly!* (1969) was being cast, and the Hollywood producers wanted Barbra Streisand, anyway. Despite its $24-million budget, its direction by Gene Kelly and the strong performance by Streisand, the film was not a success. Perhaps it was a matter of timing. Merrick had given 20th Century a contract that permitted filming only when the stage musical had closed on Broadway. By the time the film was released, the songs were no longer hits and audiences, by and large, had tired of musicals.

In the cast with Streisand were Walter Matthau as Vandergelder, Michael Crawford, Marianne McAndrew, E J Peaker, Tommy Tune and David Hurst. The film left an oddly negative impression. It had a good deal of synthetic effervescence, but very little real vitality. 'Motherhood' was eliminated, and Jerry Herman wrote two new songs for Streisand, 'Just Leave Everything to Me,' which replaced 'I Put My Hand In' and 'Love Is Only Love,' which actually was a reject from his score for *Mame*.

As the 1960s ended, fewer and fewer musical films were being made, but a solid proportion of those that were came from Broadway.

Barbra Streisand, as Dolly, in the all-stops-out 'Before the Parade Passes By' scene in the movie version of *Hello Dolly!* (1969).

THE NOSTALGIC
SEVENTIES

Hollywood musicals had worn out their welcome by 1970. It was a decade of reaction, and most musicals were looking backward: *Fiddler on the Roof, 1776, Cabaret. Grease*, with its teenagers from a casting director's dream, was a hit, while the film incarnation of *Hair*, a paean to the turbulent 1960s, was disappointing. *Jesus Christ, Superstar*, an innovative and memorable stage show, lost its faith when it got to Hollywood. Much the same could be said of the film industry.

TOP: The Crucifixion scene from *Jesus Christ, Superstar*, released in 1973.

MAIN PICTURE: John Travolta (standing) and friends in the film *Grease* (1978).

As an indication of how low the popularity of Hollywood musicals had sunk at the beginning of the 1970s, most film historians and archivists can list only five that were released in the decade's opening year. Two of them were children's musicals – Disney's *The Aristocats* (a cartoon feature) and a movie based upon a National Broadcasting Company television series for children, *Pufnstuf*, which seemed to disappear almost on its release date. One of the three remaining films that used real people was Julie Andrew's underrated *Darling Lili*. The other two movies were Broadway imports. In a bad year, two out of three isn't too bad.

On a Clear Day You Can See Forever premiered on Broadway in 1965. Its book and lyrics were by Alan Jay Lerner and the music was by Burton Lane. Directed by Robert Lewis with dances by Herbert Ross, it starred Barbara Harris, John Cullum and William Daniels, and had a run of 280 performances.

In the beginning, Richard Rodgers had had the idea for the show, and was to do the score with Lerner, but they had differences of opinion, and Rodgers dropped out of the project. With him went the original title, *I Picked a Daisy*, but this was not an important loss.

The story dealt with Daisy Gamble (Harris), who tells Dr Mark Buckner (Cullum), a psychiatrist, that she has extrasensory perception and can make flowers grow. Buckner puts her under hypnosis, and it turns out that in the eighteenth century Daisy was Melinda Wells, married to Sir Edward Moncrief. Her boy friend, Warren (Daniels), learns that she is getting interested in Buckner. In her next session with the doctor, she becomes Melinda again. Finally, Buck-

ner falls in love with Daisy, who runs back to Warren. In the end, Buckner uses mind control to win her hand.

The score was only mildly interesting. The numbers included 'On a Clear Day You Can See Forever,' 'Come Back to Me,' 'Melinda,' 'What Did I Have That I Don't Have Now?,' 'He Isn't You,' 'Go to Sleep,' 'Hurry, It's Lovely Up Here' and 'Love With All the Trimmings.'

The film version of *On A Clear Day You Can See Forever* (1970) had an all-star cast, with Barbra Streisand (Daisy), Yves Montand (Buckner), Larry Blyden (Warren), Bob Newhart and Jack Nicholson in a small role as Daisy's hippie step-brother. It was pretty much a mess that not even Streisand could save. Extensive cutting sometimes made the narrative unintelligible, and the editor even cut Nicholson's only song. On the other hand, director Vincent Minnelli was in top form, especially when mounting the sequences set amid the pomp and pageantry of eighteenth-century English aristocracy.

Operetta made a brief comeback on Broadway in 1944, with the premier of *Song of Norway*. It had a book by Milton Lazarus that was based on a play by Homer Curran. The lyrics were by Robert Wright and George 'Chet' Forrest, and the music was culled from the works of Edvard Grieg. Directed by Charles K Freeman with choreography by George Balanchine, it featured Lawrence Brooks, Irra Petina, Helena Bliss and Sig Arno. The show ran for 860 performances in New York and 526 in London.

The story was purportedly about the romance of the great Norwegian composer Edvard Grieg (Brooks), and Nina Hagerup (Bliss). It begins on Midsummer's Eve, when the poet and friend of Grieg, Rikard Nordraak, prophesies that 'Norway will find her voice and sing again. She waits for the song of one man.' That man turns out to be Grieg, of course. One of the problems with making Grieg's life into a stage musical was that he really didn't have that exciting a life. So the librettists started creating one for him. Enter Louisa Giovanni, an opera star (Petina), who lures Grieg away from Nina. Louisa and Edvard go off together to Rome, but Grieg begins to miss Nina. Upon hearing of the death of Nordraak, he runs back to Norway and his true love. It was corny, but it was effective.

Some of the numbers were 'Strange Music,' 'Wedding Day at Troldhaugen,' 'I Love You,' 'Freddy and His Fiddle,' 'Midsummer Eve,' 'Song of Norway,' 'At Christmas Time' and 'Hill of Dreams.'

It took 25 years for the film version of *Song of Norway* (1970) to be released, and the more polite critics characterized it as a bomb. By this time the public's craving for operettas had disappeared. Obviously, the film was made in an effort to emulate the success of *The Sound of Music*, but it didn't even come close. Treacly and horribly overproduced, it even included cartoon and puppet sequences. In the United Nations-style cast were 'the electrifying star of the Norwegian stage' Toralv Maurstadt (who?) as Grieg, and Florence Henderson, the veteran of so many oleomargerine

commercials, as Nina. Also in the cast were Edward G Robinson as a lovable piano salesman and Frank Poretta, Harry Secombe, Robert Morley and Oscar Homolka. But the only real star of the film was the Norwgian countryside.

Today the movie is occasionally shown in Oslo and Bergen just so the audiences can laugh at it. But it has disappeared in the United States because of public apathy and critical derision. Wolcott Gibbs said of it in *The New Yorker*, 'Everything was all right with me as long as nobody talked. Then I tried to think of something else.' Pauline Kael wrote, 'The movie is of an unbelievable badness. It brings back clichés you didn't know you knew – they're practically from the unconscious of moviegoers. You can't get angry at something this stupefying; it seems to have been made by trolls.'

Richard Schickel in *Life* called it 'Godawful. . . . The musical numbers, when not downright ugly, are ludicrous, containing all the conventions of staging that made *The Sound of Music* so easy to hate. Grieg having apparently lived a life of exemplary dullness, the only issue Stone [Andrew L Stone, the director] can trump up for dramatic purposes is his thwarted desire to create an indigenous national music for Norway – hardly a matter to keep us on the edge of our chairs. In the ineptitude of his writing, Mr Stone matches the clumsiness of his direction, unconsciously creating a double parody of both the operetta and biographical forms – truly an amazing work of unintentional humor.'

Fiddler on the Roof first appeared on Broadway in 1964. The book was by Joseph Stein, based on stories by Sholem Aleichem, with lyrics by Sheldon Harnick and music by Jerry Bock. Directed and choreographed by Jerome Robbins, it starred Zero Mostel, Maria Karnilova and Beatrice Arthur. It stayed for a remarkable 3242 performances in New York and, starring Chaim Topol and later Alfie Bass, 2030 in London.

LEFT: Austin Pendleton, as Motel the tailor, Zero Mostel as Tevye the dairyman and Joanna Merlin as the daughter who wants to marry Motel in the Broadway production of *Fiddler on the Roof* (1964).

OPPOSITE TOP: In the movie version of *Fiddler on the Roof* (1971), Tevye was played by Chaim Topol. Here he sings and dances 'To Life.'

OPPOSITE BOTTOM: Mostel, Maria Karnilova as his wife (Golde), and the cast of the Broadway musical *Fiddler on the Roof* sing 'Tradition.'

The original Aleichem stories portrayed Tevye, the Russian-Jewish milkman, as simple, passive and humble. But this would not work on the stage, so he was given more strength. The image of the fiddler on the roof came from a Marc Chagall painting and symbolized the precarious life of the religious Jew amid a hostile Christian society.

The production was set in a small Ukrainian town, Anatevka, in 1905, and told the story of Tevye, who tried to preserve his Jewish heritage against growing odds – his daughters' desires to marry the men they want rather than those picked for them by a matchmaker – the impending Russian pogrom – the necessity to leave the village.

The musical won nine Tony Awards, including that for best musical, and became truly an international sensation. In addition to the United States and the United Kingdom, there were productions in Warsaw, Vienna, Paris, Copenhagen, Antwerp, Madrid, Geneva, Istanbul, Tel Aviv, Finland, New Zealand, Norway, Holland, South Africa, West Germany, East Germany, Czechoslovakia, Iceland, several countries in South America and even Japan. People wondered how it could appeal to the Japanese, for example, but the answer was probably that it was not solely a Russian-Jewish musical: it encompassed the feeling of 'family' all over the world.

Even today, it is presented by amateur groups everywhere, possibly every day.

The musical numbers were glorious. Among them were 'Prologue – Fiddler on the Roof,' 'Tradition,' 'Matchmaker, Matchmaker,' 'If I Were a Rich Man,' 'Sabbath Prayer,' 'To Life,' 'Miracle of Miracles,' 'Tevye's Dream,' 'Sunrise, Sunset,' 'Wedding Celebration and Bottle Dance,' 'Do You Love Me?,' 'Far From the Home I Love,' 'Chava Ballet' and 'Anatevka.'

The world awaited the film version of *Fiddler on the Roof* (1971) and it was not disappointed. Of course shooting it in wide-screen Panavision 70 caused it to lose the intimacy of the stage production, but who cared? Of course Chaim Topol, the Israeli actor, could not match the exuberance of Zero Mostel, the original Tevye, but no one else would have been able to do that, either. The supporting cast included Molly Picon, Norma Crane and Leonard Frey, with an assist on the sound track from Isaac Stern playing his violin as 'The Fiddler.'

The Broadway opening of the musical *1776* was in 1969. It had a book by Peter Stone and lyrics and music by Sherman Edwards. Directed by Peter Hunt with choreography by Onna White, it starred William Daniels, Paul Hecht, Clifford David, Roy Poole and Howard Da Sylva and ran for 1217 performances. It also was the first musical comedy ever presented in its entirety at the White House.

It was a unique show. No chorus line. Only two female roles. Lyrical singing roles for such personages as Benjamin Franklin, Thomas Jefferson and John Adams. Unabashed

ABOVE: A scene from the film version of *1776* (1972).

RIGHT: Ken Howard (center) is Jefferson in the movie *1776*.

OPPOSITE BOTTOM: da Silva and Daniels in Broadway's *1776* (1969).

OPPOSITE TOP: Crane and Picon in the movie *Fiddler* (1971).

patriotism. But it worked. The Pulitzer Prize-winning musical about America's first Congress trying to come up with a Declaration of Independence from Britain had audiences on the edge of their seats. Will they or won't they agree? The final scene, which re-created the actual signing of the Declaration to the accompaniment of the calling of the roll and the ringing of the Liberty Bell, was memorable.

The score was excellent, the songs furthering the action and fleshing out the characters. Among the numbers were: 'Sit Down, John,' 'Piddle, Twiddle and Resolve,' 'The Lees of Virginia,' 'But, Mr Adams,' 'Yours, Yours, Yours,' 'He Plays the Violin,' 'Cool, Cool Considerate Men,' 'Momma Look Sharp,' 'Molasses To Rum' and 'Is Anybody There?'

The film version of *1776* (1972) featured William Daniels (Adams), Howard Da Sylva (Franklin) and Ken Howard (Jefferson), who had been in the show on Broadway. The stage version was confined to the Philadelphia meeting room, but the movie had the advantage of being able to send the camera outdoors to the Philadelphia streets or to Adams's home in Massachusetts. Unfortunately, the film score eliminated 'Cool, Cool Considerate Men,' a song that made an important point in the story line by illustrating the conservatism of the Southern members of the Congress.

Cabaret premiered on Broadway in 1966. Its book was by Joe Materoff and was based on a play by John Van Druten, *I Am A Camera*, which, in turn, was based on Christopher Isherwood's semi-autobiographical Berlin stories in his book *Goodbye to Berlin.* It had lyrics by Fred Ebb and music by John Kander. Directed by Harold Prince with dances by Ronald Field, it starred Lotte Lenya, Jill Haworth, Jack Gilford, Joel Grey and Bert Convy and ran for 1166 performances in New York and 316 in London.

One of the most interesting things about the stage show was that it was a total rejection of the principle that a musical must be integrated. *Cabaret* stated that there was nothing wrong with an unintegrated musical – one in which songs and dances were separated from the story. It was also a tough, stinging, satirical and acid play. None of the sweetness of Rodgers and Hammerstein; none of the wholesome goodness in which life is depicted with utter falsity as one big, happy, rollicking songfest.

With the exception of *The Threepenny Opera*, perhaps, which it resembled, it was the first musical to exploit the notion that life is fascinating because it is ambiguous. It confronted the facts that people use each other, homosexuality exists, Nazism had its seductions and decadence can be fun. *Cabaret* used music in an exciting new way. Characters did not burst into song to express their emotions; a

OPPOSITE: Lotte Lenya, as Fräulein Schneider, dances with some sailors in the Broadway production of *Cabaret* (1966).

RIGHT: Joel Grey was the cynical MC at the Kit Kat Klub in the stage *Cabaret*.

BELOW: Some members of the Broadway cast of *Cabaret*. In the front row are Bert Convy (Clifford Bradshaw), Joel Grey (the master of ceremonies) and Jill Haworth. Jack Gilford and Lotte Lenya are in the rear to the left.

sleazy night club, the Kit Kat Klub, became a place where satirical comment on the lives and problems of the characters was made in striking, entertaining and savage dances and songs. The club was a logical place for music, unlike a meadow in the Austrian Alps or a diction professor's study. It was a clearly artificial show, of course, but no attempt was made to convince the audience that this was a slice of real life.

On stage, *Cabaret* told the stories of two romances. One was between Clifford Bradshaw (Convy) and Sally Bowles (Haworth). He was an American writer and teacher, she was a night-club entertainer. The other, far more poignant, love story told of the romance between Herr Schultz (Gilford), a shopkeeper, and Fräulein Schneider (Lenya), the owner of the rooming house where Schultz lives. He is Jewish – she is not, and their romance was terminated by her growing fear of the rise of the Nazi Party in Germany.

Among the numbers were '*Willkommen*,' 'So What?,' 'Don't Tell Mama,' 'Telephone Song,' 'Perfectly Marvelous,' 'Two Ladies,' 'It Couldn't Please Me More (A Pineapple),' 'Why Should I Wake Up?' 'The Money Song,' 'Married,' 'Meeskite,' 'If You Could See Her,' 'What Would You Do' and 'Cabaret.'

Cabaret won the New York Drama Critics Award and a Tony for being the best musical of the year. Just a year after its New York opening, there were companies playing in London, Iceland, Holland, Switzerland, Germany, Denmark, Austria, Finland and Sweden.

The film version of *Cabaret* was released in 1972, and the movie's handling of the political material during the time of Hitler's rise to power was done with style and integrity by Bob Fosse, who won an Academy Award as best director. The cast was close to perfect, down to the last weary transvestite

and the least of the bland, blond, open-faced Nazis in the background. Joel Grey repeated his part as the master of ceremonies, the master of ambiguity, the master of motifs at the Kit Kat Klub, and he was magnificent, earning the best-supporting-actor Academy Award.

Liza Minnelli turned in a bravura performance as Sally, and won the Academy Award as best actress. One critic said, 'As for Miss Minnelli, she is sometimes wrong in the details of her role, but so magnificently right for the film as a whole that I would prefer not to imagine it without her.'

The most valid complaint that the critics had about the film was that it jettisoned the two middle-aged characters, Schultz and Schneider, who gave the stage musical dramatic strength – these two were the ones most influenced by the rise of the Nazis. That means that it also jettisoned their songs.

Another problem was the mishandling of the 'Tomorrow Belongs to Me' number. On the stage it was done by a small group of waiters at the Kit Kat Klub after the patrons had gone home in the wee hours of the morning. It started as a solo, done as a German folk song, and, as the rest of the waiters join in one by one, it became militaristically sinister. This was the song that closed the first act, and early in the run, when the audiences didn't know what to expect, they were so stunned that it took them several seconds to decide whether or not to applaud. But applaud they did, it was such a show-stopper. In the film, Fosse took the song outdoors to a huge picnic and turned it into just another chorus number.

Man of La Mancha was the surprise stage hit of 1965. Its book was by Dale Wasserman, the lyrics were by Joe Darion

RIGHT: Joan Denier played the Aldonza-Dulcinea role in the Broadway production of *Man of La Mancha* (1965). Here she is flanked by the steeds of Don Quixote and Sancho Panza.

LEFT: Richard Kiley (left) as Don Quixote and Irving Jacobson as his page, Sancho Panza, in the stage version of *Man of La Mancha*.

and the music was by Mitch Leigh. Directed by Albert Marre with dances by Jack Cole, it starred Richard Kiley, Ray Middleton, Robert Rounseville, Irving Jacobson and Joan Denier, and ran for 2330 performances.

The idea for the musical had come to Wasserman when he read a quote from author Manuel Onamuno – 'Only he who attempts the absurd is capable of achieving the impossible.' And it certainly was a good idea. In less than five years, the hit show's backers had earned 1000 percent on their investment, and the show was being performed in London, Paris, Mexico City, Belgium, Israel, Japan and Australia. It also had

RIGHT: Kiley as Quixote, is confronted by the evil knight in Broadway's *Man of La Mancha*.

become part of the opera repertory at the Komische Oper in East Berlin.

Among the numbers in the musical were 'Man of La Mancha (I, Don Quixote),' 'It's All the Same,' 'Dulcinea,' 'I'm Only Thinking of Him,' 'I Really Like Him,' 'What Do You Want of Me?,' 'The Barber's Song (Golden Helmet),' 'To Each His Dulcinea,' 'The Impossible Dream (The Quest),' 'Little Bird, Little Bird,' 'The Dubbing,' 'The Abduction,' 'Aldonza,' 'A Little Gossip' and 'The Psalm.'

The screen version of *Man of La Mancha* (1972) was an absolute bomb. Originally, this musical about Cervantes' Don Quixote and his adventures was a rather simple tale, simply staged. But the film was a disaster. According to one critic, 'Beautiful source material has been raped, murdered and buried.'

The big problem was that the stars, Peter O'Toole (Quixote), Sophia Loren (Aldonza) and James Coco (Sancho Panza), couldn't sing. And since many of the songs bordered on the operatic and the plot was minuscule, the picture really suffered. Indeed, O'Toole's singing made audiences think that he had mistaken the songs for some of Shakespeare's soliloquies.

Rock religion or 'Jesus Rock' was a popular theme during the early 1970s. It was hard to figure out if it was an iconoclastic view of religion, or a genuine attempt to convey the message in terms that the younger generation could understand.

Jesus Christ, Superstar opened on Broadway in 1971. It was a rock musical translating the New Testament account of the Passion of Christ into contemporary terms. The music was by Andrew Lloyd Weber, and the book and lyrics by Tim Rice. It ran for 720 performances and starred Jeff Fenholt and Ben Vereen.

The show actually began as a record album that was produced in England. Then it was thought of as a possible stage musical, which opened on Broadway a year before the London company went into production. Among the songs were 'I Don't Know How to Love Him,' 'Hosanna,' 'Pilate's Dream,' 'Everything's All Right' and 'Heaven On Their Minds.'

The film version of *Jesus Christ, Superstar* (1973) was less satisfying than the stage version. It was filmed on location in Israel, but for some reason director Norman Jewison decided to turn it into a play within a play, having a troupe of actors arrive by bus on the desert location to film the Biblical

OPPOSITE: James Coco as Sancho Panza, Peter O'Toole as Don Quixote and Sophia Loren as Aldonza, in the film version of *Man of La Mancha* (1972).

RIGHT: Two members of the Sanhedrin in the film version of *Jesus Christ, Superstar* (1973).

BELOW: Jeff Fenholt, as Christ, is captured to be arraigned before Caiphas and Pontius Pilate, in the Broadway production of *Jesus Christ, Superstar* (1971).

play. He also threw in a scene of jet fighters and tanks chasing Judas Iscariot during his big production number. The result was that the magic of the stage production, in which the audience came to believe in these people, with all their faults and foibles, was destroyed because they were obviously actors doing a job.

Jesus Christ was played by Ted Neeley and Judas by Carl Anderson. Neeley didn't get the part right off the bat. First the producers wanted Mick Jagger, then David Cassidy, then John Lennon. Neeley was a product of Los Angeles supper clubs and Grand Ol' Opry warm-up bands. His was not a triumphal performance, with its shrieking, pouting, teeth-gritting, eye-rolling and twitching. *Newsweek* pointed out that 'Jesus often recalls Charles Manson.' *Playboy* exclaimed that his 'portrayal of Christ ought to fix him permanently in public memory as the Screamin' Jesus.' One critic characterized the whole production as 'one of the true fiascos of modern cinema.'

LEFT: Ben Vereen, as Judas, with Bob Bingham, in Broadway's *Jesus Christ, Superstar* (1971).

BELOW: The cast of actors in the movie version of *Jesus Christ, Superstar* (1973).

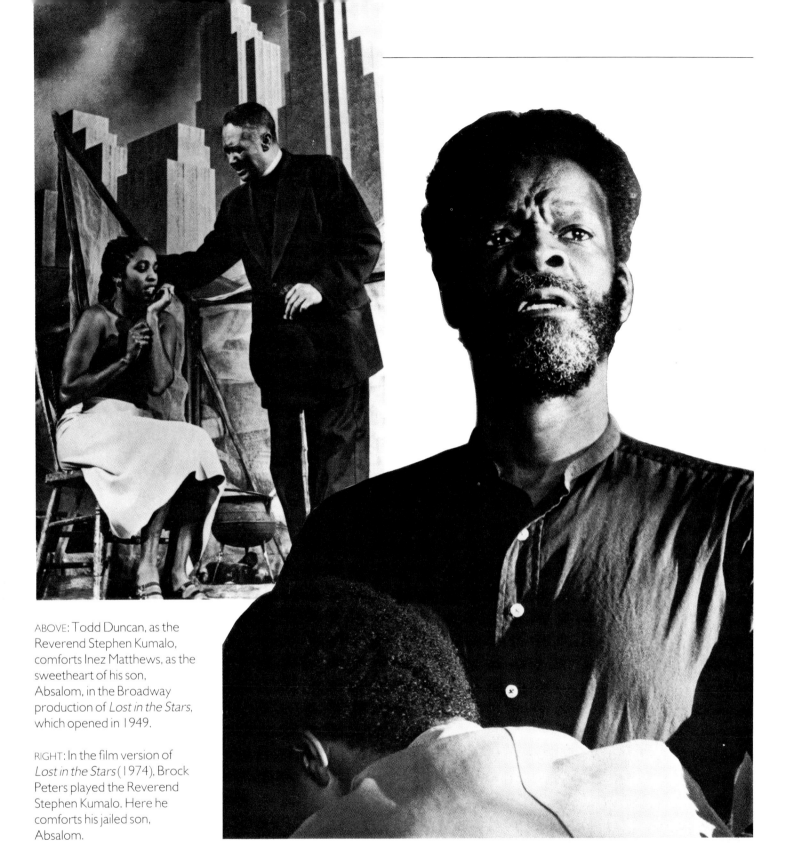

ABOVE: Todd Duncan, as the Reverend Stephen Kumalo, comforts Inez Matthews, as the sweetheart of his son, Absalom, in the Broadway production of *Lost in the Stars*, which opened in 1949.

RIGHT: In the film version of *Lost in the Stars* (1974), Brock Peters played the Reverend Stephen Kumalo. Here he comforts his jailed son, Absalom.

Lost in the Stars opened on Broadway in 1949 with a book by Maxwell Anderson, based on South African writer Alan Paton's novel *Cry, the Beloved Country*. The lyrics were by Anderson and the music by Kurt Weill. Directed by Rouben Mamoulian, it starred Todd Duncan (the original Porgy in *Porgy and Bess*), Inez Matthews and Leslie Banks, and ran for 273 performances.

The show was more like an opera than a musical, with its dramatic intensity, and, indeed, Weill thought of it as an opera. Unfortunately, he died at the age of 50, and this was his last score for the theater, or he might have gone on to become a great operatic composer. As it was, the New York City Opera revived it in its repertory in 1958.

The Reverend Stephen Kumalo (Duncan) lives in Ndotshe-ni, South Africa. He misses his son Absalom (Julian Mayfield), who is in Johannesburg earning money for his education. Kumalo and his wife have not heard from him for a long time, so they go to Johannesburg to look for him. They can't find him because he is living in the slums with his sweetheart, Irina, who is pregnant. Worried about the need for money, Absalom becomes a partner in a robbery and kills a white man. Stephen returns to Johannesburg to visit Absalom in prison, but when he learns that his son is sentenced to death, he returns home. At the end the dead man's father comes to Stephen asking for forgiveness at the exact moment that Absalom is hanged.

Some of the musical numbers were 'The Hills of Ixopo,' 'Thousands of Miles,' 'Train to Johannesburg,' 'The Little

Angela Lansbury – Broadway's
Mame (1966).

Gray House,' 'Who'll Buy?,' 'Trouble Man,' 'Murder in Parkwold,' 'Fear,' 'Lost in the Stars,' 'O Tixo, Tixo, Help Me,' 'Stay Well,' 'Cry, The Beloved Country,' 'Big Mole' and 'A Bird of Passage.'

It took 25 years to release the film version of *Lost in the Stars* (1974), and by that time it had become a dated melodrama. It also failed to get rid of a stagey production that did not take advantage of the power of the movie camera. It did lack excitement, but the basic story of bigotry remained all too relevant, and the performances of Brock Peters, Melba Moore, Raymond St Jacques and Clifton Davis were splendid.

Mame premiered on Broadway in 1966. The book was by Jerome Lawrence and Robert E Lee and was based on Patrick Dennis's novel and play *Auntie Mame*. The words and music were by Jerry Herman. Directed by Gene Saks with dances by Onna White, it starred Angela Lansbury, Frankie Michaels, Beatrice Arthur, Jane Connell and Willard Waterman, and ran for 1508 performances.

Many great ladies of the stage and the screen have played Auntie Mame in one form or another. Among them have been Angela Lansbury, Ginger Rogers, Rosalind Russell, Dolores Gray, Bea Lillie, Constance Bennett, Eve Arden, Greer Garson, Sylvia Sidney, Juliet Prowse and Lucille Ball. The life and times of Auntie Mame, of course, began with the book, but Lawrence and Lee had adapted it as a straight play and later as the movie *Auntie Mame* (1958) starring Rosalind Russell.

Mame (Lansbury) is a delightfully eccentric and boisterous woman of means who inherits an orphaned nephew, Patrick Dennis (Michaels). The show spanned the years from 1928 to 1946. During the Great Depression, Mame becomes

TOP: Lucille Ball, in Hollywoods' *Mame* leads the chorus boys in their title-song number.

ABOVE: Lucille Ball, in the film *Mame*, greets her newly arrived ward – her orphaned nephew, Patrick Dennis.

destitute and then marries a wealthy Southerner, Beauregard Jackson Pickett Burnside (Charles Braswell). Patrick grows up and gets married (he is now played by Jerry Lanning). At the end, Mame is beginning to work her off-the-wall wiles on Patrick's son.

Among the musical numbers were 'Mame,' 'If He Walked into My Life,' 'Bosom Buddies' (which was eliminated from the version seen in Great Britain), 'It's Today,' 'Loving You,' 'My Best Girl,' 'Gooch's Song (What Do I Do Now?),' 'Open a New Window,' 'St Bridget' and 'The Letter.'

The film version of *Mame* (1974) was another dilution of a smash Broadway show. Lucille Ball was Mame, Beatrice Arthur re-created her original role as Mame's actress friend, Vera Charles, and Robert Preston was Mame's Southern beau. Unfortunately, Lucille Ball didn't measure up to the sophisticated grandness and exaggerated madness of the larger-than-life character, at least not in the manner of such previous Auntie Mames as Angela Lansbury and Rosalind Russell. But the film did have its moments.

The Rocky Horror Show premiered on Broadway in 1974, and it had to be seen to be believed. The book, lyrics and music were by Richard O'Brien. It starred Tim Curry and ran for a mere three weeks.

The film version, retitled *The Rocky Horror Picture Show* (1974), was something else – an outrageously kinky horror-movie spoof, spiced with sex, transvestism and rock music. It concerned a straight couple (Susan Sarandon and Barry Bostwick) stranded in an old dark house full of weirdos from Transylvania. The songs included 'Dammit Janet,' 'Over at the Frankenstein Place,' 'Sweet Transvestite' and 'Wild and Untamed Thing.'

It became a cult flick for the younger set and was usually found on Saturday midnight bills, where all the kids who attended seemed to know the dialogue by heart and conducted a huge sing-along, often attired in the costume of their favorite creep.

A Little Night Music opened on Broadway in 1973. With a book by Hugh Wheeler and music and lyrics by Stephen Sondheim, it starred Glynis Johns, Hermione Gingold and Len Cariou. Despite the fact that one critic compared Sondheim with Franz Schubert and Gustav Mahler, the run was only 600 performances.

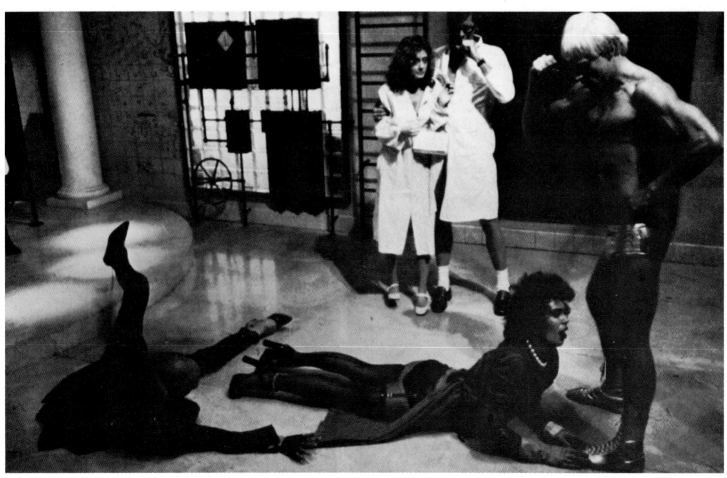

OPPOSITE TOP: Gingold, and Kahan, in Broadway's *A Little Night Music* (1973).

OPPOSITE BOTTOM: *The Rocky Horror Picture Show* (1974).

ABOVE: Cariou and Johns on stage in *Night Music*.

RIGHT: Taylor, Rigg, Guittard and Cariou in the film *A Little Night Music* (1978).

It was an operetta-type treatment of turn-of-the-century infidelities and other marital complications, based on the Ingmar Bergman film *Smiles of a Summer Night* (1955), a zingy, yet tasteful tale of wife-swapping on a country estate.

The film version of *A Little Night Music* (1978) turned out to be a laughably stilted adaptation of the stage musical. The producers went to all the trouble of casting Elizabeth Taylor, Diana Rigg (of 'The Avengers' television series), Len Cariou, as in the show, and Hermione Gingold. Naturally, in Germany the film was called *Eine Kleine Nachtmusik*. Among the numbers were 'A Weekend in the Country,' 'The Miller's Son,' 'Every Day a Little Death,' 'Liaisons' and 'Send in the Clowns.' But when Liz sang 'Send in the Clowns,' she sent out the audiences.

Grease made its Broadway debut in 1972. With a book, music and lyrics by Jim Jacobs and Warren Casey, it featured Carol Demas and Barry Bostwick, and ran for an astonishing 3388 performances – the second-longest run in the history of the Broadway theater.

It was a stock musical that fantasized the life of the young in the 1950s, an evocation of the B-picture quickies like the Beach Party films of that decade. The gang at old Rydell High

John Travolta (center) relaxes on the football-stadium bleachers in the film version of *Grease* (1978).

was unlike any high-school class that anyone had ever seen, except in the movies. For one thing, they were all a little long in the tooth to hang around malt shops. For another, they were loaded with the kind of exuberance and talent that is not often found too far from a musical stage. Some of the songs were great, such as 'It's Raining on Prom Night,' 'Beauty School Dropout,' 'Look at Me, I'm Sandra Dee' and 'There Are Worse Things I Could Do.'

The film version of *Grease* was released in 1978, and it was a triumph. John Travolta was a performer who proved the old adage that it isn't so much a star's age, as it is the age that the audience wants him to be. He played Vinnie Barbarino of the unruly bunch of Brooklyn high-school students in the television series 'Welcome Back, Kotter' when he was in his early 20s. He then went on to score a triumph in *Saturday Night Fever* (1977). A teenager is what people wanted Travolta to be, and he dutifully played one in the film, starring with Olivia Newton-John, Stockard Channing and hundreds of kids.

Several characters who were famous in the 1950s appeared in the film as a sort of inside joke. Eve Arden (the English teacher from the television series 'Our Miss Brooks') was the principal of Rydell High. Sid Caesar was the football coach. Edd Byrnes was the lecherous host of a television show. Frankie Avalon was in a dream sequence counseling an unhappy student. It was a large, funny, witty and imaginative picture, and Travolta was better than in *Saturday Night Fever*. Newton-John was funny and charming. Stockard Channing almost stole the show in her two numbers.

OPPOSITE TOP: The Broadway cast of *Grease* (1972) on stage. The musical comedy was the second-longest-running musical (after *A Chorus Line*) in the history of the New York theater.

OPPOSITE BOTTOM: Bostwick and Demas from the Broadway cast of *Grease*.

RIGHT: Cavorting members of the cast of *Grease* on stage.

BELOW: John Travolta and Olivia Newton-John in the film version of *Grease* (1978).

The Wiz first appeared on Broadway in 1975. It was a black version of *The Wizard of Oz*, with completely new music by Charlie Smalls, and starred Stephanie Mills as Dorothy, Hinton Battle as the Scarecrow, Ted Ross as the Cowardly Lion and Tiger Haynes as the Tin Man. It was directed by Geoffrey Holder, who also did the wonderful costumes.

But face it, *The Wiz* got by because of the songs, the imaginative stage images, the excellent supporting cast and a relentless television ad campaign. The book was inept. Indeed, the familiar story was told so confusingly that any child seeing it for the first time would find it impossible to follow. The story was transferred from Kansas to New York City and the dialogue was filled with street vernacular, for example when the Scarecrow kept begging Dorothy for 'spare change.'

The film version of *The Wiz* (1978) failed in spite of its talented cast, which included Diana Ross as Dorothy, Michael Jackson as the Scarecrow, Ted Ross as the Cowardly Lion, Nipsy Russell as the Tin Man, Richard Pryor as the Wizard and Lena Horne as Glinda, the Good Witch. It had a dreary ending and a dreary performance by the usually talented Ross, who, at age 34, was a bit old for the part. All in all, it missed the sense of wonder so essential to the show.

But the songs were good. They included 'Don't Bring Me No Bad News,' 'Believe in Yourself,' 'Brand New Day,' 'Home,' 'He's the Wizard,' 'The Feeling That We Have,' 'Soon As I Get Home,' 'You Can't Win,' 'What Would I Do If I Could Feel,' 'Slide Some Oil to Me,' 'I'm a Mean Old Lion,' 'Ease on Down the Road,' 'Emerald City' and 'So you Want to See the Wizard' from the original stage musical. Other songs composed by Quincy Jones were added – 'Liberation Agitato,' 'The Wiz,' 'Can I Go On?,' 'March of the Munchkins,' 'Good Witch Glinda,' 'Is This What Feeling Gets? (Dorothy's Theme),' 'Now Watch Me Dance,' 'Popper Girls,' 'End of the Yellow Brick Road' and 'A Sorry Phoney.'

BELOW: Mills and Battle in Broadway's *The Wiz* (1975).

RIGHT: A scene from the film *The Wiz* (1978).

OPPOSITE: A symbolic scene from the Broadway production of *Hair*, which opened in 1968.

Members of the cast of the motion-picture version of *Hair* (1979), frolicking through Central Park.

Hair opened on Broadway in 1968. It was an iconoclastic musical, whose approach to life, sex, drugs and rock music established a new pattern for the musical theater. The book and lyrics were by Gerome Ragni and James Rado, and the music was by Galt MacDermot. Directed by Tom O'Horgan with dances by Jule Arenal, it starred James Rado, Gerome Ragni, Shelley Plimpton, Sally Eaton and Ronald Dyson, and ran for 1750 performances in New York. The run in London was 1999 performances, and it would have passed 2000 except that the roof of the Shaftesbury Theatre caved in.

It was an instant hit. While it was playing in New York and London, there were other companies presenting it in Los Angeles, San Francisco, Chicago, Toronto, Paris, Amsterdam, Lisbon and Tokyo. As might have been expected, because of its nude scene and the off-color lyrics, censors closed the Boston company and authorities closed it after but a single performance in Acapulco, Mexico.

The story was a simple one. Claude (Rado), a long-haired hippie, leaves his Flatbush home in Brooklyn and pretends that he is from Manchester, England. He moves in with his friend, Berger (Ragni), and Berger's girl, Sheila (Lynn Kellogg). Claude is facing the military draft, to the despair of Jeanie (Eaton), although she is pregnant with somebody else's child. Claude is eventually drafted.

The songs were sensational. Among them were 'Let the Sunshine In (The Flesh Failures),' 'Aquarius,' 'Frank Mills,' 'Be-In,' 'Sodomy,' 'I Got Life,' 'White Boys,' 'Colored Spade,' 'Easy to Be Hard,' 'Where Do I Go?' and 'Good Morning Starshine.'

Hair finally made it to the screen in 1979, starring John Savage, Beverley D'Angelo and Melba Moore. Generally it was a disappointment, but the choreography by Twyla Tharp was brilliant. *Grease*, that paean to the 1950s, made it at the box office. *Hair*, eulogizing the 1960s, did not. We had *Grease 2*, but no *Hair 2*. The problem was that *Hair* turned out to be a period musical celebrating 'The Age of Aquarius,' rather than a spoof, as was *Grease*, and its impact was considerably muffled.

It was with *Hair* that the decade of the 70s ended.

THE EVOLVING EIGHTIES

Annie, the musical about the little orphan girl who wins the heart of the multi-billionaire Oliver 'Daddy' Warbucks, was the smash hit of Broadway's 1976 season. It had a book by Thomas Meehan, music by Charles Strouse and lyrics by Martin Charnin. Directed by Mike Nichols with choreography by Peter Gennaro, it starred Andrea McArdle (one of a long line of Annies who left after outgrowing the part), Reid Shelton as 'Daddy' and Dorothy Louden as Miss Hannigan, the director of the orphanage.

The story was a simple one. Annie is the bane of Miss Hannigan's existence at the orphanage because the girl is too brainy and has too much spirit. When Annie is taken to spend a few days at the palatial home of Oliver Warbucks, he grows fond of her and keeps her on under the tutelage of his secretary, Grace Farrell (Sandy Faison). Miss Hannigan, along with her brother Rooster (Robert Fitch) and his girl friend Lily (Barbara Erwin), plot to extort money from Warbucks, but their plan is thwarted.

It was a warm, intimate, pleasant show, with songs to match. Among them were 'Maybe,' 'It's The Hard-knock Life,' 'Tomorrow,' 'We'd Like to Thank You,' 'Little Girls,' 'I Think I'm Gonna Like It Here,' 'N. Y. C,' 'Easy Street,' 'You Won't Be an Orphan for Long,' 'You're Never Fully Dressed Without a Smile,' 'Something Was Missing,' 'I Don't Need Anything but You,' 'Annie' and 'A New Deal for Christmas,'

The film version of *Annie* (1982) missed the point of intimacy and was turned into an overblown production by director John Huston, who was filming his first musical. It cost more than $40 million and had a cast of thousands cavorting around a mansion that would have given the Taj Mahal a run for its money. Aileen Quinn, as Annie, and Albert Finney, as Warbucks, turned in appealing performances, but the rest of the cast (including, amazingly enough, Carol Burnett, who grossly overacted her role as Miss Hannigan) was uninspired. But, still, the music was there.

The 1980s found Hollywood a bit leery of importing Broadway musicals to film. But there is hope that another cycle may be starting. *A Chorus Line* has been on the drawing boards since 1975, when producers Cy Feuer and Ernest Martin offered $150,000 for the film rights even before the musical opened. A new offer of $400,000 was made by Peter Gruber of Columbia Pictures on opening night – 21 May 1975. Within a few weeks the offers escalated to $3 million. All were turned down. Finally, in February of 1976, a contract was signed for $5.5 million – the same price that *My Fair Lady* had gone for. The film, directed by Richard Attenborough, is scheduled to be released in December 1985, ten years and seven months after the play opened on Broadway.

It should be a smash. Millions of people have been waiting a long time to see it. And if it is a smash, perhaps the new cycle will begin. Waiting in the wings will be *Cats, Dreamgirls, La Cage au Folles, My One and Only, Sunday in the Park with George, The Tap Dance Kid* and, who knows, maybe even a remake of *42nd Street*.

Aileen Quinn and Sandy in the film version of *Annie* (1982). INSET: Carol Burnett, Quinn and Ann Reinking in *Annie*.

INDEX

Listings are in three sections:
Stage productions; Screen
productions; Personalities.
Numerals in italics refer to
illustrations.

254

ACKNOWLEDGMENTS AND CREDITS

Culver Collection: 38 (bottom).
Fred Fehl: 182, 183, 184, 192, 199 (bottom), 223 (bottom).
Theatre Collection of the Museum of the City of New York: 7 (top), 32, 34 (top), 45, 47 (bottom), 48 (left), 50, 51 (left), 62 (top), 72, 79 (top), 87, 92, 93, 103 (top), 125 (bottom), 141 (top), 145, 159, 175 (top).
Museum of Modern Art: 15, 17, 19 (bottom), 24, 29, 26 (bottom), 27, 36 (bottom), 37 (bottom), 42, 43, 44, 58, 60, 65, 74, (bottom), 75 (top), 79 (bottom), 82, 88 (bottom), 89 (right), 94, 96, 102, 103 (bottom), 110 (center and bottom), 119, 125 (top), 135 (bottom), 139, 154 (bottom), 158 (bottom), 171, 172 (bottom), 179, 185 (top), 189 (bottom), 193, 239 (bottom).
National Film Archives: 7 (bottom), 73, 153 (bottom), 170, 195, 212 (top), 217, 220 (top), 235 (top), 249.
New York Public Library Picture Collection: 12 (top left), 13 (ctr), 167 (top).
The Billy Rose Theater Collection of the New York Public Library at Lincoln Center, Lenox and Tilden Foundations: 5, 8 (bottom), 13 (top right, bottom right, bottom left), 18, 20 (bottom), 21 (bottom), 22 (top), 26 (center and top), 30 (top), 31 (top left), 38 (top), 39 (bottom), 52 (bottom), 55 (center and bottom), 56 (top and center), 57, 62 (bottom), 63 (top), 64 (bottom), 66, 68, 69 (top), 70, 70–71, 75 (bottom), 76 (bottom), 83, 86 (top and bottom right), 91 (top), 98,

99, 101 (top), 106 (top), 107 (bottom left and right), 109 (top), 110 (top), 111 (top), 115 (top), 116 (top), 118, 120, 121 (bottom), 122 (bottom), 123 (bottom), 124 (bottom), 126 (top), 127, 129 (top), 131 (top and bottom left), 132 (bottom), 133 (top), 134, 135 (top), 138, 142 (top), 146 (top), 148 (top), 149 (bottom), 150 (bottom), 151 (bottom), 153 (top), 154 (bottom), 155 (top), 157, 160 (top), 163 (top), 165, 168, 169, 172 (top), 173, 178, 180, 186, 188, 189 (top), 191 (top), 194, 196, 197, 198, 200, 201, 203 (bottom), 204, 206, 208, 209 (top), 210 (bottom), 211, 212 (bottom), 214, 215, 222 (top), 224, 225 (bottom), 226 (bottom), 228, 229, 230 (bottom), 232, 233, 235 (bottom), 236 (top), 237 (top), 238, 240 (top), 241 (top), 244, 245, (top), 246, 248.
Phototeque: 14, 16 (bottom), 19 (top), 20 (top), 22 (bottom), 23, 24–5, 25, 28, 30 (center and bottom), 31 (top right and bottom), 33 (bottom), 34 (bottom), 35, 37 (top), 38, 39 (top), 40, 41, 46, 47 (top), 48 (right), 49, 51 (right), 52 (top), 53, 54, 55 (top), 56 (bottom), 61, 63 (top), 67, 76 (top), 81, 89 (left), 90, 91 (bottom), 100, 105, 106 (bottom), 107 (top right), 108 (top), 109 (bottom), 111 (bottom), 113, 115 (bottom), 123 (top), 126 (bottom), 128, 129 (bottom), 130, 141 (bottom), 161, 174, 175 (bottom), 186-7, 213 (bottom), 216, 222 (bottom), 223 (top), 245 (bottom).